STUDENT LECTURE NOTEBOOK

Sixth Edition

Biology

LIFE ON EARTH

Teresa Audesirk

Gerald Audesirk

Bruce E. Byers

D1247325

Prentice
Hall

Upper Saddle River, NJ 07458

Editor in Chief: Sheri Snavely
Executive Editor: Teresa Chung
Project Manager: Travis Moses-Westphal
Executive Managing Editor: Kathleen Schiaparelli
Assistant Managing Editor: Dinah Thong
Production Editor: Francesca Daniele
Supplement Cover Management/Design: Paul Gourhan
Manufacturing Manager: Trudy Pisciotti
Manufacturing Buyer: Alan Fischer

Weaver bird building nest, Maasai Mara national Reserve, Kanya/Manoj Shah

© 2003 by Pearson Education, Inc.
Pearson Education, Inc.
Upper Saddle River, NJ 07458

All rights reserved. No part of this book may be reproduced in any form or
by any means, without permission in writing from the publisher.

Printed in the United States of America

10 9 8 7 6 5 4 3 2 1

ISBN 0-13-100106-X

Pearson Education Ltd., *London*
Pearson Education Australia Pty. Ltd., *Sydney*
Pearson Education Singapore, Pte. Ltd.
Pearson Education North Asia Ltd., *Hong Kong*
Pearson Education Canada, Inc., *Toronto*
Pearson Educación de Mexico, S.A. de C.V.
Pearson Education—Japan, *Tokyo*
Pearson Education Malaysia, Pte. Ltd.
Pearson Education, *Upper Saddle River, New Jersey*

Contents

CHAPTER 1   An Introduction to Life on Earth

Multiple Choice

1. *Which of the following is paired incorrectly?*
 a. organ—a structure formed of cells of similar types
 b. cell—the smallest unit of life
 c. genes—units of heredity
 d. cytoplasm—watery substance within cells that contains organelles
 e. plasma membrane—surrounds each cell

2. *A scientist examines an organism and finds that it is eukaryotic, heterotrophic, and multicellular and that it absorbs nutrients. She concludes that the organism is a member of the kingdom*
 a. Bacteria
 b. Protista
 c. Plantae
 d. Fungi
 e. Animalia

3. *Which statement is correct?*
 a. Eukaryotic cells are simpler than prokaryotic cells.
 b. *Heterotroph* means "self-feeder."
 c. Mutations are accidental changes in genes.
 d. A scientific theory is similar to an educated guess.
 e. Genes are proteins that produce DNA.

4. *Choose the answer that best describes the scientific method.*
 a. observation, hypothesis, experiment, absolute proof
 b. guess, hypothesis, experiment, conclusion
 c. observation, hypothesis, experiment, conclusion
 d. hypothesis, experiment, observation, conclusion
 e. experiment, observation, hypothesis, conclusion

5. *Which of the following are characteristics of living things?*
 a. They reproduce.
 b. They respond to stimuli.
 c. They are complex and organized.
 d. They acquire energy.
 e. all of the above

6. *The three natural processes that form the basis for evolution are*
 a. adaptation, natural selection, and inheritance
 b. predation, genetic variation, and natural selection
 c. mutation, genetic variation, and adaptation
 d. fossils, natural selection, and adaptation
 e. genetic variation, inheritance, and natural selection

? Review Questions

1. What are the differences between a salt crystal and a tree? Which is living? How do you know? How would you test your "knowledge"? What controls would you use?

2. What is the difference between a scientific theory and a hypothesis? Explain how each is used by scientists.

3. Define and explain the terms *natural selection, evolution, mutation, creationism,* and *population.*

4. Starting with the cell, list the hierarchy of organization of life, briefly explaining each level.

5. Define *homeostasis.* Why must organisms continuously acquire energy and materials from the external environment to maintain homeostasis?

6. Describe the scientific method. In what ways do you use the scientific method in everyday life?

7. What is evolution? Briefly describe how evolution occurs.

1. In the heavily populated state of California, natural occurrences, including earthquakes, heavy rains, and grass and forest wildfires, have reduced the quality of life for many Californians. Look at it another way for a moment. What ecosystems are found in this state? What impacts have humans had on these natural ecosystems? Are changes in these areas the reason for fires and floods and mudslides? What needs to be done to alter the balance of "humans and nature"?

2. Design an experiment to test the effects of a new dog food, "Super Dog," on the thickness and water-shedding properties of the coats of golden retrievers. Include all the parts of a scientific experiment. Design objective methods to assess coat thickness and water-shedding ability.

3. Science is based on principles, including uniformity in space and time and common perception. Assume that humans one day encounter intelligent beings from a planet in another galaxy who evolved under very different conditions. Discuss the two principles mentioned above and how they would affect (1) the nature of scientific observations on the different planets and (2) communications about these observations.

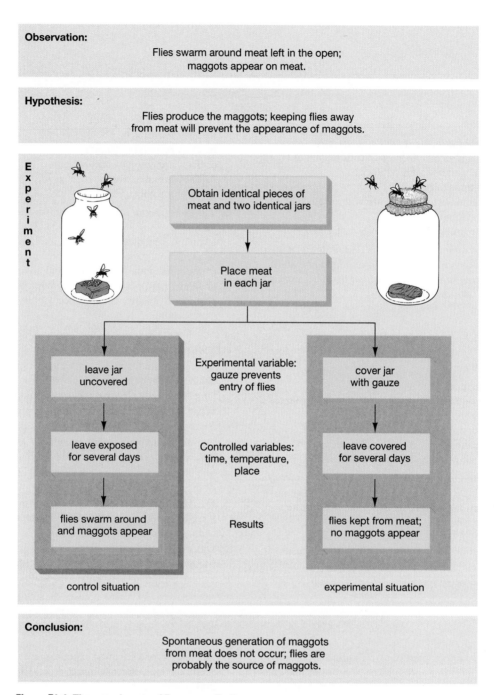

Observation:

Flies swarm around meat left in the open;
maggots appear on meat.

Hypothesis:

Flies produce the maggots; keeping flies away
from meat will prevent the appearance of maggots.

Experiment

Obtain identical pieces of
meat and two identical jars

Place meat
in each jar

leave jar
uncovered

Experimental variable:
gauze prevents
entry of flies

cover jar
with gauze

leave exposed
for several days

Controlled variables:
time, temperature,
place

leave covered
for several days

flies swarm around
and maggots appear

Results

flies kept from meat;
no maggots appear

control situation

experimental situation

Conclusion:

Spontaneous generation of maggots
from meat does not occur; flies are
probably the source of maggots.

Figure E1-1 The experiments of Francesco Redi

© 2003 Prentice Hall, Inc.

NOTES

CHAPTER 2   Atoms, Molecules, and Life

Thinking Through the Concepts

Multiple Choice

1. *What is the purest form of matter that cannot be separated into different substances by chemical means?*
   a. compounds
   b. molecules
   c. atoms
   d. elements
   e. electrons

2. *Which phrase best describes chemical bonds?*
   a. physical bridges
   b. attractive forces
   c. shared protons
   d. atomic reactions
   e. all of these phrases are equally descriptive

3. *When an atom ionizes, what happens?*
   a. It shares one or more electrons with another atom.
   b. It emits energy as it loses extra neutrons.
   c. It gives up or takes up one or more electrons.
   d. It shares a hydrogen atom with another atom.
   e. none of the above

4. *If electrons in water molecules were equally attracted to hydrogen nuclei and oxygen nuclei, water molecules would be*
   a. more polar
   b. less polar
   c. unchanged
   d. triple bonded
   e. unable to form

5. *A covalent bond forms*
   a. when two ions are attracted to one another
   b. between adjacent water molecules, producing surface tension
   c. when one atom gives up its electron to another atom
   d. when two atoms share electrons
   e. between water molecules and fat globules

6. *What is the defining characteristic of an acid?*
   a. It donates hydrogen ions.
   b. It accepts hydrogen ions.
   c. It will donate or accept hydrogen ions, depending on the pH.
   d. It has an excess of hydroxide ions.
   e. It has a pH greater than 7.

? Review Questions

1. What are the six most abundant elements that occur in living organisms?

2. Distinguish among atoms and molecules; elements and compounds; and protons, neutrons, and electrons.

3. Compare and contrast covalent bonds and ionic bonds.

4. Why can water absorb a great amount of heat with little increase in its temperature?

5. Describe how water dissolves a salt. How does this phenomenon compare with the effect of water on a hydrophobic substance such as corn oil?

6. Define *acid*, *base*, and *buffer*. How do buffers reduce changes in pH when hydrogen ions or hydroxide ions are added to a solution? Why is this phenomenon important in organisms?

Applying the Concepts

1. Many "over-the-counter" substances are sold to bring relief from "acid stomach" or "heartburn." What is the chemical basis for these compounds? Why do they work?

2. Fats and oils do not dissolve in water; polar and ionic molecules dissolve easily in water. Detergents and soaps help clean by dispersing fats and oils in water so that they can be rinsed away. From your knowledge of the structure of water and the hydrophobic nature of fats, what general chemical structures (for example, polar or nonpolar parts) must a soap or detergent have, and why?

3. What would the effects be for aquatic life if the density of ice were greater than that of liquid water? What would be the impact on terrestrial organisms?

4. How does sweating help you regulate your body temperature? Why do you feel hotter and more uncomfortable on a hot, humid day than on a hot, dry day?

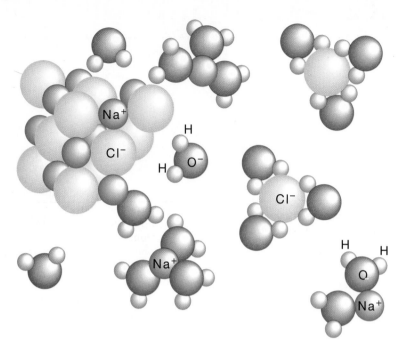

Figure 2-6 Water as a solvent

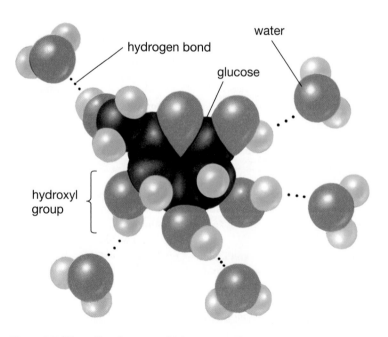

Figure 2-7 Water dissolves many biological molecules

© 2003 Prentice Hall, Inc.

NOTES

CHAPTER 3 Biological Molecules

Thinking Through the Concepts

Multiple Choice

1. Which of the following is not a function of polysaccharides in organisms?
   a. energy storage
   b. storage of hereditary information
   c. formation of cell walls
   d. structural support
   e. formation of exoskeletons

2. Characteristics of carbon that contribute to its ability to form an immense diversity of organic molecules include its
   a. tendency to form covalent bonds
   b. ability to bond with up to four other atoms
   c. capacity to form single and double bonds
   d. ability to bond together to form extensive, branched or unbranched carbon skeletons
   e. all of the above

3. Foods that are high in fiber are most likely to be derived from
   a. plants
   b. dairy products
   c. meat
   d. fish
   e. all of the above

4. Proteins differ from one another because
   a. the peptide bonds linking amino acids differ from protein to protein
   b. the sequence of amino acids in the polypeptide chain differs from protein to protein
   c. each protein molecule contains its own unique sequence of sugar molecules
   d. the number of nucleotides in each protein varies from molecule to molecule
   e. the number of nitrogen atoms in each amino acid differs from the number in all others

5. Which, if any, of the following choices does not properly pair an organic compound with one of its building blocks (subunits)?
   a. polysaccharide–monosaccharide
   b. fat–fatty acid

   c. nucleic acid–glycerol
   d. protein–amino acid
   e. all are paired correctly

6. Which of the following statements about lipids is false?
   a. A wax is a lipid.
   b. Unsaturated fats are liquid at room temperature.
   c. The body doesn't need any cholesterol.
   d. Both male and female sex hormones are steroids.
   e. Beef fat is highly saturated.

? Review Questions

1. Which elements are common components of biological molecules?

2. List the four principal types of biological molecules, and give an example of each.

3. What roles do nucleotides play in living organisms?

4. One way to convert corn oil to margarine (solid at room temperature) is to add hydrogen atoms, decreasing the number of double bonds in the molecules of oil. What is this process called? Why does it work?

5. Describe and compare dehydration synthesis and hydrolysis. Give an example of a substance formed by each chemical reaction, and describe the specific reaction in each instance.

6. Distinguish among the following: monosaccharide, disaccharide, and polysaccharide. Give two examples of each and their functions.

7. Describe the synthesis of a protein from amino acids. Then describe primary, secondary, tertiary, and quaternary structures of a protein.

8. Most structurally supportive materials in plants and animals are polymers of special sorts. Where would we find cellulose? Chitin? In what way(s) are these two polymers similar? Different?

9. Which kinds of bonds or bridges between keratin molecules are altered when hair is (a) wet and allowed to dry on curlers and (b) given a permanent wave?

Applying the Concepts

1. A preview question for Chapter 4: In Chapter 2 you learned that hydrophobic molecules tend to cluster when immersed in water. In this chapter, you discovered that a phospholipid has a hydrophilic head and hydrophobic tails. What do you think would be the configuration of phospholipids that are immersed in water?

2. Many birds must store large amounts of energy to power flight during migration. Which type of organic molecule would be the most advantageous for energy storage? Why?

3. Remember the nuclear accident at Chernobyl in 1986? A scientist suspects that the food in a nearby ecosystem may have been contaminated with radioactive nitrogen over a period of months. Which substances in plants and animals could be examined for radioactivity to test his hypothesis?

4. Fat contains twice as many calories per unit weight as carbohydrate does, so fat is an efficient way for animals, who must move about, to store energy. Compare the way fat and carbohydrates interact with water, and explain why this interaction also gives fat an advantage for weight-efficient energy storage.

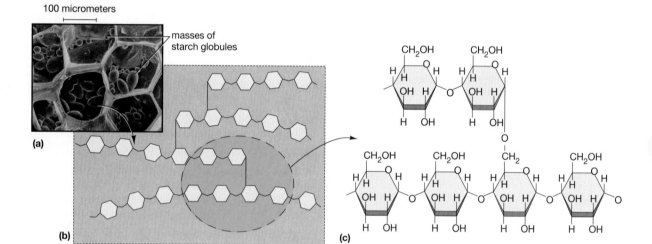

Figure 3-2 **Starch is an energy-storage polysaccharide made of glucose subunits**

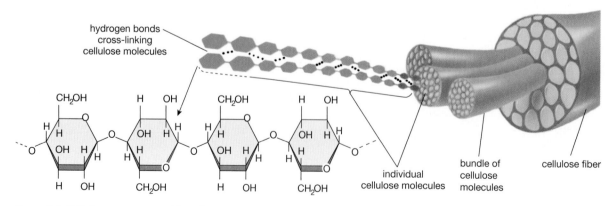

Figure 3-3 **Cellulose structure and function**

© 2003 Prentice Hall, Inc.

NOTES

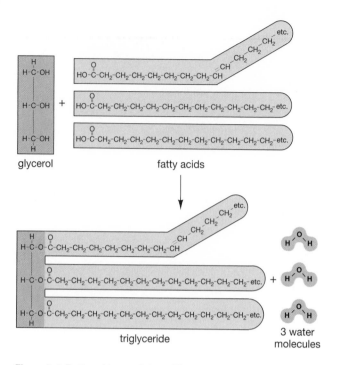

Figure 3-4 Fatty acids → triglycerids

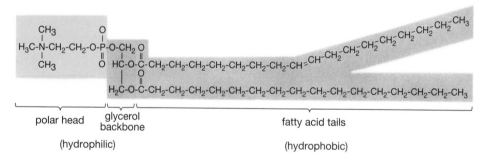

polar head · glycerol backbone · fatty acid tails

(hydrophilic) · (hydrophobic)

Figure 3-6 Phospholipids

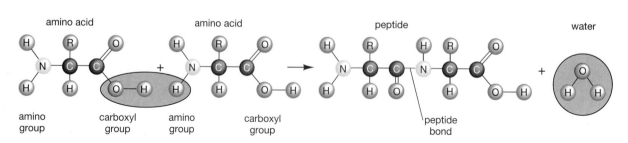

Figure 3-10 Protein synthesis

© 2003 Prentice Hall, Inc.

NOTES

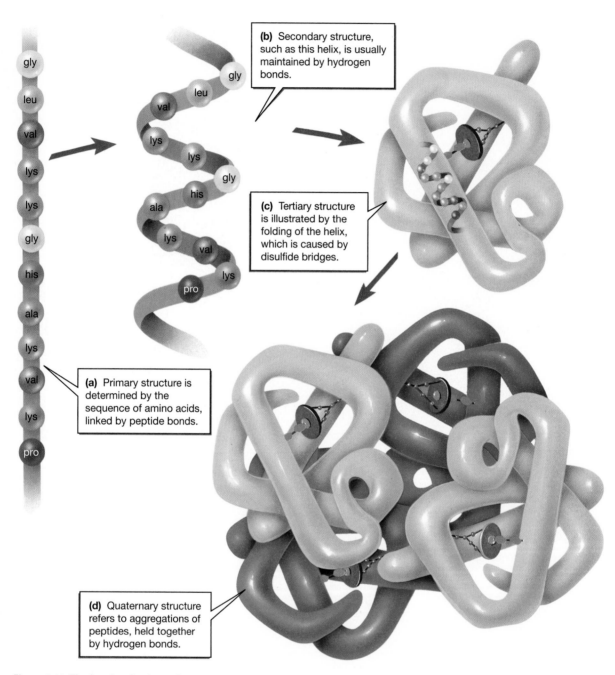

(b) Secondary structure, such as this helix, is usually maintained by hydrogen bonds.

(c) Tertiary structure is illustrated by the folding of the helix, which is caused by disulfide bridges.

(a) Primary structure is determined by the sequence of amino acids, linked by peptide bonds.

(d) Quaternary structure refers to aggregations of peptides, held together by hydrogen bonds.

Figure 3-11 **The four levels of protein structure**

© 2003 Prentice Hall, Inc.

NOTES

CHAPTER 4 Cell Membrane Structure and Function

Thinking Through the Concepts

Multiple Choice

1. *Active transport through the plasma membrane occurs through the action of*
a. diffusion
b. membrane proteins
c. DNA
d. water
e. osmosis

2. *The following is a characteristic of a plasma membrane:*
a. It separates the cell contents from its environment.
b. It is permeable to certain substances.
c. It is a lipid bilayer with embedded proteins.
d. It contains pumps for moving molecules against their concentration gradient.
e. all of the above

3. *If an animal cell is placed into a solution whose concentration of dissolved substances is higher than that inside the cell,*
a. the cell will swell
b. the cell will shrivel
c. the cell will remain the same size
d. the solution is described as hypertonic
e. both (b) and (d) are correct

4. *Small, nonpolar hydrophobic molecules such as fatty acids*
a. pass readily through a membrane's lipid bilayer
b. diffuse very slowly through the lipid bilayer
c. require special channels to enter a cell
d. are actively transported across cell membranes
e. must enter the cell via endocytosis

5. *Which of the following would be least likely to diffuse through a lipid bilayer?*
a. water
b. oxygen
c. carbon dioxide
d. sodium ions
e. the small, nonpolar molecule butane

6. *Which of the following processes causes substances to move across membranes without the expenditure of cellular energy?*
a. endocytosis
b. exocytosis
c. active transport
d. diffusion
e. pinocytosis

? Review Questions

1. Describe and diagram the structure of a plasma membrane. What are the two principal types of molecules in plasma membranes? What are the four principal functions of plasma membranes?

2. What are the three categories of proteins commonly found in plasma membranes, and what is the function of each?

3. Define *diffusion*, and compare that process to osmosis. How do these two processes help plant leaves remain firm?

4. Define *hypotonic*, *hypertonic*, and *isotonic*. What would be the fate of an animal cell immersed in each of the three types of solution?

5. Describe the following types of transport processes: simple diffusion, facilitated diffusion, active transport, pinocytosis, receptor-mediated endocytosis, phagocytosis, and exocytosis.

6. Name four types of cell-to-cell junctions and the function of each. Which junctions allow communication between the interiors of adjacent cells?

Applying the Concepts

1. Different cells have somewhat different plasma membranes. The plasma membrane of a *Paramecium*, for example, is only about 1% as permeable to water as the plasma membrane of a human red blood cell. Referring back to our discussion of the effects of osmosis on red blood cells and the role of contractile vacuoles in *Paramecium*, what do you think is the function of the low water permeability of *Paramecium*? What molecular differences do you think might account for this low water permeability?

2. A preview question for Chapter 31: The integrity of the plasma membrane is essential for cellular survival. Could the immune system utilize this fact to destroy foreign cells that have invaded the body? How might cells of the immune system disrupt membranes of foreign cells? (Two hints: Virtually all cells can secrete proteins, and some proteins form pores in membranes.)

3. A preview question for Chapter 23: Plant roots take up minerals (inorganic ions such as potassium) that are dissolved in the water of the soil. The concentration of such ions is usually much lower in the soil water than in the cytoplasm of root cells. Design the plasma membrane of a hypothetical mineral-absorbing cell, with special reference to mineral-permeable channel proteins and mineral-transporting active transport proteins. Justify your choice of channels and active-transport proteins.

4. Red blood cells will swell up and burst when placed in a hypotonic solution such as pure water. Why don't we swell up and burst when we swim in water that is hypotonic to our cells and body fluids?

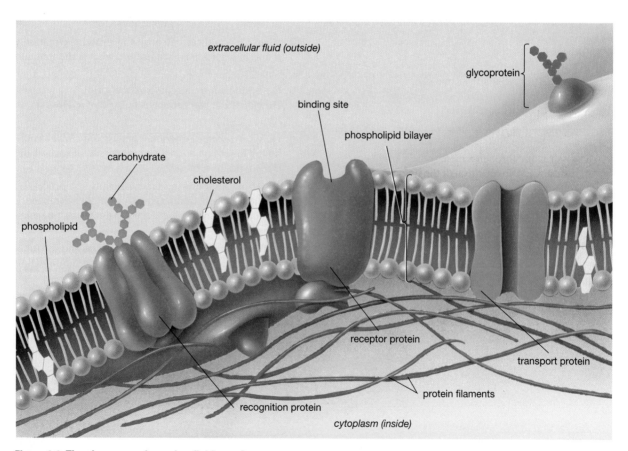

Figure 4-1 The plasma membrane is a fluid mosaic

© 2003 Prentice Hall, Inc.

NOTES

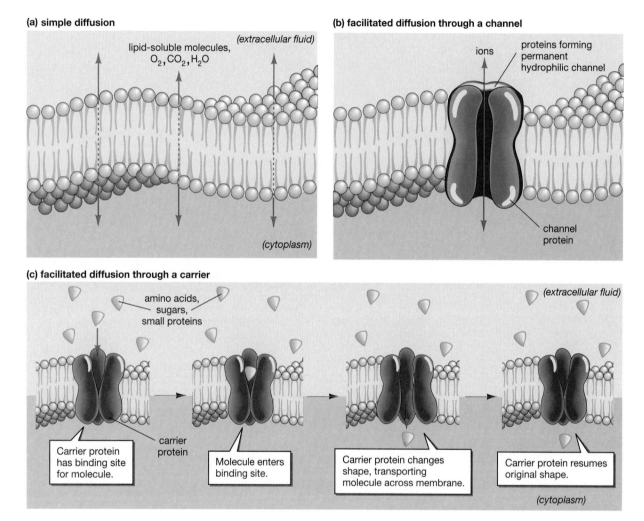

(a) simple diffusion

lipid-soluble molecules, O_2, CO_2, H_2O

(extracellular fluid)

(cytoplasm)

(b) facilitated diffusion through a channel

ions

proteins forming permanent hydrophilic channel

channel protein

(c) facilitated diffusion through a carrier

amino acids, sugars, small proteins

(extracellular fluid)

carrier protein

Carrier protein has binding site for molecule.

Molecule enters binding site.

Carrier protein changes shape, transporting molecule across membrane.

Carrier protein resumes original shape.

(cytoplasm)

Figure 4-3 Diffusion through the plasma membrane

© 2003 Prentice Hall, Inc.

NOTES

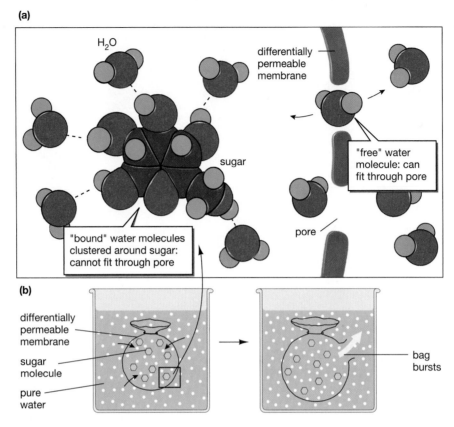

(a)

H₂O

differentially permeable membrane

"free" water molecule: can fit through pore

sugar

pore

"bound" water molecules clustered around sugar: cannot fit through pore

(b)

differentially permeable membrane

sugar molecule

pure water

bag bursts

Figure 4-4 Osmosis

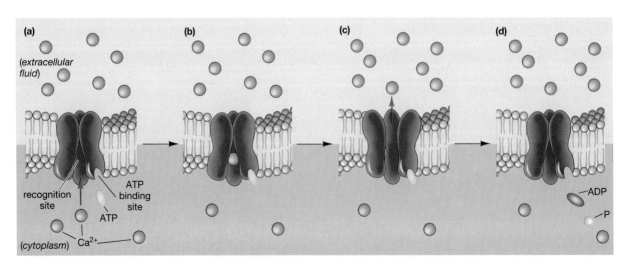

(a)

(extracellular fluid)

recognition site

ATP binding site

ATP

(cytoplasm) Ca²⁺

(b)

(c)

(d)

ADP

P

Figure 4-6 Active transport

© 2003 Prentice Hall, Inc.

NOTES

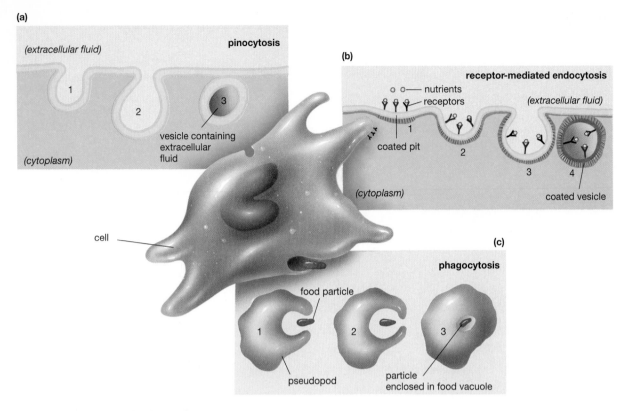

Figure 4-7 Three types of endocytosis

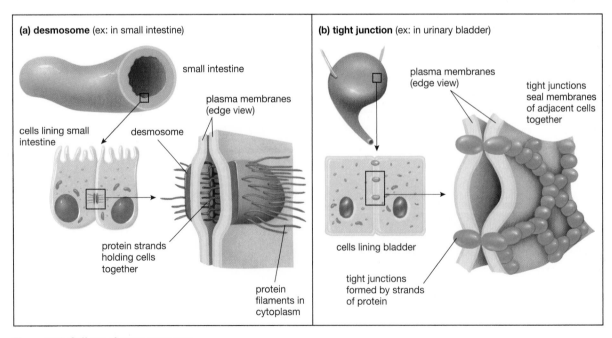

Figure 4-10 Cell attachment structures

© 2003 Prentice Hall, Inc.

NOTES

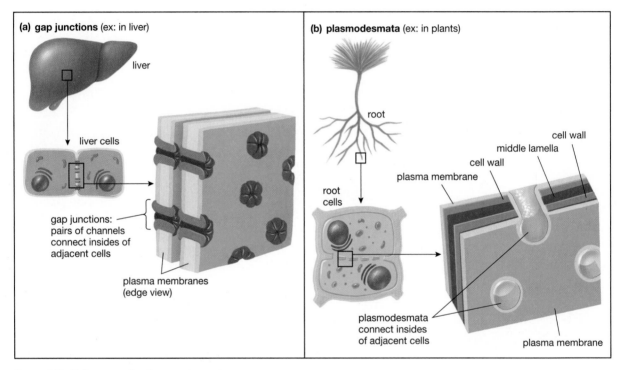

(a) gap junctions (ex: in liver)

liver

liver cells

gap junctions:
pairs of channels
connect insides of
adjacent cells

plasma membranes
(edge view)

(b) plasmodesmata (ex: in plants)

root

root
cells

plasma membrane

cell wall

middle lamella

cell wall

plasmodesmata
connect insides
of adjacent cells

plasma membrane

Figure 4-11 Cell communication structures

© 2003 Prentice Hall, Inc.

NOTES

CHAPTER 5 Cell Structure and Function

Multiple Choice

1. *The outermost boundary of an animal cell is the*
   a. plasma membrane
   b. nucleus
   c. cytoplasm
   d. cytoskeleton
   e. cell wall

2. *Which organelle contains a eukaryotic cell's chromosomes?*
   a. Golgi complex
   b. ribosomes
   c. nucleus
   d. mitochondria
   e. chloroplast

3. *Most of the cell's ATP is synthesized in the*
   a. Golgi complex
   b. ribosomes
   c. nucleus
   d. mitochondria
   e. chloroplast

4. *Which organelle sorts, chemically modifies, and packages newly synthesized protein?*
   a. Golgi complex
   b. ribosomes
   c. nucleus
   d. mitochondria
   e. chloroplast

5. *Membrane-enclosed digestive organelles that contain enzymes are called*
   a. lysosomes
   b. smooth endoplasmic reticulum
   c. cilia
   d. Golgi complex
   e. mitochondria

6. *A series of membrane-enclosed channels studded with ribosomes are called*
   a. lysosomes
   b. Golgi complex
   c. rough endoplasmic reticulum
   d. mitochondria
   e. smooth endoplasmic reticulum

? Review Questions

1. Diagram "typical" prokaryotic and eukaryotic cells, and describe their important similarities and differences.
2. Which organelles are common to both plant and animal cells, and which are unique to each?
3. Define *stroma* and *matrix*.
4. Describe the nucleus, including the nuclear envelope, chromatin, chromosomes, DNA, and the nucleolus.
5. What are the functions of mitochondria and chloroplasts? Why do scientists believe that these organelles arose from prokaryotic cells?
6. What is the function of ribosomes? Where in the cell are they typically found?
7. Describe the structure and function of the endoplasmic reticulum and Golgi complex.
8. How are lysosomes formed? What is their function?
9. Diagram the structure of cilia and flagella.

1. If muscle biopsies (samples of tissue) were taken from the legs of a world-class marathon runner and a typical couch potato, which would you expect to have a higher density of mitochondria? Why? What about a muscle biopsy from the biceps of a weight lifter?

2. One of the functions of the cytoskeleton in animal cells is to give shape to the cell. Plant cells have a fairly rigid cell wall surrounding the plasma membrane. Does this mean that a cytoskeleton is superfluous for a plant cell? Defend your answer in terms of other functions of the cytoskeleton.

3. Most cells are very small. What physical and metabolic constraints limit cell size? What problems would an enormous cell encounter? What adaptations might help a very large cell survive?

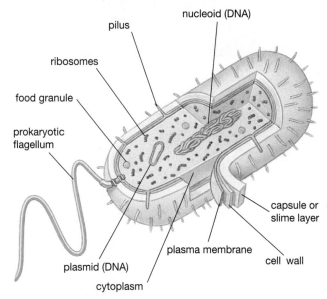

pilus

nucleoid (DNA)

ribosomes

food granule

prokaryotic
flagellum

capsule or
slime layer

plasmid (DNA)

plasma membrane

cell wall

cytoplasm

Figure 5-2 A generalized prokaryotic cell

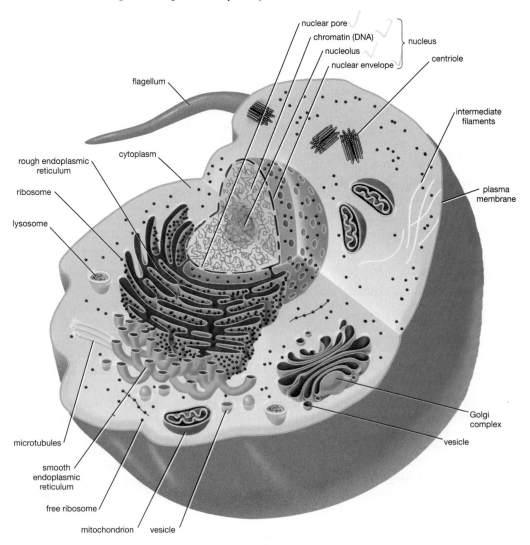

nuclear pore

chromatin (DNA)

nucleolus

nuclear envelope

nucleus

centriole

flagellum

intermediate
filaments

rough endoplasmic
reticulum

cytoplasm

plasma
membrane

ribosome

lysosome

Golgi
complex

microtubules

vesicle

smooth
endoplasmic
reticulum

free ribosome

mitochondrion

vesicle

Figure 5-3 A generalized animal cell

© 2003 Prentice Hall, Inc.

NOTES

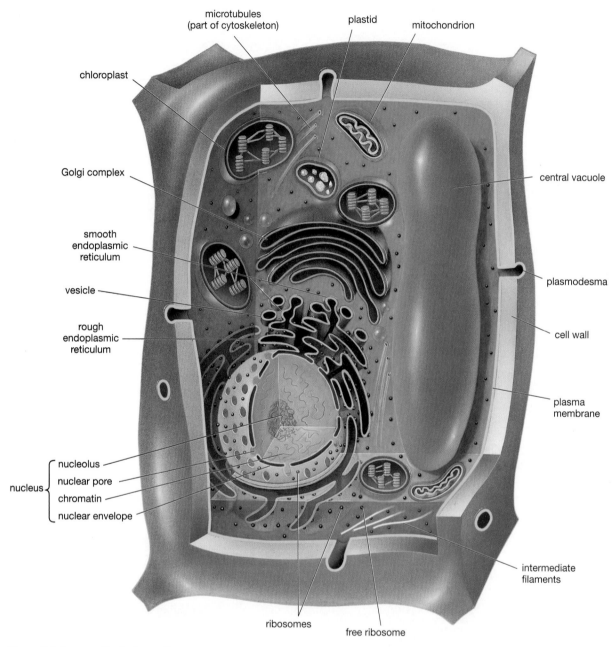

microtubules
(part of cytoskeleton)

plastid

mitochondrion

chloroplast

Golgi complex

smooth
endoplasmic
reticulum

vesicle

rough
endoplasmic
reticulum

central vacuole

plasmodesma

cell wall

plasma
membrane

nucleus
nucleolus
nuclear pore
chromatin
nuclear envelope

intermediate
filaments

ribosomes

free ribosome

Figure 5-4 A generalized plant cell

© 2003 Prentice Hall, Inc.

NOTES

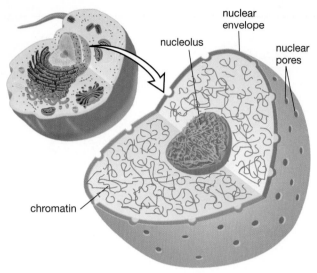

Figure 5-5 **The nucleus**

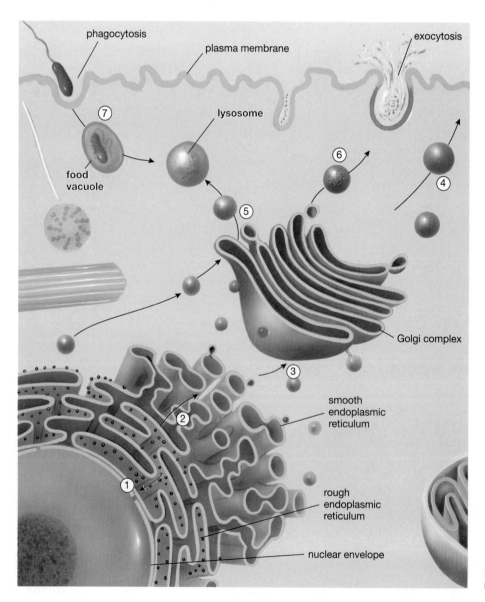

Figure 5-10 **The flow of membrane within the cell**

© 2003 Prentice Hall, Inc.

NOTES

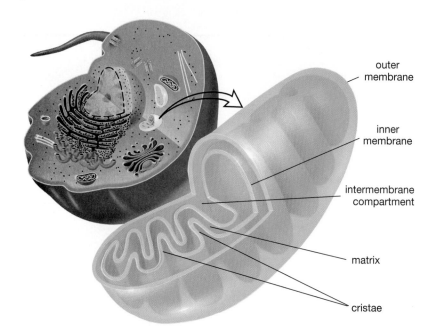

Figure 5-13 **A mitochondrion**

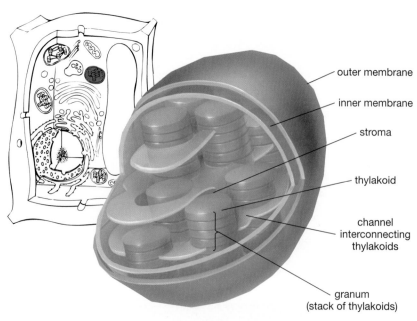

Figure 5-14 **A chloroplast**

© 2003 Prentice Hall, Inc.

NOTES

CHAPTER 6 Energy Flow in the Life of a Cell

Thinking Through the Concepts

Multiple Choice

1. *According to the first law of thermodynamics, the total amount of energy in the universe*
  a. is always increasing
  b. is always decreasing
  c. varies up and down
  d. is constant
  e. cannot be determined

2. *What is predicted by the second law of thermodynamics?*
  a. Energy is always decreasing.
  b. Disorder cannot be created or destroyed.
  c. Systems always tend toward greater states of disorder.
  d. All potential energy exists as chemical energy.
  e. all of the above

3. *Which statement about exergonic reactions is true?*
  a. The products have more energy than do the reactants.
  b. The reactants have more energy than do the products.
  c. They will not proceed spontaneously.
  d. Energy input reverses entropy.
  e. none of the above

4. *ATP is important in cells because*
  a. it transfers energy from exergonic reactions to endergonic reactions
  b. it is assembled into long chains that make up cell membranes
  c. it acts as an enzyme
  d. it accelerates diffusion
  e. all of the above

5. *How does an enzyme increase the speed of a reaction?*
  a. by changing an endergonic to an exergonic reaction
  b. by providing activation energy
  c. by lowering activation energy requirements
  d. by decreasing the concentration of reactants
  e. by increasing the concentration of products

6. *Which of the following statements about enzymes is (are) true?*
  a. They interact with specific reactants (substrates).
  b. Their three-dimensional shapes are closely related to their activities.
  c. They change the shape of the reactants.
  d. They have active sites.
  e. all of the above

? Review Questions

1. Explain why organisms do not violate the second law of thermodynamics. What is the ultimate energy source for most forms of life on Earth?

2. Define *metabolism*, and explain how reactions can be coupled to one another.

3. What is activation energy? How do catalysts affect activation energy? How does this change the rate of reactions?

4. Describe some exergonic and endergonic reactions that occur in plants and animals very regularly.

5. Describe the structure and function of enzymes. How is enzyme activity regulated?

Applying the Concepts

1. A preview question for ecology: When a brown bear eats a salmon, does the bear acquire all the energy contained in the body of the fish? Why or why not? What implications do you think this answer would have for the relative abundance (by weight) of predators and their prey? Does the second law of thermodynamics help explain the title of the book *Why Big Fierce Animals Are Rare*?

2. Many people in sub-Saharan Africa have experienced the effects of malnutrition and starvation, but the very young are most severely affected. Some individuals suffer permanent disability even if food is provided. How could a lack of food intake interfere with functions of individual cells and tissues? Which tissues are likely to suffer the most irreversible damage?

3. As you learned in Chapter 3, the subunits of virtually all organic molecules are joined by condensation reactions and can be broken apart by hydrolysis reactions. Why, then, does your digestive system produce separate enzymes to digest proteins, fats, and carbohydrates—in fact, several of each type?

4. Suppose someone tried to disprove the existence of evolution with the following argument: "According to evolutionary theory, organisms have increased in complexity through time. However, evolution of increased biological complexity contradicts the second law of thermodynamics. Therefore, evolution is impossible." How would you respond to this argument in support of evolution?

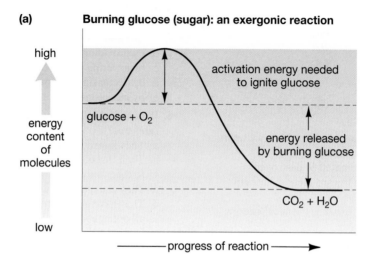

(a)   **Burning glucose (sugar): an exergonic reaction**

high

energy content of molecules

low

activation energy needed to ignite glucose

glucose + O_2

energy released by burning glucose

$CO_2 + H_2O$

progress of reaction

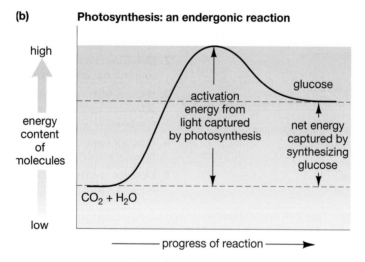

(b)   **Photosynthesis: an endergonic reaction**

high

energy content of molecules

low

activation energy from light captured by photosynthesis

glucose

net energy captured by synthesizing glucose

$CO_2 + H_2O$

progress of reaction

Figure 6-2 **Energy relations in exergonic and endergonic reactions**

© 2003 Prentice Hall, Inc.

NOTES

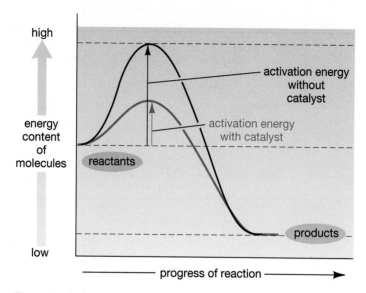

Figure 6-8 Activation energy controls the rate of chemical reactions

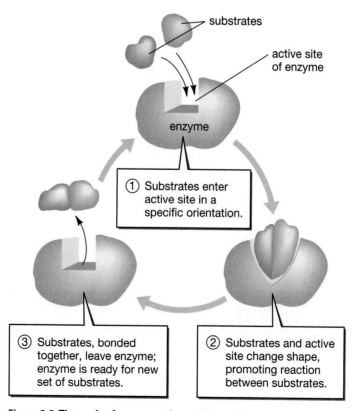

Figure 6-9 The cycle of enzyme–substrate interactions

© 2003 Prentice Hall, Inc.

NOTES

CHAPTER 7 Capturing Solar Energy: Photosynthesis

Thinking Through the Concepts

Multiple Choice

1. *Photosynthesis is measured in the leaf of a green plant exposed to different wavelengths of light. Photosynthesis is*
   a. highest in green light
   b. highest in red light
   c. highest in blue light
   d. highest in red and blue light
   e. the same at all wavelengths

2. *Where do the light-dependent reactions of photosynthesis occur?*
   a. in the stomata
   b. in the chloroplast stroma
   c. within the thylakoid membranes of the chloroplast
   d. in the leaf cell cytoplasm
   e. in leaf cell mitochondria

3. *The oxygen produced during photosynthesis comes from*
   a. the breakdown of CO_2
   b. the breakdown of H_2O
   c. the breakdown of both CO_2 and H_2O
   d. the breakdown of oxaloacetate
   e. photorespiration

4. *The role of accessory pigments is to*
   a. provide an additional photosystem to generate more ATP
   b. allow photosynthesis to occur in the dark
   c. prevent photorespiration
   d. donate electrons to chlorophyll reaction centers
   e. capture additional light energy and transfer it to the chlorophyll reaction centers

5. *The generation of ATP by electron transport in photosynthesis and cellular respiration depends on*
   a. a proton gradient across a membrane
   b. proton pumps driven by electron transport chains
   c. an ATP-synthesizing enzyme complex
   d. a, b, and c are all required for ATP generation
   e. none of the above are required for ATP generation

6. *Where do the light-independent, carbon-fixing reactions occur?*
   a. in the guard cell cytoplasm
   b. in the chloroplast stroma
   c. within the thylakoid membranes
   d. at night in the thylakoids
   e. in mitochondria

? Review Questions

1. Write the overall equation for photosynthesis. Does the overall equation differ between C_3 and C_4 plants?

2. Draw a diagram of a chloroplast, and label it. Explain specifically how chloroplast structure is related to its function.

3. Briefly describe the light-dependent and light-independent reactions. In what part of the chloroplast does each occur?

4. What is the difference between carbon fixation in C_3 and in C_4 plants? Under what conditions does each mechanism of carbon fixation work most effectively?

5. Describe the process of chemiosmosis in chloroplasts, tracing the flow of energy from sunlight to ATP.

Applying the Concepts

1. Many lawns and golf courses are planted with bluegrass, a C_3 plant. In the spring, the bluegrass grows luxuriously. In the summer, crabgrass, a weed and a C_4 plant, often appears and spreads rapidly. Explain this sequence of events, given the normal weather conditions of spring and summer and the characteristics of C_3 versus C_4 plants.

2. Suppose an experiment is performed in which plant I is supplied with normal carbon dioxide but with water that contains radioactive oxygen atoms. Plant II is supplied with normal water but with carbon dioxide that contains radioactive oxygen atoms. Each plant is allowed to perform photosynthesis, and the oxygen gas and sugars produced are tested for radioactivity. Which plant would you expect to produce radioactive sugars, and which plant would you expect to produce radioactive oxygen gas? Why?

3. You continuously monitor the photosynthetic oxygen production from the leaf of a plant illuminated by white light. Explain what will happen (and why) if you place (a) red, (b) blue, and (c) green filters between the light source and the leaf.

4. A plant is placed in a CO_2-free atmosphere in bright light. Will the light-dependent reactions continue to generate ATP and NADPH indefinitely? Explain how you reached your conclusion.

5. You are called before the Ways and Means Committee of the House of Representatives to explain why the U.S. Department of Agriculture should continue to fund photosynthesis research. How would you justify the expense of producing, by genetic engineering, the enzyme that catalyzes the reaction of RuBP with CO_2 and prevents RuBP from reacting with oxygen as well as CO_2? What are the potential applied benefits of this research?

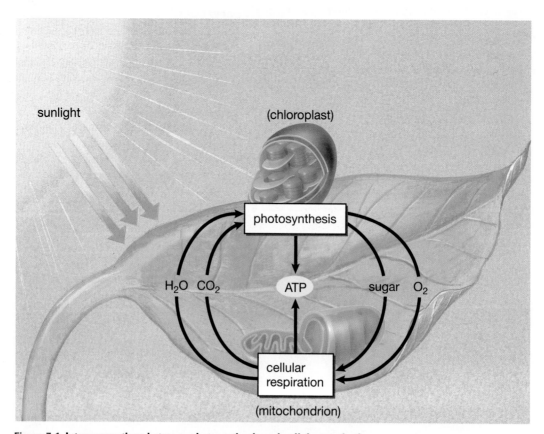

Figure 7-1 Interconnections between photosynthesis and cellular respiration

© 2003 Prentice Hall, Inc.

NOTES

chloroplast in mesophyll cell

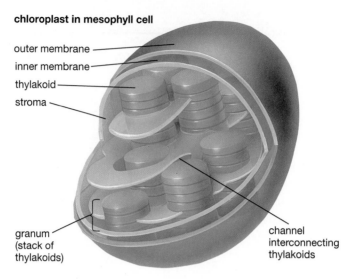

outer membrane
inner membrane
thylakoid
stroma

granum
(stack of
thylakoids)

channel
interconnecting
thylakoids

Figure 7-2 An overview of photosynthetic structures

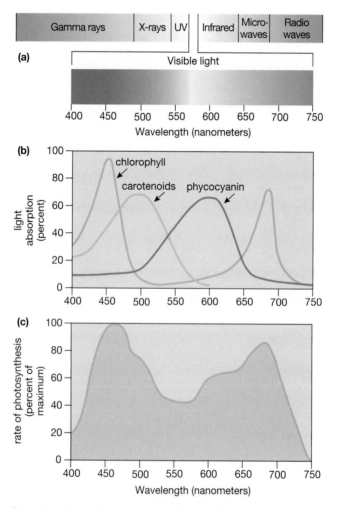

Figure 7-3 Light, chloroplast pigments, and photosynthesis

© 2003 Prentice Hall, Inc.

NOTES

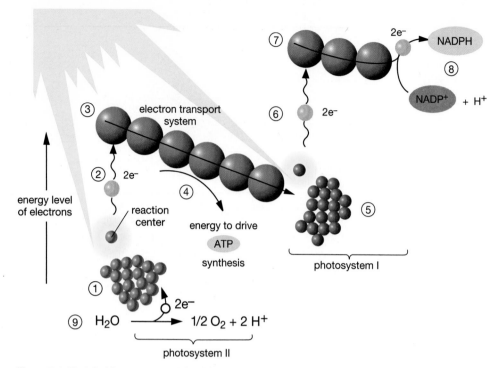

Figure 7-4 Thylakoid structure and the light-dependent reactions of photosynthesis

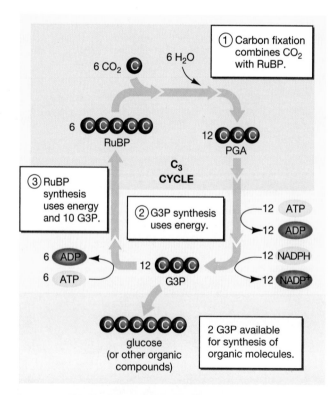

Figure 7-6 The C₃ cycle of carbon fixation

© 2003 Prentice Hall, Inc.

NOTES

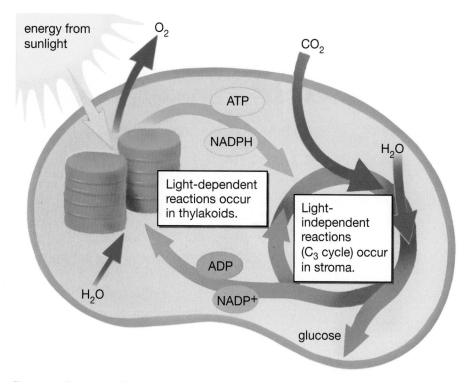

energy from sunlight

O_2

CO_2

ATP

NADPH

H_2O

Light-dependent reactions occur in thylakoids.

Light-independent reactions (C_3 cycle) occur in stroma.

ADP

NADP+

H_2O

glucose

Figure 7-7 **A summary diagram of photosynthesis**

© 2003 Prentice Hall, Inc.

NOTES

CHAPTER 8 Harvesting Energy: Glycolysis and Cellular Respiration

Thinking Through the Concepts

Multiple Choice

1. *Where does glycolysis occur?*
   a. cytoplasm
   b. matrix of mitochondria
   c. inner membrane of mitochondria
   d. outer membrane of mitochondria
   e. stroma of chloroplast

2. *Where does respiratory electron transport occur?*
   a. cytoplasm
   b. matrix of mitochondria
   c. inner membrane of mitochondria
   d. outer membrane of mitochondria
   e. stroma of chloroplast

3. *What is the product of the fermentation of sugar by yeast in bread dough that is essential for the rising of the dough?*
   a. lactate   b. ATP
   c. ethanol   d. CO_2
   e. O_2

4. *The majority of ATP produced in aerobic respiration comes from*
   a. glycolysis   b. the Krebs cycle
   c. chemiosmosis   d. fermentation
   e. photosynthesis

5. *The process that converts glucose into two molecules of pyruvate is*
   a. glycolysis   b. fermentation
   c. the Krebs cycle
   d. respiratory electron transport
   e. the Calvin-Benson cycle

6. *The process that causes lactate buildup in muscles during strenuous exercise is*
   a. glycolysis   b. fermentation
   c. the Krebs cycle
   d. respiratory electron transport
   e. the Calvin-Benson cycle

? Review Questions

1. Starting with glucose $(C_6H_{12}O_6)$, write the overall reactions for (a) aerobic respiration and (b) fermentation in yeast.

2. Draw a labeled diagram of a mitochondrion, and explain how its structure is related to its function.

3. What role do the following play in respiratory metabolism: (a) glycolysis, (b) mitochondrial matrix, (c) inner membrane of mitochondria, (d) fermentation, and (e) NAD^+?

4. Outline the major steps in (a) aerobic and (b) anaerobic respiration, indicating the sites of ATP production. What is the overall energy harvest (in terms of ATP molecules generated per glucose molecule) for each?

5. Describe the Krebs cycle. In what form is most of the energy harvested?

6. Describe the mitochondrial electron transport system and the process of chemiosmosis.

7. Why is oxygen necessary for cellular respiration to occur?

Applying the Concepts

1. Some years ago a freight train overturned, spilling a load of grain. Because the grain was unusable, it was buried in the embankment. Yeasts are common in the soil. Although there is no shortage of other food locally, the local bear population has created a nuisance by continually uncovering the grain. What do you think has happened to the grain to make them do this, and how is it related to human cultural evolution?

2. In detective novels, "the odor of bitter almonds" is the telltale clue to murder by cyanide poisoning. Cyanide works by attacking the enzyme that transfers electrons from respiratory electron transport to O_2. Why is it not possible for the victim to survive by using anaerobic respiration? Why is cyanide poisoning almost immediately fatal?

3. More than a century ago, French biochemist Louis Pasteur described a phenomenon, now called "the Pasteur effect," in the wine-making process. He observed that in a sealed container of grape juice containing yeast, the yeast will consume the sugar very slowly as long as oxygen remains in the container. As soon as the oxygen is gone, however, the rate of sugar consumption by the yeast increases greatly and the alcohol content in the container rises. Discuss the Pasteur effect on the basis of what you know about aerobic and anaerobic cellular respiration.

4. Some species of bacteria that live at the surface of sediment on the bottom of lakes are facultative anaerobes; that is, they are capable of either aerobic or anaerobic respiration. How will their metabolism change during the summer when the deep water becomes anoxic (deoxygenated)? If the bacteria continue to grow at the same rate, will glycolysis increase, decrease, or remain the same after the lake becomes anoxic? Explain why.

5. The dumping of large amounts of raw sewage into rivers or lakes typically leads to massive fish kills, although sewage itself is not toxic to fish. Similar fish kills also occur in shallow lakes that become covered in ice during the winter. What kills the fish? How might you reduce fish mortality after raw sewage is accidentally released into a small pond containing large bass?

6. Although respiration occurs in all living cells, different cells respire at different rates. Explain why. How could you predict the relative respiratory rates of different tissues in a fish by microscopic examination of cells?

7. Imagine that a starving cell reached the stage where every bit of its ATP was depleted and converted to ADP plus phosphate. If that cell were placed in fresh nutrient broth at this point, will it recover and survive? Explain your answer based on what you know of glucose breakdown.

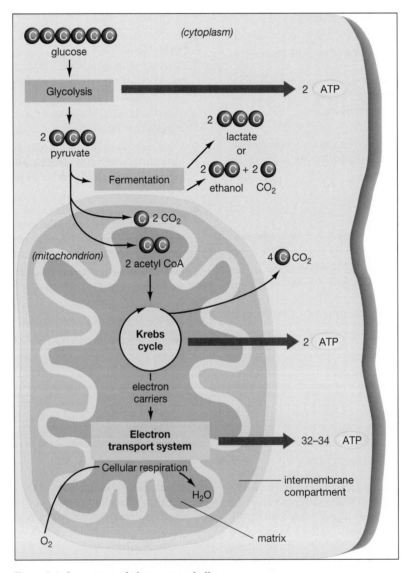

Figure 8-1 A summary of glucose metabolism

© 2003 Prentice Hall, Inc.

NOTES

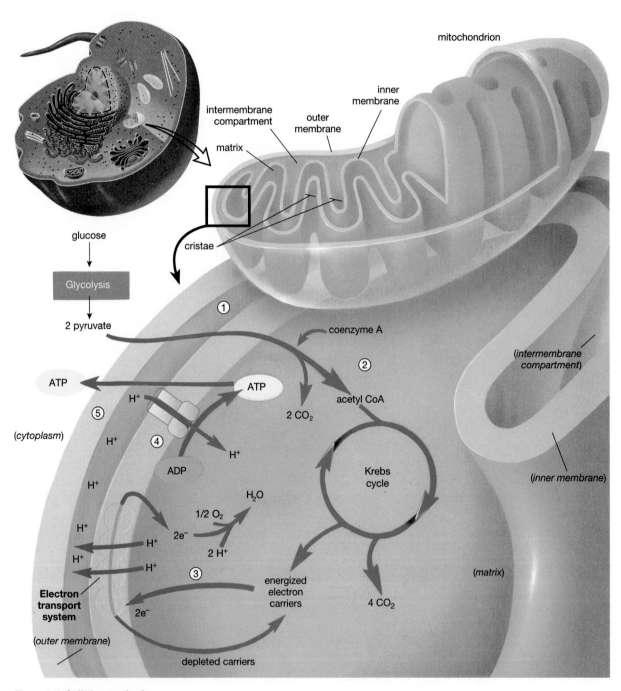

Figure 8-4 Cellular respiration

© 2003 Prentice Hall, Inc.

NOTES

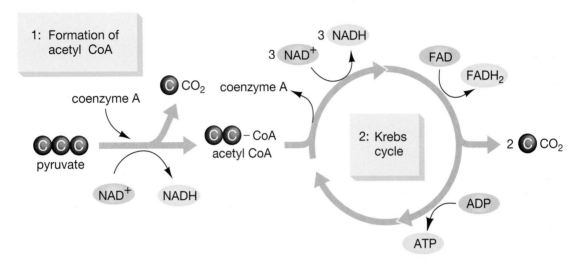

Figure 8-5 **The essential reactions in the mitochondrial matrix**

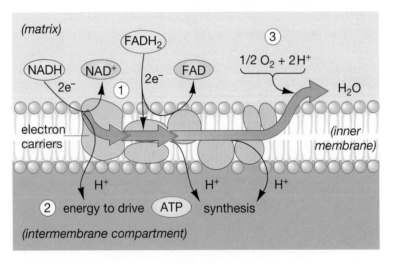

Figure 8-6 **The electron transport system of mitochondria**

© 2003 Prentice Hall, Inc.

NOTES

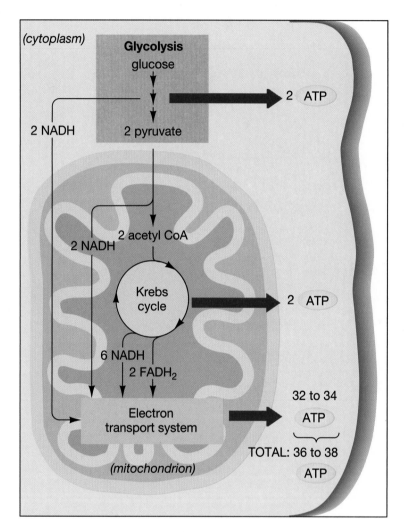

Figure 8-7 The energy harvest from the complete metabolism of one glucose molecule

© 2003 Prentice Hall, Inc.

NOTES

CHAPTER 9 DNA: The Molecule of Heredity

Multiple Choice

1. *How many different possible base sequences are there in a nucleotide chain three nucleotides in length?*
   a. 1
   b. 3
   c. 9
   d. 64
   e. more than 64

2. *Because each base pairs with a complementary base, in every DNA molecule the amount of*
   a. cytosine equals that of guanine
   b. cytosine equals that of thymine
   c. cytosine equals that of adenine
   d. each nucleotide is unrelated to all others
   e. each nucleotide is equal to all others

3. *Semiconservative replication refers to the fact that*
   a. each new DNA molecule contains two new single DNA strands
   b. DNA polymerase uses free nucleotides to synthesize new DNA molecules
   c. certain bases pair with specific bases
   d. each parental DNA strand is joined with a new strand containing complementary base pairs
   e. mistakes are made during DNA replication

4. *DNA helicase*
   a. cleaves hydrogen bonds that join the two strands of DNA
   b. converts two single strands of DNA into a double helix
   c. is a unique form of DNA
   d. adds nucleotides to newly forming DNA molecules
   e. proofreads the newly formed DNA strand

5. *DNA polymerase*
   a. can advance in either direction along a single strand of DNA
   b. cleaves hydrogen bonds that join the two strands of DNA
   c. creates a polymer that consists of many molecules of DNA
   d. adds appropriate nucleotides to a newly forming DNA strand
   e. is the protein found in conjunction with DNA in eukaryotic chromosomes

6. *Which of the following are incorrectly matched?*
   a. complementary base pairs ↔ adenine and cytosine
   b. bases ↔ adenine, thymine, cytosine, and guanine
   c. nucleotide ↔ phosphate and sugar and base
   d. eukaryotic chromosome ↔ DNA and protein
   e. enzymes involved in DNA replication ↔ DNA polymerase and DNA helicase

? Review Questions

1. Draw the general structure of a nucleotide. Which parts are identical in all nucleotides, and which can vary?

2. Name the four types of nitrogen-containing bases found in DNA.

3. Which bases are complementary to one another? How are they held together in the double helix of DNA?

4. Describe the structure of DNA. Where are the bases, sugars, and phosphates in the structure?

5. Describe the process of DNA replication.

Applying the Concepts

1. As you learned in "Scientific Inquiry: The Discovery of the Double Helix," scientists in different laboratories often compete with one another to make new discoveries. Do you think this competition helps promote scientific discoveries? Sometimes, researchers in different laboratories collaborate with one another. What advantages does collaboration offer over competition? What factors might provide barriers to collaboration and lead to competition?

2. Today, scientific advances are being made at an astounding rate, and nowhere is this more evident than in our understanding of the biology of heredity. Using DNA as a starting point, do you believe there are limits to the knowledge people should acquire? Defend your answer.

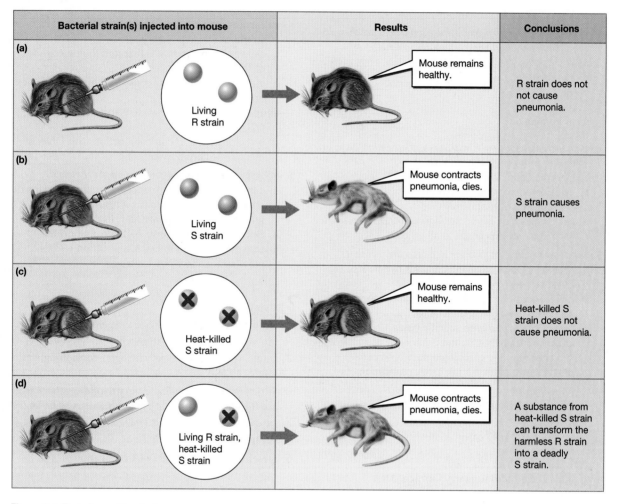

Figure 9-1 Transformed bacteria

© 2003 Prentice Hall, Inc.

NOTES

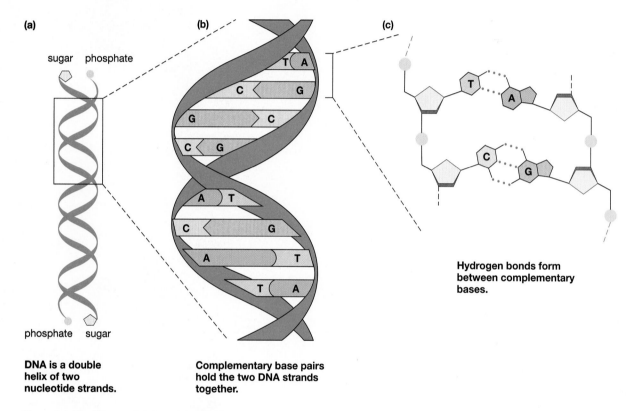

(a)

sugar   phosphate

phosphate   sugar

DNA is a double helix of two nucleotide strands.

(b)

Complementary base pairs hold the two DNA strands together.

(c)

Hydrogen bonds form between complementary bases.

Figure 9-3 The Watson-Crick model of DNA structure

© 2003 Prentice Hall, Inc.

NOTES

(a) Continuous versus segmented DNA replication

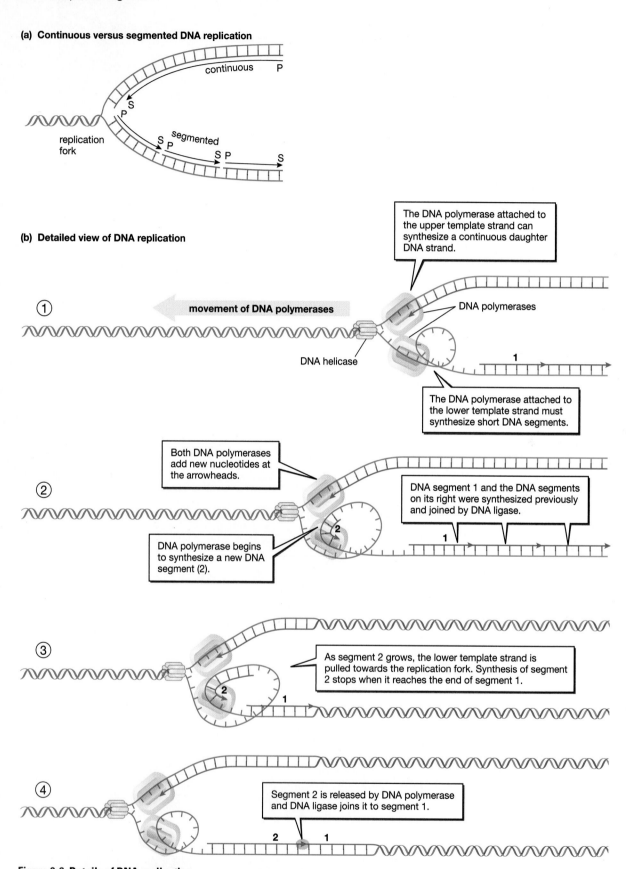

(b) Detailed view of DNA replication

The DNA polymerase attached to the upper template strand can synthesize a continuous daughter DNA strand.

① movement of DNA polymerases

DNA polymerases

DNA helicase

The DNA polymerase attached to the lower template strand must synthesize short DNA segments.

Both DNA polymerases add new nucleotides at the arrowheads.

② DNA segment 1 and the DNA segments on its right were synthesized previously and joined by DNA ligase.

DNA polymerase begins to synthesize a new DNA segment (2).

③ As segment 2 grows, the lower template strand is pulled towards the replication fork. Synthesis of segment 2 stops when it reaches the end of segment 1.

④ Segment 2 is released by DNA polymerase and DNA ligase joins it to segment 1.

Figure 9-6 Details of DNA replication

© 2003 Prentice Hall, Inc.

NOTES

CHAPTER 10 Gene Expression and Regulation

Multiple Choice

1. *A gene*
   a. is synonymous with a chromosome
   b. is composed of mRNA
   c. is a specific segment of nucleotides in DNA
   d. contains only those nucleotides required to synthesize a protein
   e. specifies the sequence of nutrients required by the body

2. *Which of the following is a single-stranded molecule that contains the information for assembly of a specific protein?*
   a. transfer RNA
   b. messenger RNA
   c. exon DNA
   d. intron DNA
   e. ribosomal RNA

3. Anticodon *is the term applied to*
   a. the list of amino acids that corresponds to the genetic code
   b. the concept that multiple codons sometimes code for a single amino acid
   c. the part of the tRNA that interacts with the codon
   d. the several three-nucleotide stretches that code for "stop"
   e. the part of the tRNA that binds to an amino acid

4. *DNA*
   a. takes part directly in protein synthesis by leaving the nucleus and being translated on the ribosome
   b. takes part indirectly in protein synthesis; the DNA itself stays in the nucleus
   c. has nothing to do with protein synthesis; it is involved only in cell division
   d. is involved in protein synthesis within the nucleus
   e. codes for mRNA but not for tRNA or rRNA

5. *Synthesis of a protein based on the sequence of messenger RNA*
   a. is catalyzed by DNA polymerase
   b. is catalyzed by RNA polymerase
   c. is called *translation*
   d. is called *transcription*
   e. occurs in the nucleus

6. *A Barr body is*
   a. a condensed X chromosome
   b. an organelle involved in protein synthesis
   c. another term for chromosomes as they are seen during cell division
   d. visible in cells of both males and females
   e. present only in males, because their female chromosomes are inactivated

? Review Questions

1. How does RNA differ from DNA?

2. What are the three types of RNA? What is the function of each?

3. Define the following terms: *genetic code*; *codon*; *anticodon*. What is the relationship among the bases in DNA, the codons of mRNA, and the anticodons of tRNA?

4. How is mRNA formed from a eukaryotic gene?

5. Diagram and describe protein synthesis.

6. Explain how complementary base pairing is involved in both transcription and translation.

7. Describe some mechanisms of gene regulation.

8. Define *mutation*, and give one example of how a mutation might occur. Would you expect most mutations to be beneficial or harmful? Explain your answer.

Applying the Concepts

1. Some antibiotics, such as erythromycin and streptomycin, bind to the small ribosomal subunit in bacteria and inhibit translation. Why do these drugs kill bacteria? How might bacteria evolve so that they become resistant to such antibiotics?

2. Although they are rare, male calico cats do occur. In fact, about 1 in 3000 calico cats is a male. Can you come up with an explanation that explains the origin of male calico cats? Most male calico cats are infertile. Why? About 1 in 10,000 male calico cats is fertile. Considering chromosomes, genes, and mutations, can you explain the differences between infertile and fertile male calico cats?

3. As you have learned in this chapter, many factors influence gene expression, including hormones. The use of anabolic steroids and growth hormones among athletes has created controversy in recent years. Hormones certainly affect gene expression, but, in the broadest sense, so do vitamins and foods. What do you think are appropriate guidelines for the use of hormones? Should athletes take steroids or growth hormones? Should children at risk of being unusually short be given growth hormones? Should parents be allowed to request growth hormones for their children of normal height in the hope of producing a future basketball player?

(a) Growth characteristics of normal and mutant *Neurospora* on simple medium with different supplements show that defects in a single gene lead to defects in a single enzyme.

		Supplements Added to Medium				CONCLUSIONS
		none	Arginine	Citrulline	Ornithine	
Normal *Neurospora*						Normal *Neurospora* can synthesize arginine, citrulline, and ornithine.
Mutants with single gene defect	A					Mutant A grows only if arginine is added. It cannot synthesize arginine because it has a defect in enzyme 2; gene A is needed for synthesis of arginine.
	B					Mutant B grows if either arginine or citrulline are added. It cannot synthesize arginine because it has a defect in enzyme 1. Gene B is needed for synthesis of citrulline.

(b) The biochemical pathway for synthesis of the amino acid arginine involves two steps, each catalyzed by a different enzyme.

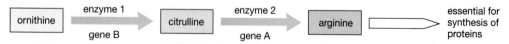

Figure 10-1 **Beadle and Tatum's experiments with *Neurospora* mutants**

© 2003 Prentice Hall, Inc.

NOTES

(a) mRNA

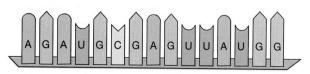

(b) ribosome (contains rRNA)

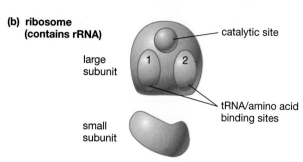

catalytic site

large subunit

tRNA/amino acid binding sites

small subunit

(c) transfer RNA

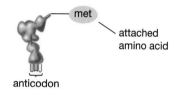

met

attached amino acid

anticodon

Figure 10-2 Cells synthesize three major types of RNA

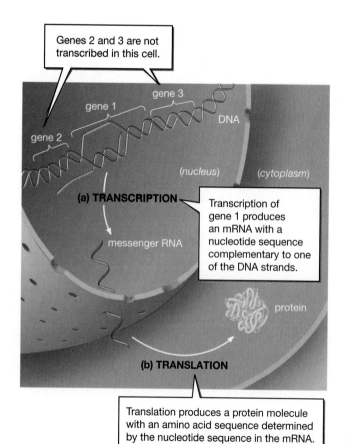

Genes 2 and 3 are not transcribed in this cell.

gene 2   gene 1   gene 3

DNA

(nucleus)   (cytoplasm)

(a) TRANSCRIPTION

Transcription of gene 1 produces an mRNA with a nucleotide sequence complementary to one of the DNA strands.

messenger RNA

protein

(b) TRANSLATION

Translation produces a protein molecule with an amino acid sequence determined by the nucleotide sequence in the mRNA.

Figure 10-3 Genetic information flows from DNA to RNA to protein

© 2003 Prentice Hall, Inc.

NOTES

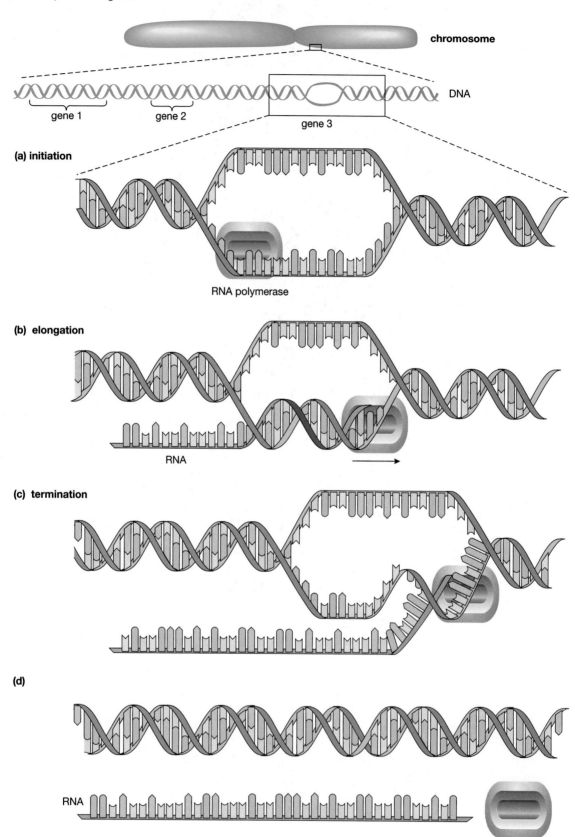

chromosome

DNA

gene 1   gene 2   gene 3

(a) initiation

RNA polymerase

(b) elongation

RNA

(c) termination

(d)

RNA

Figure 10-4 Transcription occurs in three steps

© 2003 Prentice Hall, Inc.

NOTES

_____

INITIATION:

(a) A tRNA with an attached methionine amino acid binds to a small ribosomal subunit, forming an initiation complex.

(b) The initiation complex binds to the end of an mRNA and travels down until it encounters an AUG codon in the mRNA. The anticodon of the tRNA in the initiation complex forms base pairs with the AUG codon.

(c) The large ribosomal subunit binds to the small subunit, with the mRNA between the two subunits. The methionine tRNA is in the first tRNA site on the large subunit.

ELONGATION:

(d) The second tRNA enters the second tRNA site on the large ribosomal subunit. Which tRNA binds depends on the ability of its anticodon (CAA in this example) to base pair with the codon (GUU in this example) in the mRNA. tRNAs with a CAA anticodon carry an attached valine amino acid, which was added to it by enzymes in the cytoplasm.

(e) The catalytic site on the large subunit catalyzes the formation of a peptide bond linking the amino acids methionine to valine. The two amino acids are now attached to the tRNA in the second binding position.

(f) The "empty" tRNA is released and the ribosome moves down the mRNA, one codon to the right. The tRNA that is attached to the two amino acids is now in the first tRNA binding site and the second tRNA binding site is empty.

ribosome moves one codon to right

TERMINATION:

(g) Another tRNA enters the second tRNA binding site carrying its attached amino acid. The tRNA has an anticodon that can base pair with the codon. In this example, the CAU mRNA codon pairs with a GUA tRNA anticodon. The tRNA molecule carries the amino acid histidine (his).

(h) The catalytic site forms a new peptide bond, in this example, between the valine and the histidine. A three-amino acid chain is now attached to the tRNA in the second tRNA binding site. The empty tRNA in the first site is released and the ribosome moves one codon to the right.

(i) The binding of appropriate tRNAs and formation of peptide bonds between the amino acids continues until the ribosome reaches one of three STOP codons, in this example, UAG. No tRNA binds to STOP codons. Instead, protein "release factors" signal the ribosome to release the newly made protein. The mRNA is also released and the large and small subunits separate.

Figure 10-6 Translation is the process of protein synthesis

© 2003 Prentice Hall, Inc.

NOTES

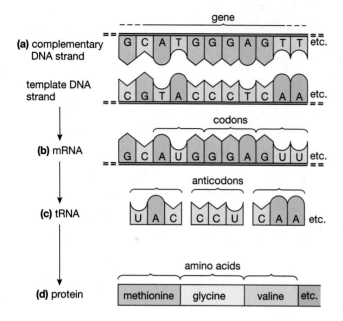

Figure 10-7 Complementary base pairing is critical at each step in decoding genetic information

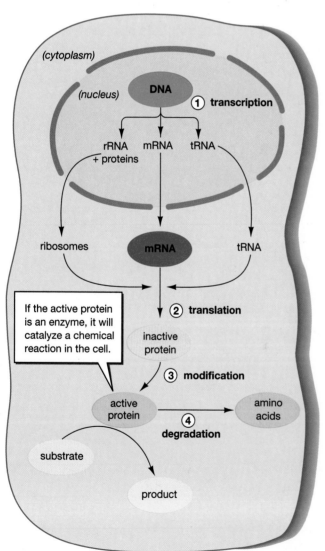

Figure 10-8 An overview of "information flow" in a cell

© 2003 Prentice Hall, Inc.

NOTES

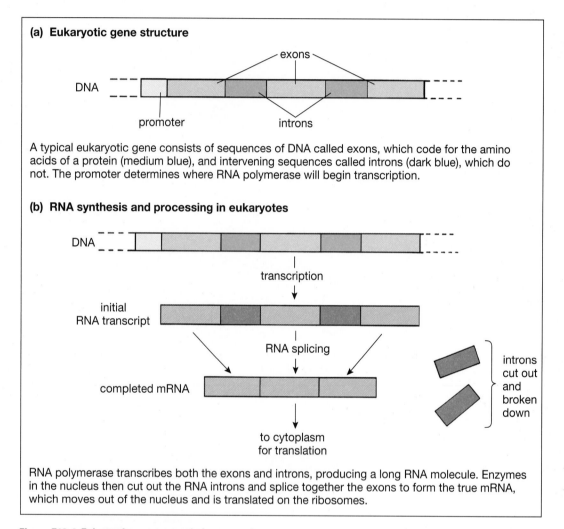

(a) Eukaryotic gene structure

A typical eukaryotic gene consists of sequences of DNA called exons, which code for the amino acids of a protein (medium blue), and intervening sequences called introns (dark blue), which do not. The promoter determines where RNA polymerase will begin transcription.

(b) RNA synthesis and processing in eukaryotes

RNA polymerase transcribes both the exons and introns, producing a long RNA molecule. Enzymes in the nucleus then cut out the RNA introns and splice together the exons to form the true mRNA, which moves out of the nucleus and is translated on the ribosomes.

Figure E10-4 Eukaryotic genes contain introns and exons

© 2003 Prentice Hall, Inc.

NOTES

CHAPTER 11 The Continuity of Life: Cellular Reproduction

Thinking Through the Concepts

Multiple Choice

1. *At which stage of mitosis are chromosomes arranged along a plane at the midline of the cell?*
   a. anaphase
   b. telophase
   c. metaphase
   d. prophase
   e. interphase

2. *A diploid cell contains in its nucleus*
   a. an even number of chromosomes
   b. an odd number of chromosomes
   c. one copy of each homologue
   d. either an even or an odd number of chromosomes
   e. two sister chromatids of each chromosome during G_1

3. *Synthesis of new DNA occurs during*
   a. prophase
   b. interphase
   c. mitosis
   d. cytokinesis
   e. formation of the cell plate

4. *Which statement is most correct?*
   a. All mutations are harmful.
   b. Both mitosis and meiosis add to genetic diversity.
   c. Crossing over helps each gamete get a different set of alleles in meiosis.
   d. Mitosis always makes diploid daughter cells; meiosis always produces gametes.
   e. The only haploid cells are gametes.

5. *When do homologous chromosomes pair up?*
   a. only in mitosis
   b. only in meiosis I
   c. only in meiosis II
   d. in both mitosis and meiosis
   e. in neither mitosis nor meiosis

6. *Curiously, there is no crossing over of any chromosome in the male fruit fly* Drosophila, *which has four pairs of chromosomes. How many different combinations of maternal vs. paternal chromosomes are possible in a male fruit fly's sperm?*
   a. 2
   b. 4
   c. 8
   d. 16
   e. many more than the above

? Review Questions

1. Diagram and describe the eukaryotic cell cycle. Name the various phases, and briefly describe the events that occur during each. What is the role of the cell cycle in a human?

2. Define *mitosis* and *cytokinesis*. What changes in cell structure result when cytokinesis does not occur after mitosis?

3. Diagram the stages of mitosis. How does mitosis ensure that each daughter nucleus receives a full set of chromosomes?

4. Define the following terms: *homologous chromosome, centromere, kinetochore, chromatid, diploid, haploid.*

5. Describe and compare the process of cytokinesis in animal cells and in plant cells.

6. Diagram the events of meiosis. At which stage do homologous chromosomes separate?

7. Describe homologue pairing and crossing over. At which stage of meiosis do they occur? Name two functions of chiasmata.

8. In what ways are mitosis and meiosis similar? In what ways are they different?

9. Describe how meiosis provides for genetic variability. If an animal had a haploid number of 2 (no sex chromosomes), how many genetically different types of gametes could it produce? (Assume no crossing over.) If it had a haploid number of 5?

Applying the Concepts

1. Nerve cells in the adult human central nervous system, as well as heart muscle cells, remain in the G_0 portion of interphase. In contrast, cells lining the inside of the small intestine divide frequently. Discuss this difference in terms of why damage to the nervous system and heart muscle cells (such as caused by a stroke or heart attack) is so dangerous. What do you think might happen to tissues such as the intestinal lining if some disorder or drug blocked mitoses in all cells of the body?

2. Cancer cells divide out of control. Side effects of chemotherapy and radiation therapy that fight cancers include loss of hair and of the gastrointestinal lining, producing severe nausea. Note that cells in hair follicles and intestinal lining divide frequently. What can you infer about the mechanisms of these treatments? What would you look for in an improved cancer therapy?

3. Some animal species can reproduce either asexually or sexually, depending on the state of the environment. Asexual reproduction tends to occur in stable, favorable environments; sexual reproduction is more common in unstable and/or unfavorable circumstances. Discuss the advantages or disadvantages this behavior might have on survival of the species in an evolutionary sense or on survival of individuals.

4. Would you predict that a clone produced as Dolly was would be a carbon copy of the animal from which the nucleus was obtained? What factors might cause the two sheep to differ? What variables might cause a human clone to differ from the individual who donated the genetic material?

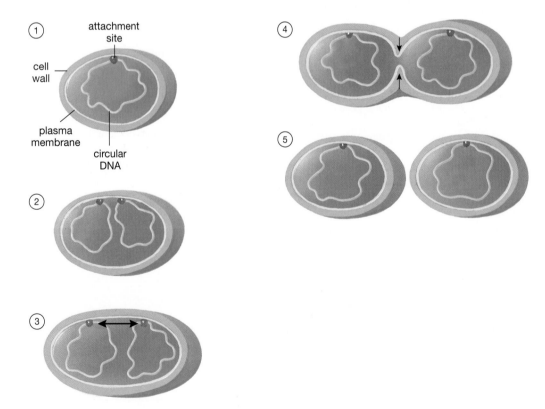

Figure 11-1 Prokaryotic cells divide by binary fission

© 2003 Prentice Hall, Inc.

NOTES

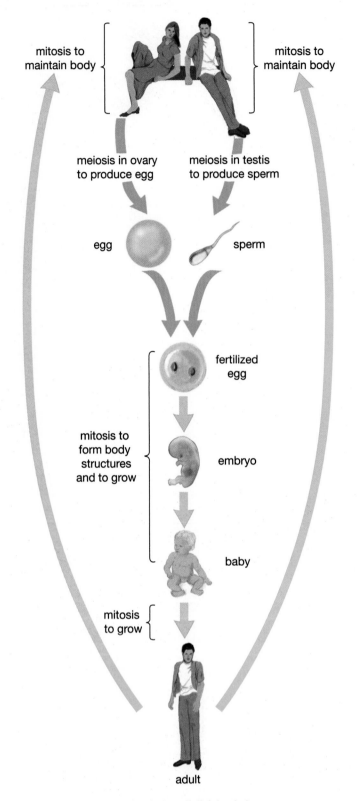

mitosis to
maintain body

mitosis to
maintain body

meiosis in ovary
to produce egg

meiosis in testis
to produce sperm

egg

sperm

fertilized
egg

mitosis to
form body
structures
and to grow

embryo

baby

mitosis
to grow

adult

Figure 11-5 Mitotic and meiotic cell division in humans

© 2003 Prentice Hall, Inc.

NOTES

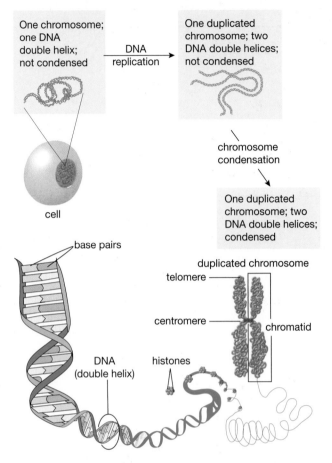

Figure 11-6 Chromosome condensation

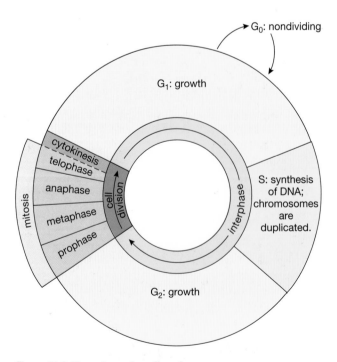

Figure 11-9 The eukaryotic cell cycle

© 2003 Prentice Hall, Inc.

NOTES

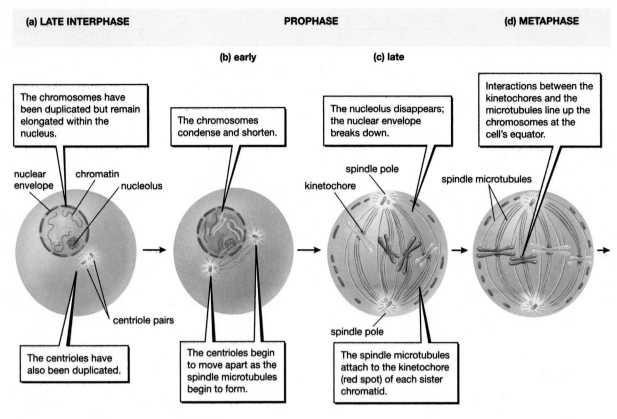

(a) LATE INTERPHASE

PROPHASE

(d) METAPHASE

(b) early

(c) late

The chromosomes have been duplicated but remain elongated within the nucleus.

The chromosomes condense and shorten.

The nucleolus disappears; the nuclear envelope breaks down.

Interactions between the kinetochores and the microtubules line up the chromosomes at the cell's equator.

nuclear envelope

chromatin

nucleolus

spindle pole

kinetochore

spindle microtubules

centriole pairs

The centrioles have also been duplicated.

The centrioles begin to move apart as the spindle microtubules begin to form.

spindle pole

The spindle microtubules attach to the kinetochore (red spot) of each sister chromatid.

Figure 11-11 **The cell cycle in an animal cell**

© 2003 Prentice Hall, Inc.

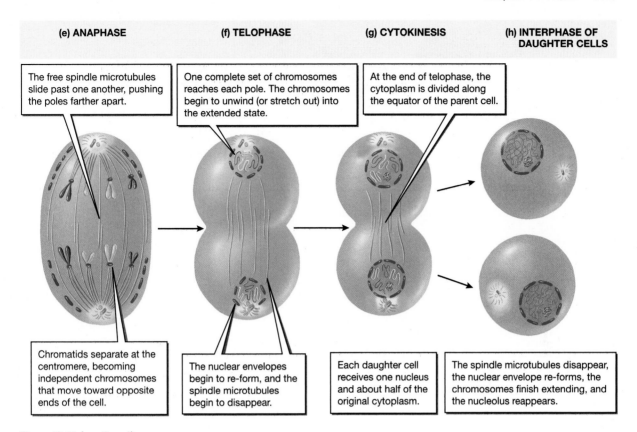

| (e) ANAPHASE | (f) TELOPHASE | (g) CYTOKINESIS | (h) INTERPHASE OF DAUGHTER CELLS |

The free spindle microtubules slide past one another, pushing the poles farther apart.

One complete set of chromosomes reaches each pole. The chromosomes begin to unwind (or stretch out) into the extended state.

At the end of telophase, the cytoplasm is divided along the equator of the parent cell.

Chromatids separate at the centromere, becoming independent chromosomes that move toward opposite ends of the cell.

The nuclear envelopes begin to re-form, and the spindle microtubules begin to disappear.

Each daughter cell receives one nucleus and about half of the original cytoplasm.

The spindle microtubules disappear, the nuclear envelope re-forms, the chromosomes finish extending, and the nucleolus reappears.

Figure 11-11 *(continued)*

NOTES

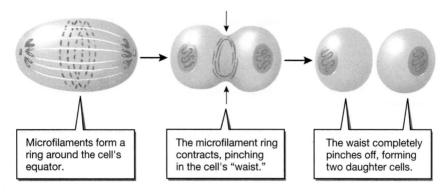

Microfilaments form a ring around the cell's equator.

The microfilament ring contracts, pinching in the cell's "waist."

The waist completely pinches off, forming two daughter cells.

Figure 11-12 **Cytokinesis in an animal cell**

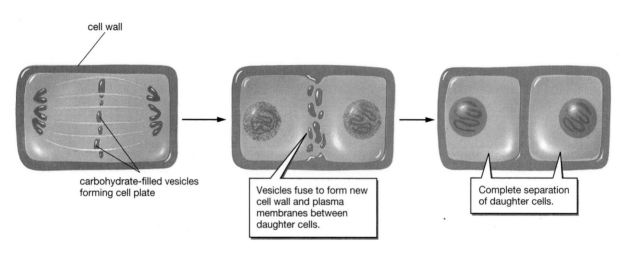

cell wall

carbohydrate-filled vesicles forming cell plate

Vesicles fuse to form new cell wall and plasma membranes between daughter cells.

Complete separation of daughter cells.

Figure 11-13 **Cytokinesis in a plant cell**

© 2003 Prentice Hall, Inc.

NOTES

MEIOSIS I

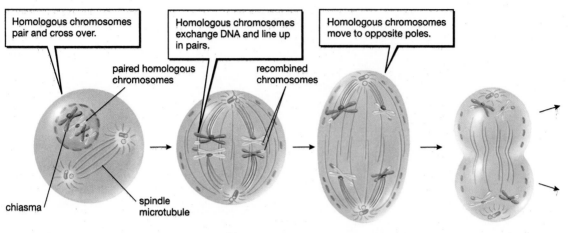

Homologous chromosomes pair and cross over.

Homologous chromosomes exchange DNA and line up in pairs.

Homologous chromosomes move to opposite poles.

paired homologous chromosomes

recombined chromosomes

chiasma

spindle microtubule

(a) Prophase I. Duplicated chromosomes condense. Homologous chromosomes pair up and chiasmata occur as chromatids of homologues exchange parts. The nuclear envelope disintegrates, and spindle microtubules form.

(b) Metaphase I. Paired homologous chromosomes line up along the equator of the cell. One homologue of each pair faces each pole of the cell and attaches to spindle microtubules via its kinetochore (red).

(c) Anaphase I. Homologues separate, one member of each pair going to each pole of the cell. Sister chromatids do not separate.

(d) Telophase I. Spindle microtubules disappear. Two clusters of chromosomes have formed, each containing one member of each pair of homologues. The daughter nuclei are therefore haploid. Cytokinesis commonly occurs at this stage. There is little or no interphase between meiosis I and meiosis II.

Figure 11-14 The details of meiotic cell division

© 2003 Prentice Hall, Inc.

MEIOSIS II

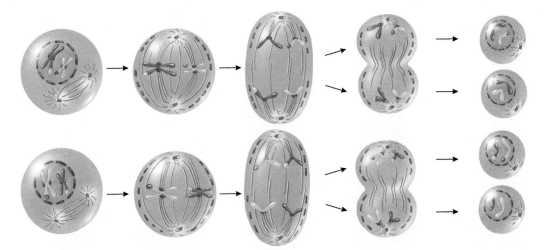

(e) Prophase II.
If chromosomes
have relaxed after
telophase I, they
recondense. Spindle
microtubules re-form
and attach to the
sister chromatids.

(f) Metaphase II.
Chromosomes line
up along the equator,
with sister chromatids
of each chromosome
attached to spindle
microtubules that lead
to opposite poles.

(g) Anaphase II.
Chromatids separate
into independent
daughter chromosomes,
one former chromatid
moving toward each
pole.

(h) Telophase II.
Chromosomes finish
moving to opposite
poles. Nuclear
envelopes re-form,
and the chromosomes
become extended
again (not shown here).

(i) Four haploid cells.
Cytokinesis results in
four haploid cells, each
containing one member
of each pair of
homologous
chromosomes (shown
here in condensed state).

Figure 11-14 *(continued)*

NOTES

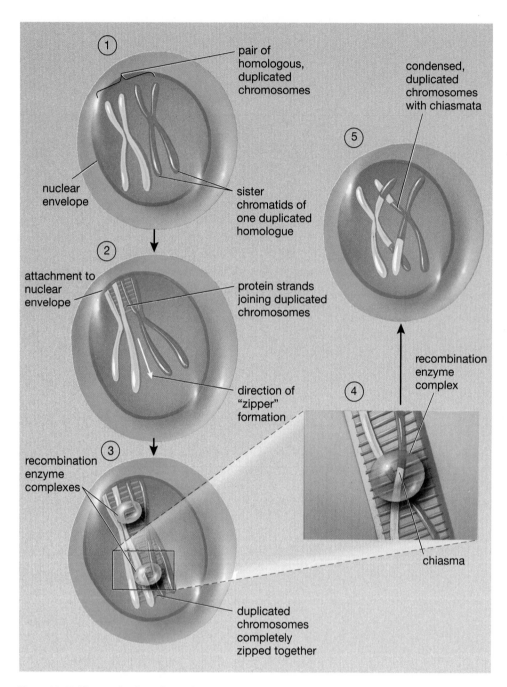

Figure 11-15 **The mechanism of crossing over**

© 2003 Prentice Hall, Inc.

NOTES

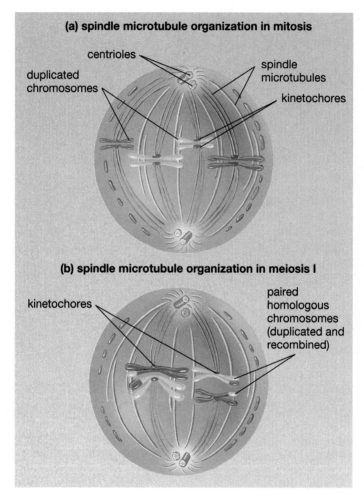

Figure 11-16 A comparison of the spindles formed during mitosis and meiosis I

© 2003 Prentice Hall, Inc.

NOTES

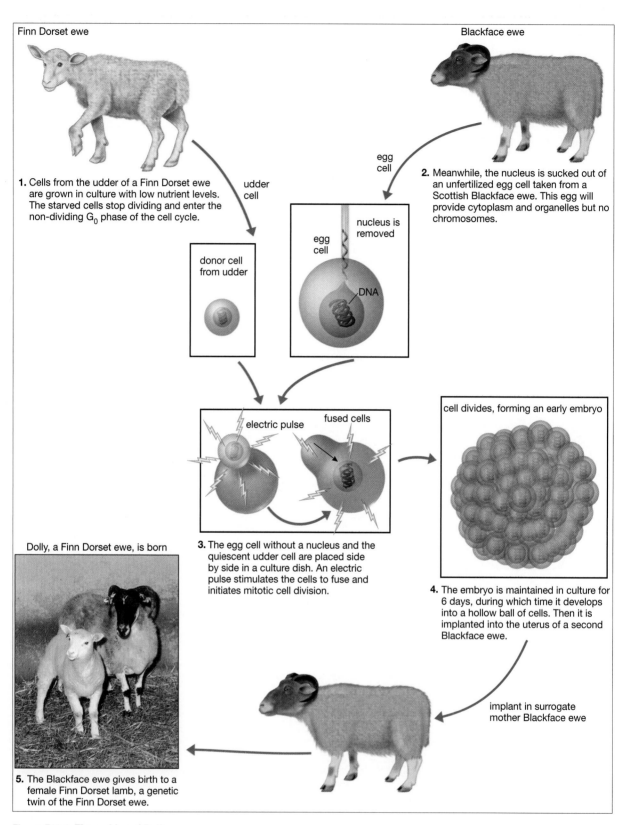

Finn Dorset ewe

Blackface ewe

1. Cells from the udder of a Finn Dorset ewe are grown in culture with low nutrient levels. The starved cells stop dividing and enter the non-dividing G_0 phase of the cell cycle.

udder cell

egg cell

2. Meanwhile, the nucleus is sucked out of an unfertilized egg cell taken from a Scottish Blackface ewe. This egg will provide cytoplasm and organelles but no chromosomes.

donor cell from udder

egg cell

nucleus is removed

DNA

cell divides, forming an early embryo

electric pulse   fused cells

Dolly, a Finn Dorset ewe, is born

3. The egg cell without a nucleus and the quiescent udder cell are placed side by side in a culture dish. An electric pulse stimulates the cells to fuse and initiates mitotic cell division.

4. The embryo is maintained in culture for 6 days, during which time it develops into a hollow ball of cells. Then it is implanted into the uterus of a second Blackface ewe.

implant in surrogate mother Blackface ewe

5. The Blackface ewe gives birth to a female Finn Dorset lamb, a genetic twin of the Finn Dorset ewe.

Figure E11-1 The making of Dolly

© 2003 Prentice Hall, Inc.

NOTES

CHAPTER 12 Patterns of Inheritance

Thinking Through the Concepts

Multiple Choice

1. *An organism is described as* Rr:red. *The* Rr *is the organism's [A]; red is the organism's [B]; and the organism is [C].*
   a. [A] phenotype; [B] genotype; [C] degenerate
   b. [A] karyotype; [B] hybrid; [C] recessive
   c. [A] genotype; [B] phenotype; [C] heterozygous
   d. [A] gamete; [B] linkage; [C] pleiotropic
   e. [A] zygote; [B] phenotype; [C] homozygous

2. *The 9:3:3:1 ratio is a ratio of*
   a. phenotypes in a test cross
   b. phenotypes in a cross of individuals that differ in one trait
   c. phenotypes in a cross of individuals that differ in two traits
   d. genotypes in a cross of individuals that differ in one trait
   e. genotypes in a cross of individuals that differ in two traits

3. *A lawyer tells a male client that blood type cannot be used to his advantage in a paternity suit against the client because the child could, in fact, be the client's, according to blood type. Which of the following is the only possible combination supporting this hypothetical circumstance? (Answers are in the order mother:father:child.)*
   a. A:B:O
   b. A:O:B
   c. AB:A:O
   d. AB:O:AB
   e. B:O:A

4. *A heterozygous red-eyed female* Drosophila *mated with a white-eyed male would produce*
   a. red-eyed females and white-eyed males in the F_1
   b. white-eyed females and red-eyed males in the F_1
   c. half red- and half white-eyed females and all white-eyed males in the F_1
   d. all white-eyed females and half red- and half white-eyed males in the F_1
   e. half red- and half white-eyed females as well as males in the F_1

5. *Which is NOT true of sickle-cell anemia?*
   a. It is most common in African Americans.
   b. It involves a one-amino-acid change in hemoglobin.
   c. It involves red blood cells.
   d. It is lethal in heterozygotes because it is dominant.
   e. It confers some resistance to malaria.

6. *Sex-linked disorders such as color blindness and hemophilia are*
   a. caused by genes on the X chromosome
   b. caused by genes on the autosome
   c. caused by genes on the Y chromosome
   d. expressed only in men
   e. expressed only when two chromosomes are homozygous recessive

? Review Questions

1. Define the following terms: *gene, allele, dominant, recessive, true-breeding, homozygous, heterozygous, cross-fertilization, self-fertilization.*

2. Explain why genes located on the same chromosome are said to be linked. Why do alleles of linked genes sometimes separate during meiosis?

3. Define *polygenic inheritance.* Why could polygenic inheritance allow parents to produce offspring that are notably different in eye or skin color than either parent?

4. What is sex linkage? In mammals, which sex would be most likely to show recessive sex-linked traits?

5. What is the difference between a phenotype and a genotype? Does knowledge of an organism's phenotype always allow you to determine the genotype? What type of experiment would you perform to determine the genotype of a phenotypically dominant individual?

6. If one (heterozygous) parent of a couple has Huntington disease, calculate the fraction of that couple's children that would be expected to develop the disease. What if both parents were heterozygous?

7. Why are most genetic diseases inherited as recessives rather than dominants?

8. Define *nondisjunction*, and describe the common syndromes caused by nondisjunction of sex chromosomes and autosomes.

Applying the Concepts

1. Sometimes the term *gene* is used rather casually. Compare and contrast use of the terms *allele* and *locus* as alternatives to *gene*.

2. Using the information in the chapter, explain why AB individuals are referred to as "universal recipients" in terms of blood transfusions and why people with type O blood are called "universal donors."

3. Mendel's numbers seemed almost too perfect to be real; some believe he may have cheated a bit on his data. Perhaps he continued to collect data until the numbers matched his predicted ratios, then stopped. Recently, there has been much publicity over violations of scientific ethics, including researchers' plagiarizing others' work, using other scientists' methods to develop lucrative patents, or just plain fabricating data. How important an issue is this for society? What are the boundary lines of ethical scientific behavior? How should the scientific community or society "police" scientists? What punishments would be appropriate for violations of scientific ethics?

4. Although American society has been described as a "melting pot," people often engage in "assortative mating," in which they marry others of similar height, socioeconomic status, race, and IQ. Discuss the consequences to society of assortative mating among humans. Would society be better off if people mated more randomly? Discuss why or why not.

5. *Eugenics* is the term applied to the notion that the human condition might be improved by improving the human genome. Do you think there are both good and bad sides to eugenics? What examples can you think of to back up your stand? What would a eugenicist think of the medical advances that have ameliorated the problems of hemophilia?

6. Think about some of the personal, religious, and economic issues related to prenatal counseling and diagnosis. Would you avoid having children if you knew that both you and your spouse were heterozygous for a recessive disorder that is fatal at an early age and may involve considerable suffering? What would you do if you or your spouse were pregnant and learned that your offspring, if born, would be homozygous for such a disorder? Is the situation qualitatively different for Down syndrome? (Down syndrome children have a life expectancy of 20 to 30 years with mental retardation but can have productive lives.) If you were heterozygous for Huntington disease, would you want to avail yourself of the medical diagnostic tests now available to find out? Would your answer be different if you were planning to have a baby?

© 2003 Prentice Hall, Inc.

Genetics Problems

(Note: An extensive group of genetics problems, with answers, can be found in the Study Guide.)

1. In certain cattle, hair color can be red (homozygous *RR*), white (homozygous *R'R'*), or roan (a mixture of red and white hairs, heterozygous *RR'*).

   a. When a red bull is mated to a white cow, what genotypes and phenotypes of offspring could be obtained?

   b. If one of the offspring in (a) were mated to a white cow, what genotypes and phenotypes of offspring could be produced? In what proportion?

2. The palomino horse is golden in color. Unfortunately for horse fanciers, palominos do not breed true. In a series of matings between palominos, the following offspring were obtained:

   > 65 palominos, 32 cream-colored,
   > 34 chestnut (reddish brown)

   What is the probable mode of inheritance of palomino coloration?

3. In the edible pea, tall (*T*) is dominant to short (*t*), and green pods (*G*) are dominant to yellow pods (*g*). List the types of gametes and offspring that would be produced in the following crosses:

   a. *TtGg × TtGg*   b. *TtGg × TTGG*   c. *TtGg × Ttgg*

4. In tomatoes, round fruit (*R*) is dominant to long fruit (*r*), and smooth skin (*S*) is dominant to fuzzy skin (*s*). A true-breeding round, smooth tomato (*RRSS*) was cross-bred with a true-breeding long, fuzzy tomato (*rrss*). All the F$_1$ offspring were round and smooth (*RrSs*). When these F$_1$ plants were bred, the following F$_2$ generation was obtained:

   > Round, smooth: 43   Long, fuzzy: 13

   Are the genes for skin texture and fruit shape likely to be on the same chromosome or on different chromosomes? Explain your answer.

5. In the tomatoes of problem 4, an F$_1$ offspring (*RrSs*) was mated with a homozygous recessive (*rrss*). The following offspring were obtained:

   > Round, smooth: 583   Round, fuzzy: 21
   > Long, fuzzy: 602   Long, smooth: 16

   What is the most likely explanation for this distribution of phenotypes?

6. In humans, hair color is controlled by two interacting genes. The same pigment, melanin, is present in both brown-haired and blond-haired people, but brown hair has much more of it. Brown hair (*B*) is dominant to blond (*b*). Whether any melanin can be synthesized depends on another gene. The dominant form (*M*) allows melanin synthesis; the recessive form (*m*) prevents melanin synthesis. Homozygous recessives (*mm*) are albino. What will be the expected proportions of phenotypes in the children of the following parents?

   a. *BBMM × BbMm*

   b. *BbMm × BbMm*

   c. *BbMm × bbmm*

7. In humans, one of the genes determining color vision is located on the X chromosome. The dominant form (*C*) produces normal color vision; red-green color blindness (*c*) is recessive. If a man with normal color vision marries a color-blind woman, what is the probability of their having a color-blind son? A color-blind daughter?

8. In the couple described in problem 7, the woman gives birth to a color-blind but otherwise normal daughter. The husband sues for a divorce on the grounds of adultery. Will his case stand up in court? Explain your answer.

**chromosome 1
from tomato**

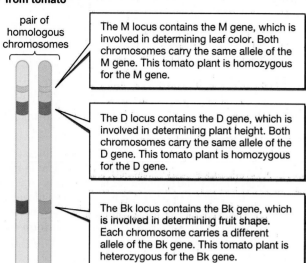

pair of homologous chromosomes

The M locus contains the M gene, which is involved in determining leaf color. Both chromosomes carry the same allele of the M gene. This tomato plant is homozygous for the M gene.

The D locus contains the D gene, which is involved in determining plant height. Both chromosomes carry the same allele of the D gene. This tomato plant is homozygous for the D gene.

The Bk locus contains the Bk gene, which is involved in determining fruit shape. Each chromosome carries a different allele of the Bk gene. This tomato plant is heterozygous for the Bk gene.

Figure 12-2 The relationships among genes, alleles, and chromosomes

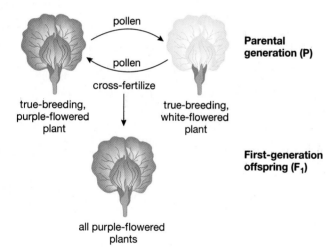

pollen

pollen

cross-fertilize

Parental generation (P)

true-breeding, purple-flowered plant

true-breeding, white-flowered plant

First-generation offspring (F$_1$)

all purple-flowered plants

Figure 12-2un01 Production of F1

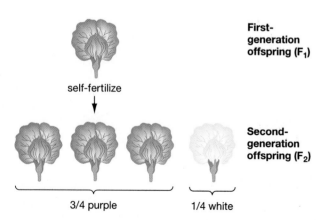

First-generation offspring (F$_1$)

self-fertilize

Second-generation offspring (F$_2$)

3/4 purple

1/4 white

Figure 12-2un02 Production of F2

© 2003 Prentice Hall, Inc.

NOTES

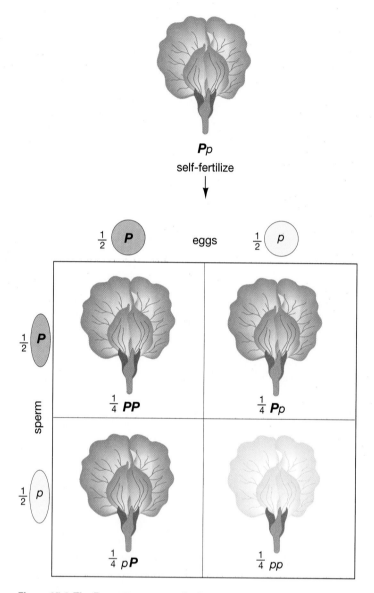

Figure 12-4 The Punnett square method

© 2003 Prentice Hall, Inc.

NOTES

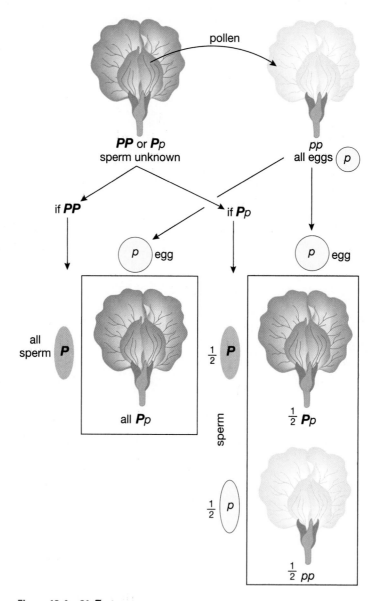

Figure 12-4un01 Test cross

© 2003 Prentice Hall, Inc.

NOTES

(a)

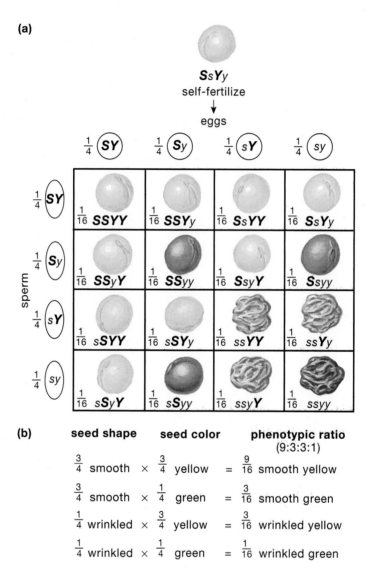

(b)

seed shape	seed color	phenotypic ratio (9:3:3:1)
$\frac{3}{4}$ smooth $\times$	$\frac{3}{4}$ yellow =	$\frac{9}{16}$ smooth yellow
$\frac{3}{4}$ smooth $\times$	$\frac{1}{4}$ green =	$\frac{3}{16}$ smooth green
$\frac{1}{4}$ wrinkled $\times$	$\frac{3}{4}$ yellow =	$\frac{3}{16}$ wrinkled yellow
$\frac{1}{4}$ wrinkled $\times$	$\frac{1}{4}$ green =	$\frac{1}{16}$ wrinkled green

Figure 12-6 Predicting genotypes and phenotypes for a cross between gametes that are heterozygous for two traits

© 2003 Prentice Hall, Inc.

NOTES

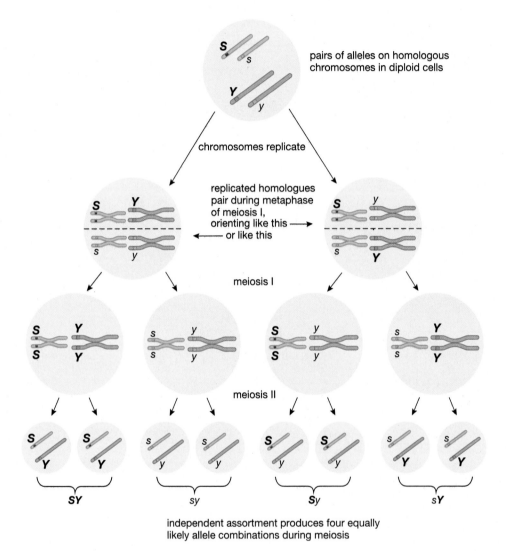

pairs of alleles on homologous chromosomes in diploid cells

chromosomes replicate

replicated homologues pair during metaphase of meiosis I, orienting like this ⟶ ⟵ or like this

meiosis I

meiosis II

SY   sy   Sy   sY

independent assortment produces four equally likely allele combinations during meiosis

Figure 12-7 Independent assortment of alleles

© 2003 Prentice Hall, Inc.

NOTES

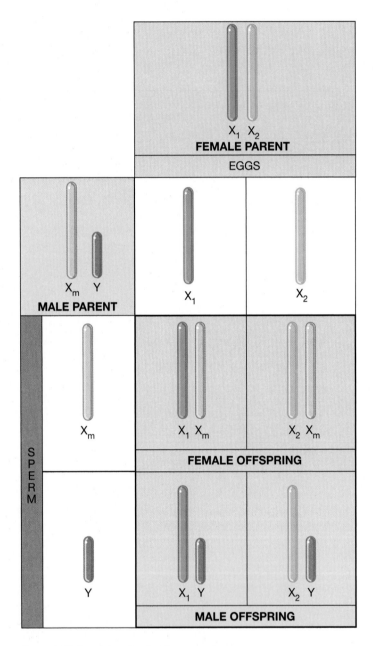

Figure 12-9 Sex determination in mammals

© 2003 Prentice Hall, Inc.

NOTES

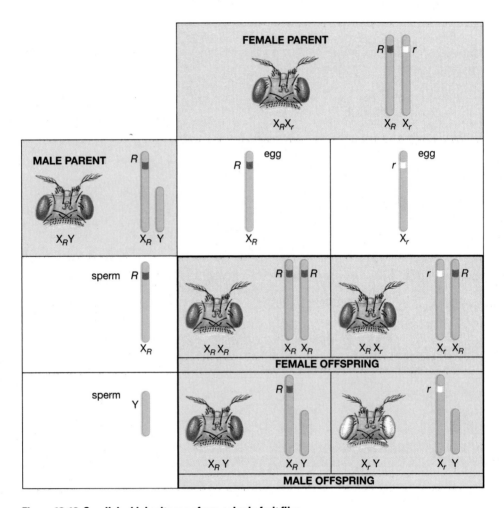

Figure 12-10 Sex-linked inheritance of eye color in fruit flies

© 2003 Prentice Hall, Inc.

NOTES

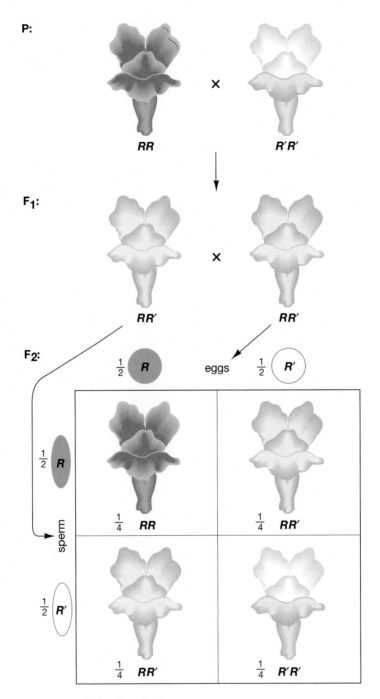

Figure 12-11 Incomplete dominance

© 2003 Prentice Hall, Inc.

NOTES

Table 12-1 Human Blood Group Characteristics

Blood Type	Genotype	Red Blood Cells	Has Plasma Antibodies to:	Can Receive Blood from:	Can Donate Blood to:	Frequency in U.S.
A	AA or Ao	A glycoprotein	B glycoprotein	A or O (no blood with B glycoprotein)	A or AB	40%
B	BB or Bo	B glycoprotein	A glycoprotein	B or O (no blood with A glycoprotein)	B or AB	10%
AB	AB	Both A and B glycoproteins	Neither A nor B glycoprotein	AB, A, B, O (universal recipient)	AB	4%
O	oo	Neither A nor B glycoprotein	Both A and B glycoproteins	O (no blood with A or B glycoprotein)	O, AB, A, B (universal donor)	46%

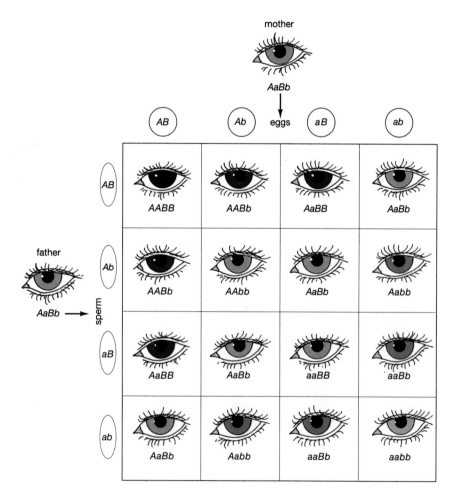

Figure 12-12 Human eye color

© 2003 Prentice Hall, Inc.

NOTES

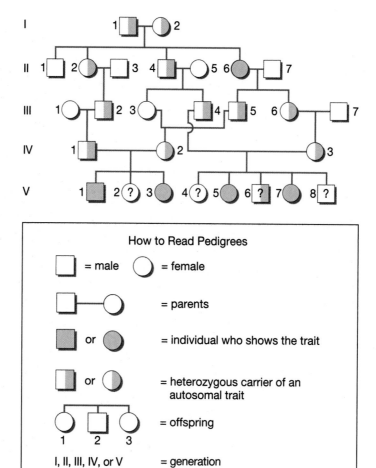

Figure 12-14 **A family pedigree**

© 2003 Prentice Hall, Inc.

NOTES

CHAPTER 13 Biotechnology

Thinking Through the Concepts

Multiple Choice

1. *Restriction enzymes are*
   a. isolated from bacterial cells
   b. used to produce DNA fingerprints
   c. used to create recombinant plasmids
   d. used to create a DNA library
   e. all of the above

2. *Restriction fragment length polymorphisms*
   a. all of the following
   b. can be used to detect differences in DNA among individuals
   c. have been used to identify human genes
   d. can be used to analyze fetal cells to detect disorders prenatally
   e. are produced through the use of restriction enzymes

3. *The polymerase chain reaction*
   a. is a method of synthesizing human protein from human DNA
   b. takes place naturally in bacteria
   c. can produce billions of copies of a DNA fragment in several hours
   d. uses restriction enzymes
   e. is relatively slow and expensive compared with other types of DNA purification

4. *Knock-out mice*
   a. are a particularly aggressive strain
   b. have been genetically engineered to produce a human protein
   c. produce human proteins
   d. have been genetically engineered to lack a specific mouse gene
   e. are naturally produced mutant mice

5. *DNA fingerprinting*
   a. requires large amounts of DNA
   b. is useful only for forensic analysis
   c. can involve analysis of RFLPs
   d. can only prove guilt, never innocence
   e. is a constitutional right

6. *A child with a single allele for sickle-cell anemia*
   a. is likely to die before age 30 from this disease
   b. will have difficulty getting enough oxygen at high altitudes
   c. will have difficulty participating in sports
   d. will need immediate treatment at birth
   e. will be able to lead a perfectly normal life

? Review Questions

1. Describe three natural forms of genetic recombination, and discuss the similarities and differences between recombinant DNA technology and these natural forms of genetic recombination.

2. What is a plasmid? How are plasmids involved in bacterial transformation?

3. What is a restriction enzyme? How can restriction enzymes be used to splice a piece of human DNA within a plasmid?

4. What is a DNA library? Briefly describe the steps involved in creating a DNA library of a mouse genome.

5. What is a restriction fragment length polymorphism (RFLP)? Describe how it might be useful in proving innocence of a murder suspect or determining relatedness among people.

6. Describe the polymerase chain reaction.

7. Describe several uses of genetic engineering in agriculture.

8. Describe several uses of genetic engineering in human medicine.

9. Describe amniocentesis and chorionic villus sampling, including the advantages and disadvantages of each. What are their medical uses?

Applying the Concepts

1. Discuss the ethical issues that surround the release of bioengineered organisms (plants, animals, or bacteria) into the environment. What could go wrong? What precautions might prevent the problems you listed from occurring? What benefits do you think would justify the risks?

2. Do you think that using recombinant DNA technologies to change the genetic composition of a human egg cell is ever justified? If so, what restrictions should be placed on such a use? What about human cloning?

3. Are there any conditions under which insurance companies or employers should be allowed access to the results of tests for genetic defects? Discuss this issue from the standpoint of the company or employer, the individual who was tested, and society as a whole.

4. In what ways was the program to test for sickle-cell anemia in the 1970s flawed? What criteria should be met (education, privacy guarantees, etc.) before any genetic screening test is administered to the general public?

5. If you were contemplating having a child, would you want both yourself and your spouse tested for the cystic fibrosis gene? If both of you were carriers, how would you deal with this decision?

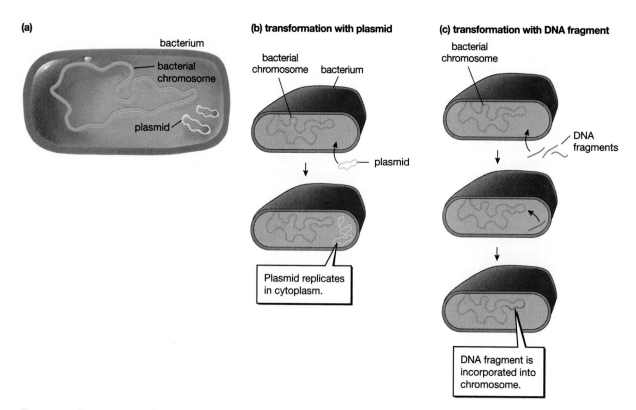

Figure 13-1 Recombination in bacteria

© 2003 Prentice Hall, Inc.

NOTES

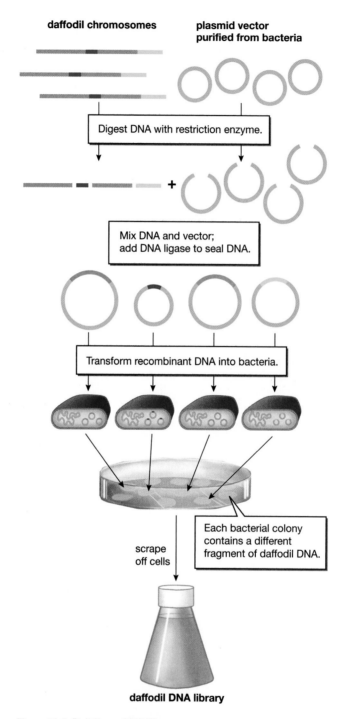

daffodil chromosomes

plasmid vector
purified from bacteria

Digest DNA with restriction enzyme.

+

Mix DNA and vector;
add DNA ligase to seal DNA.

Transform recombinant DNA into bacteria.

Each bacterial colony
contains a different
fragment of daffodil DNA.

scrape
off cells

daffodil DNA library

Figure 13-3 **Building a DNA library**

© 2003 Prentice Hall, Inc.

NOTES

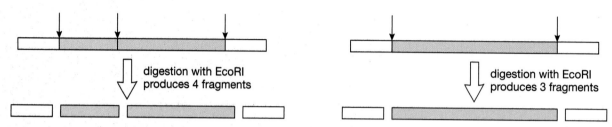

Figure 13-3un01 Restriction digestion

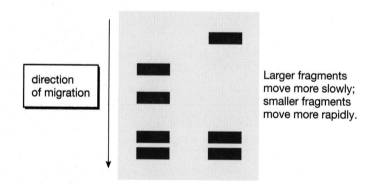

Figure 13-3un02 Separation of DNA fragments

© 2003 Prentice Hall, Inc.

NOTES

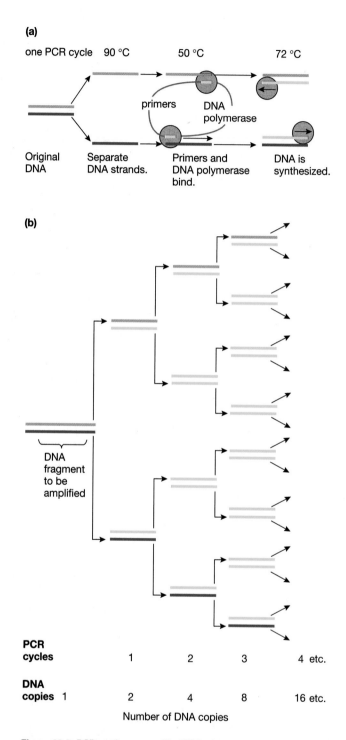

Figure 13-5 **PCR copies a specific DNA sequence**

© 2003 Prentice Hall, Inc.

NOTES

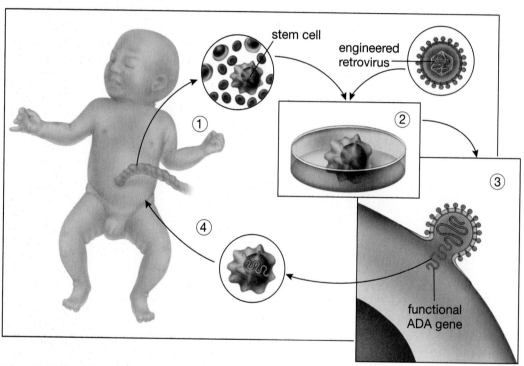

Figure 13-11 Hope through gene therapy

© 2003 Prentice Hall, Inc.

NOTES

CHAPTER 14

Principles of Evolution

Thinking Through the Concepts

Multiple Choice

1. *Your arm is homologous with*
a. a seal flipper
b. an octopus tentacle
c. a bird wing
d. a sea star arm
e. both a and c

2. *All organisms share the same genetic code. This commonality is evidence that*
a. evolution is occurring now
b. convergent evolution has occurred
c. evolution occurs gradually
d. all organisms are descended from a common ancestor
e. life began a long time ago

3. *Which of the following are fossils?*
a. pollen grains buried in the bottom of a peat bog
b. the petrified cast of a clam's burrow
c. the impression a clam shell made in mud, preserved in mudstone
d. an insect leg sealed in plant resin
e. all of the above

4. *In Africa, there is a species of bird called the yellow-throated longclaw. It looks almost exactly like the meadowlark found in North America, but they are not closely related. This is an example of*
a. uniformitarianism
b. artificial selection
c. gradualism
d. vestigial structures
e. convergent evolution

5. *Which of the following are examples of vestigial structures?*
a. your tailbone
b. your ear lobes
c. sixth fingers found in some humans
d. your kneecap
e. none of the above

6. *Which of the following would stop evolution by natural selection from occurring?*
a. if humans became extinct because of a disease epidemic
b. if a thermonuclear war killed most living organisms and changed the environment drastically
c. if ozone depletion led to increased ultraviolet radiation, which caused many new mutations
d. if all individuals in a population were genetically identical, and there was no genetic recombination, sexual reproduction, or mutation
e. all of the above

? Review Questions

1. Selection acts on individuals, but only populations evolve. Explain why this is true.

2. Distinguish between catastrophism and uniformitarianism. How did these hypotheses contribute to the development of evolutionary theory?

3. Describe Lamarck's theory of inheritance of acquired characteristics. Why is it invalid?

4. What is natural selection? Describe how natural selection might have caused differential reproduction among the ancestors of a fast-swimming predatory fish, such as the barracuda.

5. Describe how evolution occurs through the interactions among the reproductive potential of a species, the normally constant size of natural populations, variation among individuals of a species, natural selection, and inheritance.

6. What is convergent evolution? Give an example.

7. How do biochemistry and molecular genetics contribute to the evidence that evolution occurred?

Applying the Concepts

1. Does evolution through natural selection produce "better" organisms in an absolute sense? Are we climbing the "ladder of Nature"? Defend your answer.

2. Both the study of fossils and the idea of special creation have had an impact on evolutionary thought. Discuss why one is considered scientific endeavor and the other not scientific.

3. In evolutionary terms, "success" can be defined in many different ways. What are the most successful organisms you can think of in terms of (a) persistence over time, (b) sheer numbers of individuals alive now, (c) numbers of species (for a lineage), and (d) geographical range?

4. In what sense are humans currently acting as "agents" of selection on other species? Name some organisms that are *favored* by the environmental changes humans cause.

5. Darwin and Wallace's discovery of natural selection is one of the great revolutions in scientific thought. Some scientific revolutions spill over and affect the development of philosophy and religion. Is this true of evolution? Does (or should) the idea of evolution by natural selection affect the way humans view their place in the world?

6. In your mind, what scientific question currently represents the "mystery of mysteries"?

① eggs in nest

② skin impression

③ bones

④ fossilized feces (coprolites)

⑤ footprint

Figure 14-2 Types of fossils

© 2003 Prentice Hall, Inc.

NOTES

(a) large ground finch, beak suited to large seeds

(b) small ground finch, beak suited to small seeds

(c) warbler finch, beak suited to insects

(d) vegetarian tree finch, beak suited to leaves

Figure 14-4 Darwin's finches, residents of the Galapagos Islands

© 2003 Prentice Hall, Inc.

NOTES

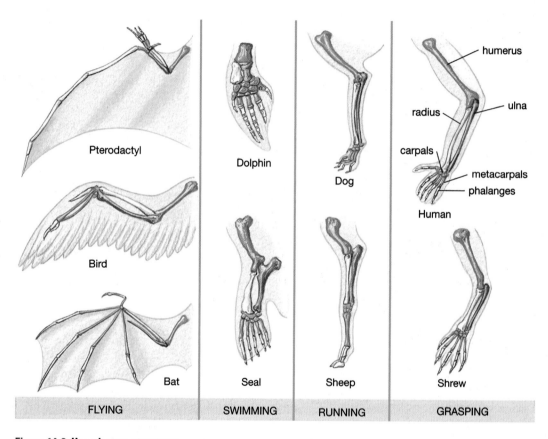

Figure 14-8 **Homologous structures**

© 2003 Prentice Hall, Inc.

NOTES

CHAPTER 15 How Organisms Evolve

Thinking Through the Concepts

Multiple Choice

1. *Genetic drift is a _____ process.*
   a. random
   b. directed
   c. selection-driven
   d. coevolutionary
   e. uniformitarian

2. *Most of the 700 species of fruit flies found in the Hawaiian archipelago are each restricted to a single island. One hypothesis to explain this pattern is that each species diverged after a small number of flies had colonized a new island. This mechanism is called*
   a. sexual selection
   b. genetic equilibrium
   c. disruptive selection
   d. the founder effect
   e. assortative mating

3. *You are studying leaf size in a natural population of plants. The second season is particularly dry, and the following year the average leaf size in the population is smaller than the year before. But the amount of overall variation is the same, and the population size hasn't changed. Also, you've done experiments that show that small leaves are better adapted to dry conditions than are large leaves. Which of the following has occurred?*
   a. genetic drift
   b. directional selection
   c. stabilizing selection
   d. disruptive selection
   e. the founder effect

4. *You have bacteria thriving in your gastrointestinal tract. This is an example of*
   a. inclusive fitness
   b. balanced polymorphism
   c. symbiosis
   d. kin selection
   e. altruism

5. *Lamarckian evolution, the inheritance of acquired characteristics, could occur*
   a. if each gene had only one allele
   b. if individuals had different phenotypes
   c. if the genotype was altered by the same environmental changes that altered the phenotype
   d. if the phenotype was altered by the environment
   e. under none of these conditions

6. *Of the following possibilities, the best way to estimate an organism's evolutionary fitness is to measure the*
   a. size of its offspring
   b. number of eggs it produces
   c. number of eggs it produces over its lifetime
   d. number of offspring it produces over its lifetime
   e. number of offspring it produces over its lifetime that survive to breed

? Review Questions

1. What is a gene pool? How would you determine the allele frequencies in a gene pool?

2. Define *equilibrium population*. Outline the conditions that must be met for a population to stay in genetic equilibrium.

3. How does population size affect the likelihood of changes in allele frequencies by chance alone? Can significant changes in allele frequencies (that is, evolution) occur as a result of genetic drift?

4. If you measured the allele frequencies of a gene and found large differences from the proportions predicted by the Hardy-Weinberg principle, would that prove that natural selection is occurring in the population you are studying? Review the conditions that lead to an equilibrium population, and explain your answer.

5. People like to say that "you can't prove a negative." Study the experiment in Figure 15-1 again, and comment on what it demonstrates.

6. Describe the three ways in which natural selection can affect a population over time. Which way(s) is (are) most likely to occur in stable environments, and which way(s) might occur in rapidly changing environments?

7. What is sexual selection? How is sexual selection similar to and different from other forms of natural selection?

8. Briefly describe competition, symbiosis, and altruism, and give an example of each.

9. Define *kin selection* and *inclusive fitness*. Can these concepts help explain the evolution of altruism?

Applying the Concepts

1. In North America the average height of adult humans has been increasing steadily for decades. Is directional selection occurring? What data would justify your answer?

2. Malaria is rare in North America. In populations of African Americans, what would you predict is happening to the frequency of the hemoglobin allele that leads to sickling in red blood cells? How would you go about determining if your prediction is true?

3. By the 1940s the whooping crane population had been reduced to fewer than 50 individuals. Thanks to conservation measures, their numbers are now increasing. What special evolutionary problems do whooping cranes have now that they have passed through a population bottleneck?

4. In many countries, conservationists are trying to design national park systems so that "islands" of natural area (the big parks) are connected by thin "corridors" of undisturbed habitat. The idea is that this arrangement will allow animals and plants to migrate between refuges. Why would such migration be important?

5. A preview question for Chapter 16: A species is all the populations of organisms that potentially interbreed with one another but that are reproductively isolated from (cannot interbreed with) other populations. Using the five assumptions of the Hardy-Weinberg principle as a starting point, what factors do you think would be important in the splitting of a single ancestral species into two modern species?

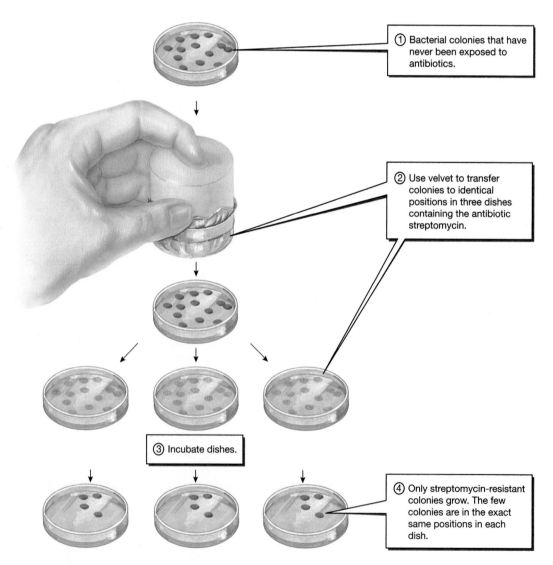

① Bacterial colonies that have never been exposed to antibiotics.

② Use velvet to transfer colonies to identical positions in three dishes containing the antibiotic streptomycin.

③ Incubate dishes.

④ Only streptomycin-resistant colonies grow. The few colonies are in the exact same positions in each dish.

Figure 15-1 Mutations occur spontaneously

© 2003 Prentice Hall, Inc.

NOTES

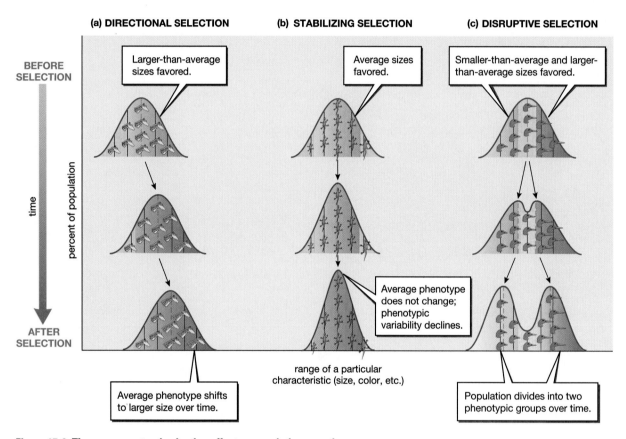

Figure 15-8 Three ways natural selection affects a population over time

© 2003 Prentice Hall, Inc.

NOTES

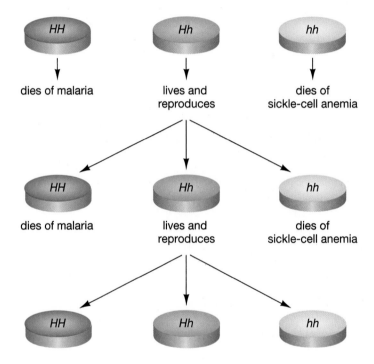

Figure 15-10 **Stabilizing selection can produce balanced polymorphism**

© 2003 Prentice Hall, Inc.

NOTES

CHAPTER 16 The Origin of Species

Thinking Through the Concepts

Multiple Choice

1. *Many closely related species of marine invertebrates exist on either side of the isthmus of Panama. They probably resulted from*
   a. premating isolation   b. isolation by distance
   c. postmating isolation   d. gametic incompatibility
   e. allopatric speciation

2. *Many hybrids are sterile because their chromosomes don't pair up correctly during meiosis. Why aren't polyploid plants sterile?*
   a. They backcross to the parental generation.
   b. Most are triploid.   c. They cross-pollinate.
   d. They self-fertilize, using their diploid gametes.
   e. Their eggs develop directly, without fertilization.

3. *In many species of fireflies, males flash to attract females. Each species has a different flashing pattern. This is probably an example of*
   a. ecological isolation   b. temporal isolation
   c. geographical isolation   d. premating isolation
   e. postmating isolation

4. *Under the biological-species concept, the main criterion for identifying a species is*
   a. anatomical distinctiveness
   b. behavioral distinctiveness
   c. geographic isolation
   d. reproductive isolation
   e. gametic incompatibility

5. *In terms of changes in gene frequencies, founder events result in*
   a. gradual accumulation of many small changes
   b. large, rapid changes   c. polyploidy
   d. hybridization
   e. mechanical incompatibility

6. *After the demise of the dinosaurs, mammals evolved rapidly into many new forms because of*
   a. the founder effect   b. a genetic bottleneck
   c. adaptive radiation   d. geological time
   e. genetic drift

? Review Questions

1. Define the following terms: *species*, *speciation*, *allopatric speciation*, and *sympatric speciation*. Explain how allopatric and sympatric speciations might work, and give a hypothetical example of each.

2. Many of the oak tree species in central and eastern North America hybridize (interbreed). Are they "true species"?

3. Review the material on the possibility of sympatric speciation in *Rhagoletis* varieties that breed on apples or hawthorns. What types of genotypic, phenotypic, or behavioral data would convince you that the two forms have become separate species?

4. A drug called *colchicine* affects the mitotic spindle fibers and prevents cell division after the chromosomes have doubled at the start of meiosis. Describe how you would use colchicine to produce a new polyploid species of your favorite garden flower.

5. List and describe the different types of premating and postmating isolating mechanisms.

Applying the Concepts

1. The biological-species concept has no meaning with regard to asexual organisms, and it is difficult to apply to extinct organisms that we know only as fossils. Can you devise a meaningful, useful species definition that would apply in all situations?

2. Seedless varieties of fruits and vegetables, created by breeders, are triploid. Explain why they are seedless.

3. Why do you suppose there are so many *endemic* species—that is, species found nowhere else—on islands? And why have the overwhelming majority of recent extinctions occurred on islands?

4. A contrarian biologist you've met claims that the fact that humans are pushing other species into small,

isolated populations is good for biodiversity because these are the conditions that lead to new speciation events. Comment.

5. Southern Wisconsin is home to several populations of gray squirrels (*Sciurus carolinensis*) with black fur. Design a study to determine if they are actually separate species.

6. It is difficult to gather data on speciation events in the past or to perform interesting experiments about the process of speciation. Does this difficulty make the study of speciation "unscientific"? Should we abandon the study of speciation?

Figure 16-2 Models of allopatric and sympatric speciations

© 2003 Prentice Hall, Inc.

NOTES

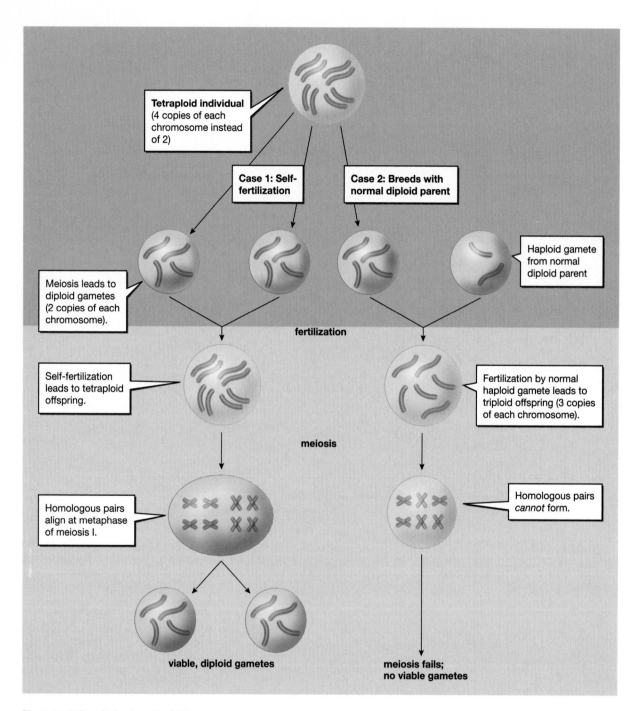

Figure 16-5 Speciation by polyploidy

© 2003 Prentice Hall, Inc.

NOTES

CHAPTER 17 The History of Life on Earth

Multiple Choice

1. *There was no free oxygen in the early atmosphere because most of it was tied up in*
   a. water
   b. ammonia
   c. methane
   d. rock
   e. radioactive isotopes

2. *RNA became a candidate for the first information-carrying molecule when Tom Cech and Sidney Altman discovered that some RNA molecules can act as enzymes that*
   a. degrade proteins
   b. turn light into chemical energy
   c. split water and release oxygen gas
   d. synthesize copies of themselves
   e. synthesize amino acids

3. *The earliest living organisms were*
   a. multicellular
   b. eukaryotes
   c. prokaryotes
   d. photosynthesizers
   e. aerobic

4. *Which three of the following observations support Lynn Margulis's endosymbiont hypothesis for the origin of chloroplasts and mitochondria from ingested bacteria?*
   a. Aerobic respiration takes place in mitochondria.
   b. Mitochondria have their own DNA.
   c. Photosynthesis takes place in chloroplasts.
   d. Chloroplasts have their own DNA.
   e. Bacterial plasma membranes are strikingly similar to the inner membrane of mitochondria.

5. *The exoskeleton of early, marine-dwelling arthropods can be considered a preadaptation for life on land because that shell*
   a. can support an animal's weight against the pull of gravity
   b. allows a wide diversity of body types
   c. resists drying
   d. absorbs light
   e. both a and c

6. *The evolution of the shelled, waterproof egg was an important event in vertebrate evolution because it*
   a. led to the Cambrian explosion
   b. was the first example of parents caring for their young
   c. allowed the colonization of freshwater environments
   d. freed organisms from having to lay their eggs in water
   e. allowed internal fertilization of eggs

? Review Questions

1. What is the evidence that life might have originated from nonliving matter on primordial Earth? What kind of evidence would you like to see before you would accept this hypothesis?

2. If they were so much more efficient at producing energy, why didn't the first cells with aerobic metabolism extinguish cells with only anaerobic metabolism?

3. Explain the endosymbiont hypothesis for the origin of chloroplasts and mitochondria.

4. Name two advantages of multicellularity in both plants and animals.

5. What advantages and disadvantages would terrestrial existence have had for the first plants to invade the land? For the first land animals?

6. Outline the major adaptations that emerged during the evolution of vertebrates, from fish to amphibians to reptiles to birds and mammals. Explain how these adaptations increased the fitness of the various groups for life on land.

7. Outline the evolution of humans from early primates. Include in your discussion such features as binocular vision, grasping hands, bipedal locomotion, social living, tool making, and brain expansion.

Applying the Concepts

1. What is cultural evolution? Is cultural evolution more or less rapid than biological evolution? Why?

2. Do you think that studying our ancestors can shed light on the behavior of modern humans? Why or why not?

3. A biologist would probably answer the age-old question "What is life?" by saying "the ability to self-replicate." Do you agree with this definition? If so, why? If not, how would you define life in biological terms?

4. Traditional definitions of humans have emphasized "the uniqueness of humans" because we possess language and use tools. But most animals can communicate with other individuals in sophisticated ways, and many vertebrates use tools to accomplish tasks. Pretend that you are a biologist from Mars, and write a taxonomic description of the species *Homo sapiens*.

5. Extinctions have occurred throughout the history of life on Earth. Why should we care if humans are causing a mass extinction event now?

6. The "out of Africa" and "multiregional" hypotheses of *Homo sapiens'* evolution make contrasting predictions about the extent and nature of genetic divergence among human races. One predicts that races are old and highly diverged genetically; the other predicts that races are young and little diverged genetically. What data would help you determine which hypothesis is closer to the truth?

7. In biological terms, what do you think was the most significant event in the history of life? Explain your answer.

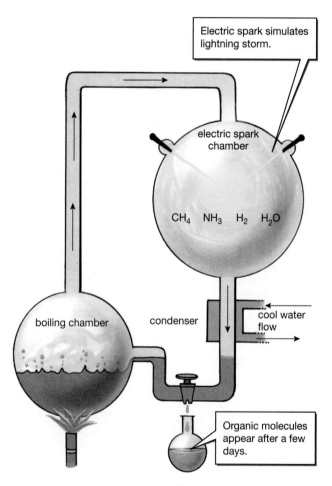

Figure 17-2 The experimental apparatus of Stanley Miller and Harold Urey

© 2003 Prentice Hall, Inc.

NOTES

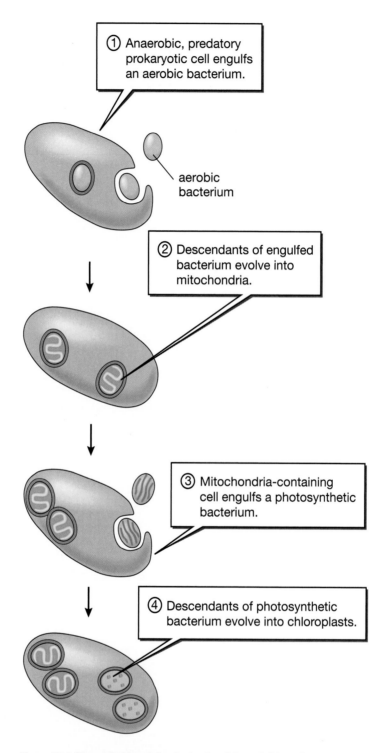

Figure 17-4 The probable origin of mitochondria and chloroplasts in eukaryotic cells

© 2003 Prentice Hall, Inc.

NOTES

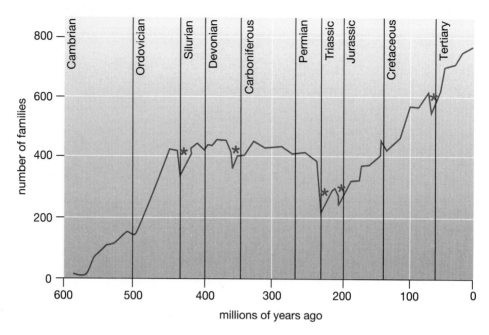

Figure 17-10 Episodes of mass extinction

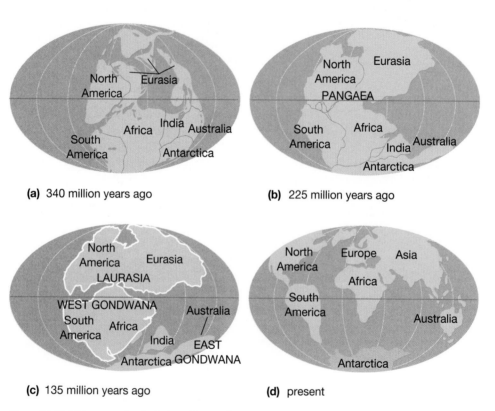

(a) 340 million years ago

(b) 225 million years ago

(c) 135 million years ago

(d) present

Figure 17-11 Plate tectonics is tied to climate change

© 2003 Prentice Hall, Inc.

NOTES

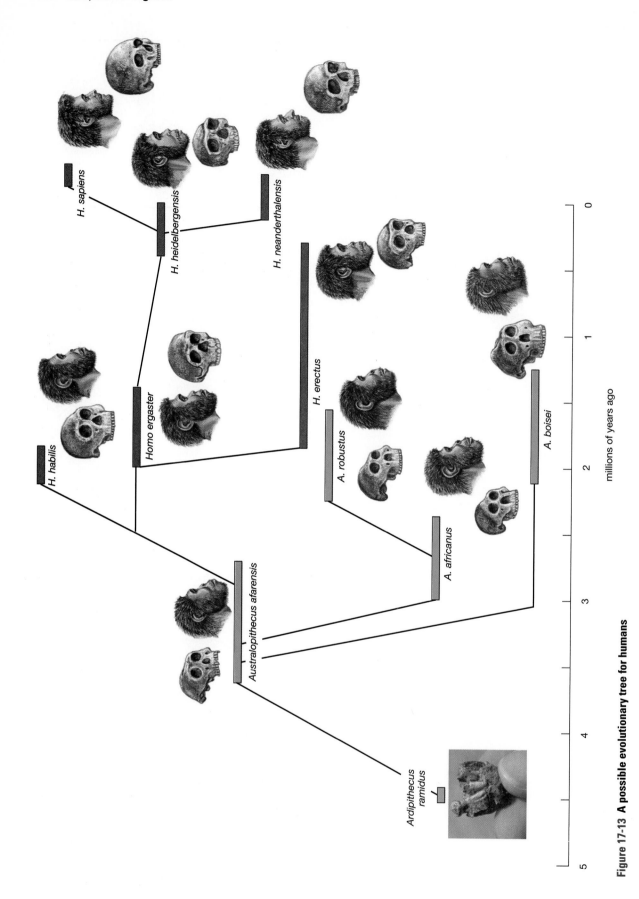

Figure 17-13 A possible evolutionary tree for humans

© 2003 Prentice Hall, Inc.

NOTES

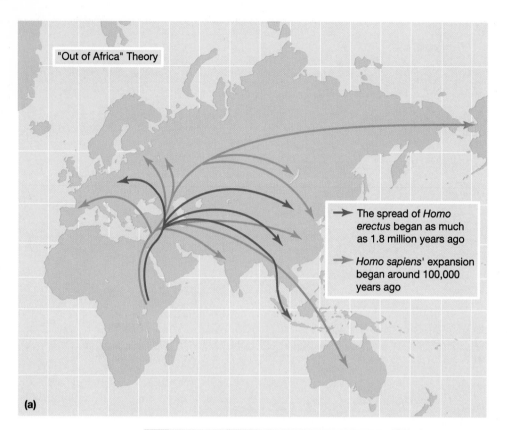

"Out of Africa" Theory

The spread of *Homo erectus* began as much as 1.8 million years ago

Homo sapiens' expansion began around 100,000 years ago

(a)

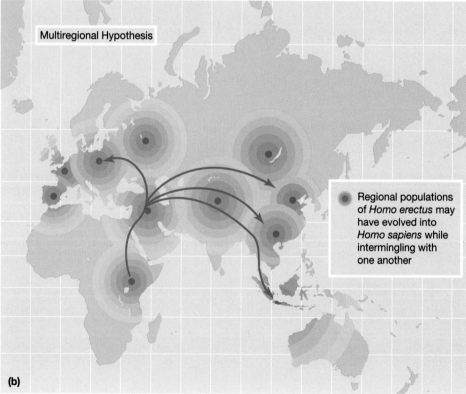

Multiregional Hypothesis

Regional populations of *Homo erectus* may have evolved into *Homo sapiens* while intermingling with one another

(b)

Figure 17-17 Competing hypotheses for the evolution of *Homo sapiens*

© 2003 Prentice Hall, Inc.

NOTES

CHAPTER 18 Systematics: Seeking Order Amidst Diversity

Thinking Through the Concepts

Multiple Choice

1. *It is possible to imagine the various levels of taxonomic classification as a kind of "family tree" for an organism. If the kingdom is analogous to the trunk of the tree, which taxonomic category would be analogous to the large limbs coming off that trunk?*
   a. class
   b. family
   c. order
   d. phylum
   e. subfamily

2. *The more taxonomic categories two organisms share, the more closely related those organisms are in an evolutionary sense. Which scientist's work led to this insight?*
   a. Aristotle
   b. Darwin
   c. Linnaeus
   d. Whittaker
   e. Woese

3. *Which of the following criteria could not be used to determine how closely related two types of organisms are?*
   a. similarities in the presence and relative abundance of specific molecules
   b. DNA sequence
   c. the presence of homologous structures
   d. developmental stages
   e. occurrence of both organisms in the same habitat

4. *Which one of the following habitats appears to have the greatest number of species?*
   a. the seafloor
   b. deserts
   c. tropical rain forests
   d. grasslands
   e. mountaintops

5. *Which of the following pairs is the most distantly related?*
   a. archaea and bacteria
   b. protists and fungi
   c. plants and animals
   d. fish and starfish
   e. fungi and plants

6. *An organism is described to you as having many nuclei-containing cells, each surrounded by a cell wall of chitin and absorbing its food. In which kingdom or domain would you place it?*
   a. Plantae
   b. Protista
   c. Animalia
   d. Fungi
   e. Archaea

? Review Questions

1. What contributions did Aristotle, Linnaeus, and Darwin each make to modern taxonomy?

2. What features would you study to determine whether a dolphin is more closely related to a fish or to a bear?

3. What techniques might you use to determine whether the extinct cave bear is more closely related to a grizzly bear or to a black bear?

4. Only a small fraction of the total number of species on Earth has been scientifically described. Why?

5. In England, "daddy long-legs" refers to a long-legged fly, but the same name refers to a spider-like animal in the United States. How do scientists attempt to avoid such confusion?

Applying the Concepts

1. There are many areas of disagreement among taxonomists. For example, there is no consensus about whether the red wolf is a distinct species or about how many kingdoms are within the domain Bacteria. What difference does it make whether biologists consider the red wolf a species, or into which kingdom a bacterial species falls? As Shakespeare put it, "What's in a name?"

2. The pressures created by human population growth and economic expansion place storehouses of biological diversity such as the Tropics in peril. The seriousness of the situation is clear when we consider that probably only 1 out of every 20 tropical species is known to science at present. What arguments can you make for preserving biological diversity in poor and developing countries? Does such preservation require that these countries sacrifice economic development? Suggest some solutions to the conflict between the growing demand for resources and the importance of conserving biodiversity.

3. During major floods, only the topmost branches of submerged trees may be visible above the water. If you were asked to sketch the branches below the surface of the water solely on the basis of the positions of the exposed tips, you would be attempting a reconstruction somewhat similar to the "family tree" by which taxonomists link various organisms according to their common ancestors (analogous to branching points). What sources of error do both exercises share? What advantages do modern taxonomists have?

4. The Florida panther, found only in the Florida Everglades, is currently classified as an endangered species, protecting it from human activities that could lead to its extinction. It has long been considered a subspecies of cougar (mountain lion), but recent mitochondrial DNA studies have shown that the Florida panther may actually be a hybrid between American and South American cougars. Should the Florida panther be protected by the Endangered Species Act?

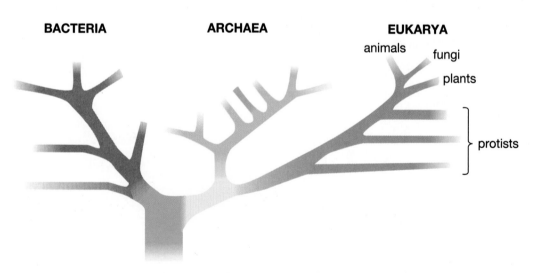

Figure 18-5 **The tree of life**

© 2003 Prentice Hall, Inc.

NOTES

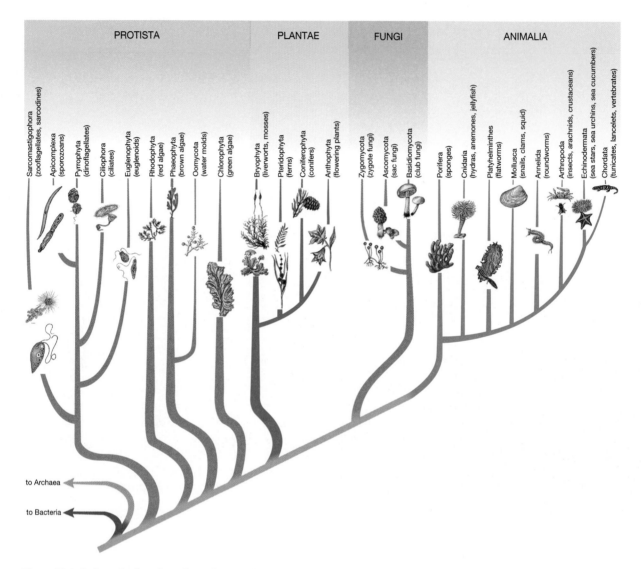

Figure 18-6 A closer look at the eukaryotic tree of life

© 2003 Prentice Hall, Inc.

NOTES

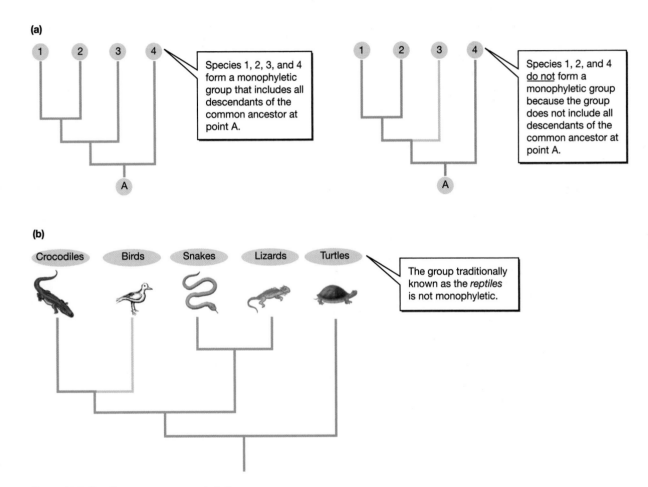

(a)

Species 1, 2, 3, and 4 form a monophyletic group that includes all descendants of the common ancestor at point A.

Species 1, 2, and 4 <u>do not</u> form a monophyletic group because the group does not include all descendants of the common ancestor at point A.

(b)

The group traditionally known as the *reptiles* is not monophyletic.

Figure 18-8 **Reptiles are not a monophyletic group**

© 2003 Prentice Hall, Inc.

NOTES

CHAPTER 19 The Hidden World of Microbes

Thinking Through the Concepts

Multiple Choice

1. *Which of the following is true?*
   a. Viruses cannot reproduce outside a host cell.
   b. Prions are infectious proteins.
   c. Viroids lack a protein coat.
   d. Some viruses cause cancer.
   e. all of the above

2. *Which structure is used to transfer genetic material between bacteria?*
   a. flagellum
   b. pilus
   c. peptidoglycan
   d. spore
   e. capsule

3. *Most pathogenic bacteria cause disease by*
   a. directly destroying individual cells of the host
   b. fixing nitrogen and depriving the host of this nutrient
   c. producing toxins that disrupt normal functions
   d. depleting the energy supply of the host
   e. depriving the host of oxygen

4. *Cyanobacteria*
   a. have chlorophyll
   b. are chemosynthetic
   c. can live without oxygen
   d. are archaea
   e. all of the above

5. *Which organisms are sometimes called the "pastures of the sea"?*
   a. dinoflagellates
   b. foraminiferans
   c. diatoms
   d. radiolarians
   e. amoebae

6. *Which of the following pairs of organism and disease is incorrect?*
   a. sporozoan: malaria
   b. prion: kuru
   c. bacterium: syphilis
   d. archaean: gonorrhea
   e. virus: AIDS

? Review Questions

1. Describe the structure of a typical virus. How do viruses replicate?

2. List the major differences between prokaryotes and protists.

3. Describe some of the ways in which bacteria obtain energy and nutrients.

4. What are nitrogen-fixing bacteria, and what role do they play in ecosystems?

5. What is an endospore? What is its function?

6. Describe some examples of bacterial symbiosis.

7. What is the importance of dinoflagellates in marine ecosystems? What happens when they reproduce rapidly?

8. What is the major ecological role played by unicellular algae?

9. What protozoan group consists entirely of parasitic forms?

10. Describe the life cycle and mode of transmission of the malarial parasite.

Applying the Concepts

1. In some developing countries, antibiotics can be purchased without a prescription. Why do you think this is done? What biological consequences would you predict?

2. Before the discovery of prions, many (perhaps most) biologists would have agreed with the statement, "It is a fact that no infectious organism or particle can exist that lacks nucleic acid (such as DNA or RNA)." What lessons do prions have to teach us about nature, science, and scientific inquiry? You may wish to review Chapter 1 to help answer this question.

3. Recent research shows that ocean water off southern California has warmed by 2–3 °F (1–1.5 °C) over the past four decades, possibly due to the greenhouse effect. This warming has led indirectly to a depletion of nutrients in the water and thus a decline in photosynthetic protists such as diatoms. What effects is this warming likely to have for the life in the oceans?

4. Argue for and against the statement, "Viruses are alive."

5. The internal structure of many protists is much more complex than that of cells of multicellular organisms. Does this mean that the protist is engaged in more complex activities than the multicellular organism? If not, why should the protistan cell be much more complicated?

6. Why would the lives of multicellular animals be impossible if prokaryotic and protistan organisms did not exist?

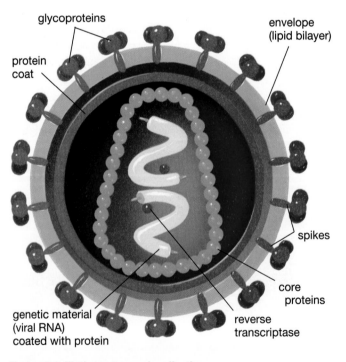

Figure 19-2 Viral structure and replication

© 2003 Prentice Hall, Inc.

NOTES

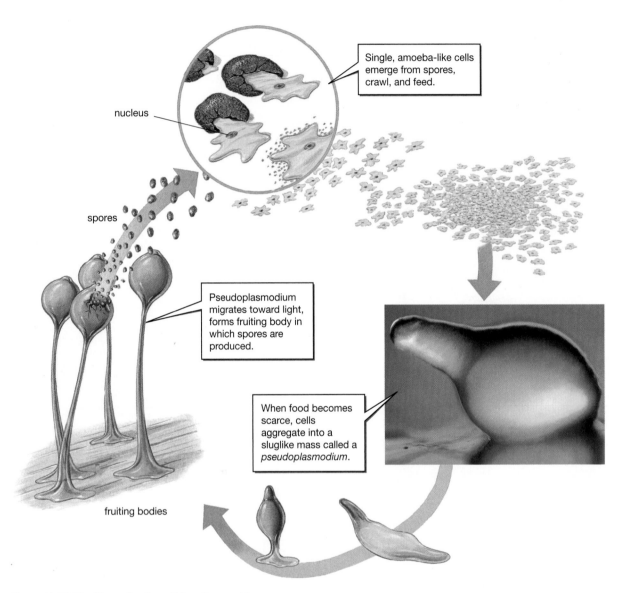

Figure 19-18 The life cycle of a cellular slime mold

© 2003 Prentice Hall, Inc.

NOTES

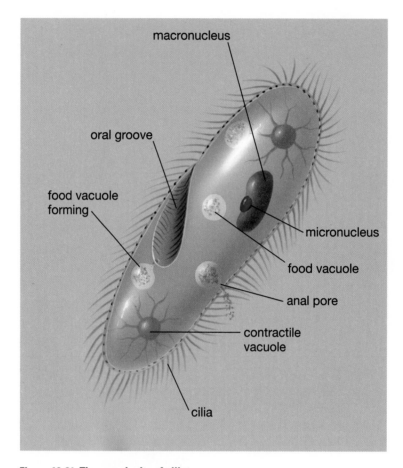

Figure 19-31 The complexity of ciliates

© 2003 Prentice Hall, Inc.

NOTES

(a) HIV virus, a retrovirus, invades a white blood cell.

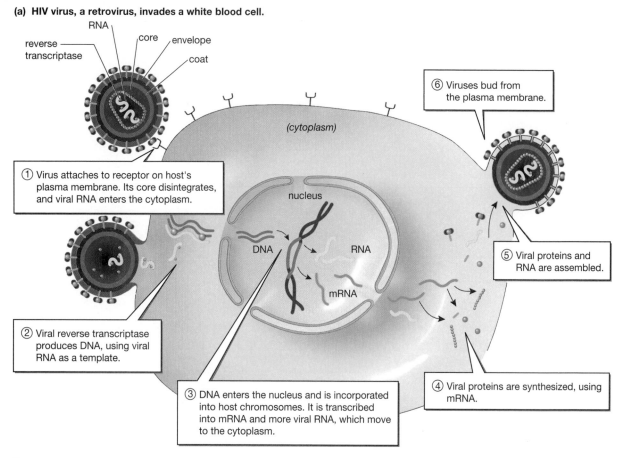

Figure E19-1a How viruses replicate

(b) Herpes virus, a double-stranded DNA virus, invades a skin cell.

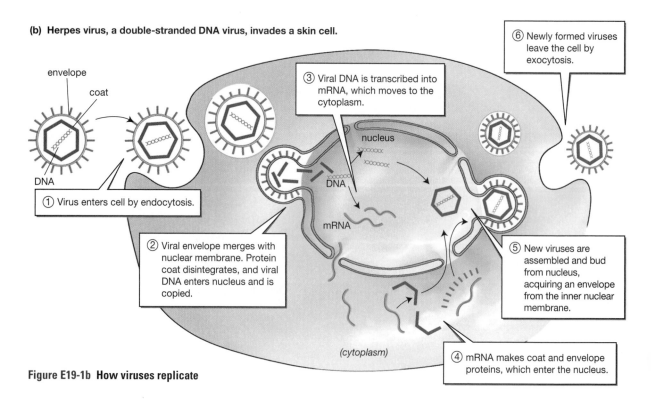

Figure E19-1b How viruses replicate

© 2003 Prentice Hall, Inc.

NOTES

CHAPTER 20   The Fungi

Thinking Through the Concepts

Multiple Choice

1. *There are no fungi that are*
   a. predators   b. photosynthetic
   c. decomposers   d. parasites
   e. symbiotic

2. *With what plant organ do mycorrhizae interact?*
   a. roots   b. leaves
   c. stems   d. fruits
   e. all parts of the plant

3. *What term refers to the mass of threads that forms the body of most fungi?*
   a. hyphae   b. mycelium
   c. sporangia   d. ascus
   e. basidium

4. *Which of the following pairs is incorrect?*
   a. fruit rot: zygote fungus
   b. edible mushroom: club fungus
   c. black bread mold: sac fungus
   d. shelf fungus: club fungus
   e. yeast: sac fungus

5. *Which of the following statements is true both of fungi and of animals?*
   a. Both photosynthesize.
   b. Both form embryos.
   c. They interact to form lichens.
   d. Both fix nitrogen.
   e. Both are heterotrophic.

6. *Which of the following structures would you expect to find in the corn smut fungus?*
   a. ascospores   b. basidiospores
   c. asci   d. zygospores
   e. fairy rings

? Review Questions

1. Describe the structure of the fungal body. How do fungal cells differ from most plant and animal cells?

2. What portion of the fungal body is represented by mushrooms, puffballs, and similar structures? Why are these structures elevated above the ground?

3. What two plant diseases, caused by parasitic fungi, have had an enormous impact on forests in the United States? In which division are these fungi found?

4. List some fungi that attack crops. In which phyla is each?

5. Describe asexual reproduction in fungi.

6. What is the major structural ingredient in fungal cell walls?

7. List the major phyla of fungi, describe the feature that gives each its name, and give one example of each.

8. Describe how a fairy ring of mushrooms is produced. Why is the diameter related to its age?

9. Describe two symbiotic associations between fungi and organisms from other kingdoms. In each case, explain how each partner in these associations is affected.

Applying the Concepts

1. Dutch elm disease in the United States is caused by an *exotic*—that is, an organism (in this case, a fungus) introduced from another part of the world. What damage has this introduction done? What other fungal pests fall into this category? Why are parasitic fungi particularly likely to be transported out of their natural habitat? What can governments do to limit this importation?

2. The discovery of penicillin revolutionized the treatment of bacterial diseases. However, penicillin is now rarely prescribed. Why is this? HINT: Refer back to Chapter 15.

3. The discovery of penicillin was the result of a chance observation by an observant microbiologist, Alexander Fleming. How would you search systematically for new antibiotics produced by fungi? Where would you look for these fungi?

4. Fossil evidence indicates that mycorrhizal associations between fungi and plant roots existed in the late Paleozoic era, when the invasion of land by plants began. This evidence suggests an important link between mycorrhizae and the successful invasion of land by plants. Why might mycorrhizae have been important fungi in the colonization of terrestrial habitats by plants?

5. General biology texts in the 1960s included fungi in the plant kingdom. Why do biologists no longer consider fungi as legitimate members of the plant kingdom?

6. What ecological consequences would occur if humans, using a new and deadly fungicide, destroyed all fungi on Earth?

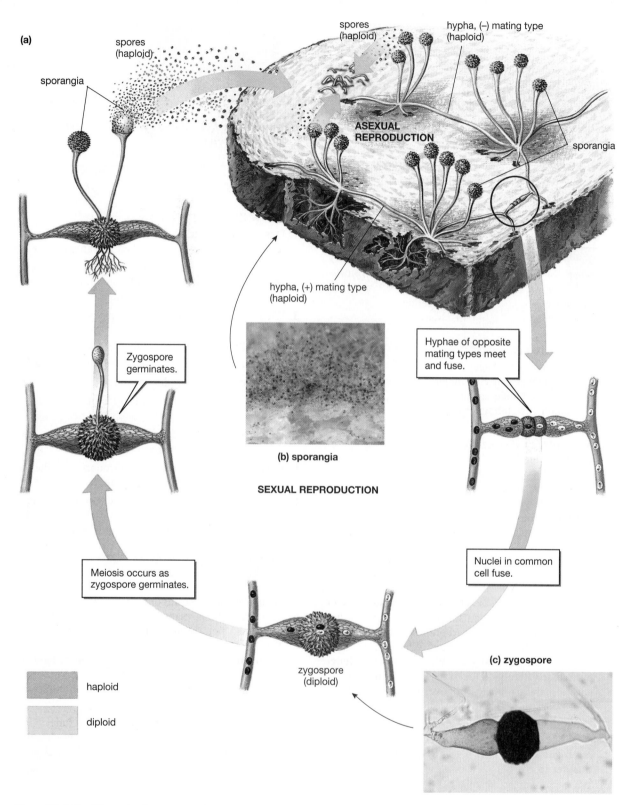

(a)

spores (haploid)

sporangia

spores (haploid)

hypha, (–) mating type (haploid)

ASEXUAL REPRODUCTION

sporangia

hypha, (+) mating type (haploid)

Zygospore germinates.

(b) sporangia

SEXUAL REPRODUCTION

Hyphae of opposite mating types meet and fuse.

Meiosis occurs as zygospore germinates.

Nuclei in common cell fuse.

(c) zygospore

zygospore (diploid)

haploid

diploid

Figure 20-4 The life cycle of a zygomycete

NOTES

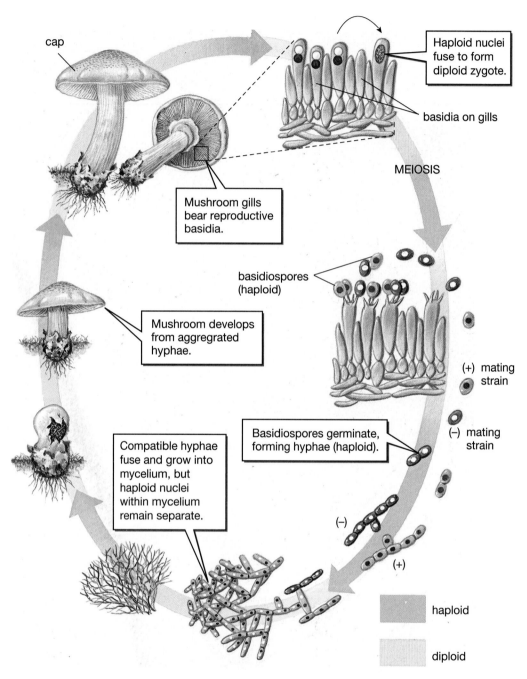

cap

Haploid nuclei fuse to form diploid zygote.

basidia on gills

Mushroom gills bear reproductive basidia.

MEIOSIS

basidiospores (haploid)

Mushroom develops from aggregrated hyphae.

(+) mating strain

(−) mating strain

Basidiospores germinate, forming hyphae (haploid).

Compatible hyphae fuse and grow into mycelium, but haploid nuclei within mycelium remain separate.

(−)

(+)

haploid

diploid

Figure 20-6 The life cycle of a "typical" basidiomycete

© 2003 Prentice Hall, Inc.

NOTES

CHAPTER 21 The Plant Kingdom

Thinking Through the Concepts

Multiple Choice

1. *Which of the following organisms bear fruit?*
   a. mosses
   b. pine trees
   c. maple trees
   d. liverworts
   e. ferns

2. *In which of the following plants is the gametophyte the dominant generation?*
   a. mosses
   b. ferns
   c. pine trees
   d. sunflowers
   e. The sporophyte is dominant in all of the above.

3. *What is the function of a fruit?*
   a. It attracts pollinators.
   b. It provides food for the developing embryo.
   c. It stores excess food produced by photosynthesis.
   d. It helps ensure seed dispersal from the parent plant.
   e. It evolved so that people would cultivate the plant, ensuring its survival.

4. *What is the function of lignin?*
   a. It provides support for the plant.
   b. It waterproofs plant surfaces.
   c. It stores food.
   d. It promotes gas exchange in plant leaves.
   e. It transports dissolved nutrients.

5. *Which of the following plants produces sperm that swim to the egg?*
   a. walnut tree
   b. Douglas fir tree, a conifer
   c. rattlesnake fern
   d. common dandelion
   e. none of the above

6. *Which of the following is the correct sequence during alternation of generations?*
   a. sporophyte—diploid spores—gametophyte—haploid gametes
   b. sporophyte—haploid spores—gametophyte—haploid gametes
   c. sporophyte—haploid gametes—gametophyte—haploid spores
   d. sporophyte—haploid gametes—gametophyte—diploid spores
   e. sporophyte—diploid gametes—gametophyte—diploid spores

? Review Questions

1. What is meant by "alternation of generations"? What two generations are involved? How does each reproduce?

2. Explain the evolutionary changes in plant reproduction that adapted plants to increasingly dry environments.

3. Describe evolutionary trends in the life cycles of plants. Emphasize the relative sizes of the gametophyte and sporophyte.

4. From which algal phylum did green plants probably arise? Explain the evidence that supports this hypothesis.

5. List the structural adaptations necessary for the invasion of dry land by plants. Which of these adaptations are possessed by bryophytes? By ferns? By gymnosperms and angiosperms?

6. The number of species of flowering plants is greater than the number of species in the rest of the plant kingdom. What feature(s) are responsible for the enormous success of angiosperms? Explain why.

7. List the adaptations of gymnosperms that have helped them become the dominant tree in dry, cold climates.

8. What is a pollen grain? What role has it played in helping plants colonize dry land?

9. The majority of all plants are seed plants. What is the advantage of a seed? How do plants that lack seeds meet the needs served by seeds?

Applying the Concepts

1. You are a geneticist working for a firm that specializes in plant biotechnology. Explain what *specific* parts (fruit, seeds, stems, roots, etc.) of the following plants you would try to alter by genetic engineering, what changes you would try to make, and why, on (a) corn, (b) tomatoes, (c) wheat, and (d) avocados.

2. Prior to the development of synthetic drugs, more than 80% of all medicines were of plant origin. Even today, indigenous tribes in remote Amazonian rain forests can provide a plant product to treat virtually any ailment. Herbal medicine is also widely and successfully practiced in China. Most of these drugs are unknown to the Western world. But the forests from which much of this plant material is obtained are being converted to agriculture. We are in danger of losing many of these potential drugs before they can be discovered. What steps can you suggest to preserve these natural resources while also allowing nations to direct their own economic development?

3. Only a few hundred of the hundreds of thousands of species in the plant kingdom have been domesticated for human use. One example is the almond. The domestic almond is nutritious and harmless, but its wild precursor can cause cyanide poisoning. The oak makes potentially nutritious seeds (acorns) that contain very bitter-tasting tannins. If we could breed the tannin out of acorns, they might become a delicacy. Why do you suppose we have failed to domesticate oaks?

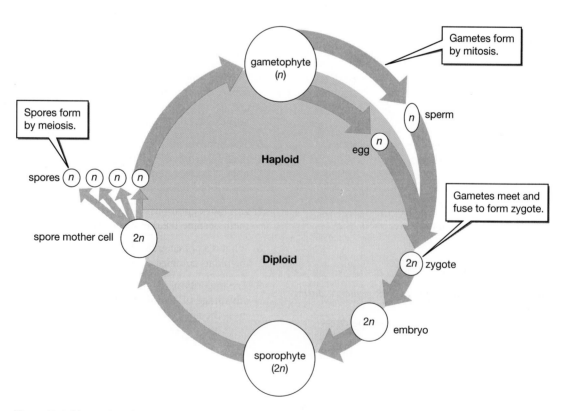

Figure 21-1 Alternation of generations in plants

© 2003 Prentice Hall, Inc.

NOTES

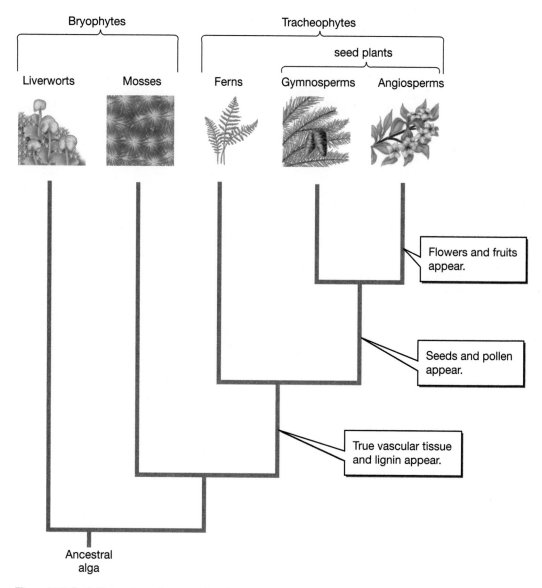

Figure 21-2 Evolutionary tree of some major plant groups

© 2003 Prentice Hall, Inc.

NOTES

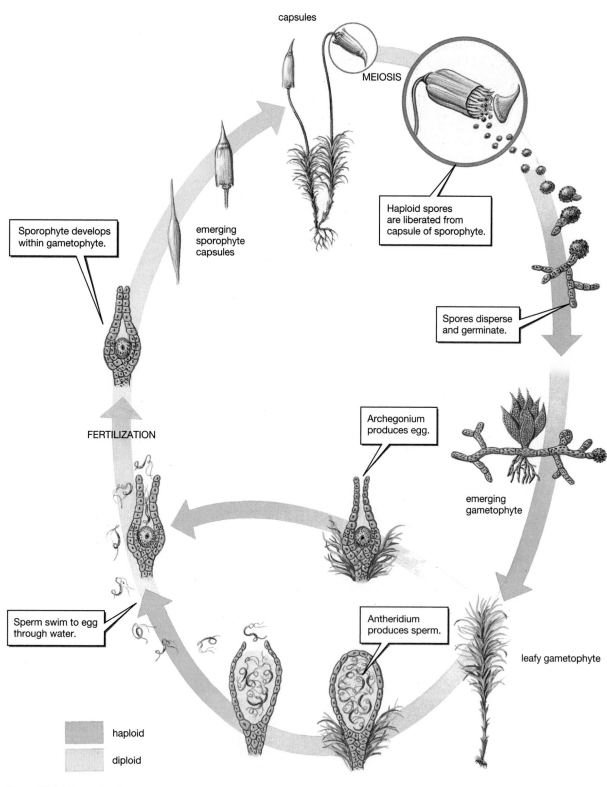

capsules

MEIOSIS

Haploid spores
are liberated from
capsule of sporophyte.

Sporophyte develops
within gametophyte.

emerging
sporophyte
capsules

Spores disperse
and germinate.

FERTILIZATION

Archegonium
produces egg.

emerging
gametophyte

Sperm swim to egg
through water.

Antheridium
produces sperm.

leafy gametophyte

haploid

diploid

Figure 21-4 Life cycle of a moss

© 2003 Prentice Hall, Inc.

NOTES

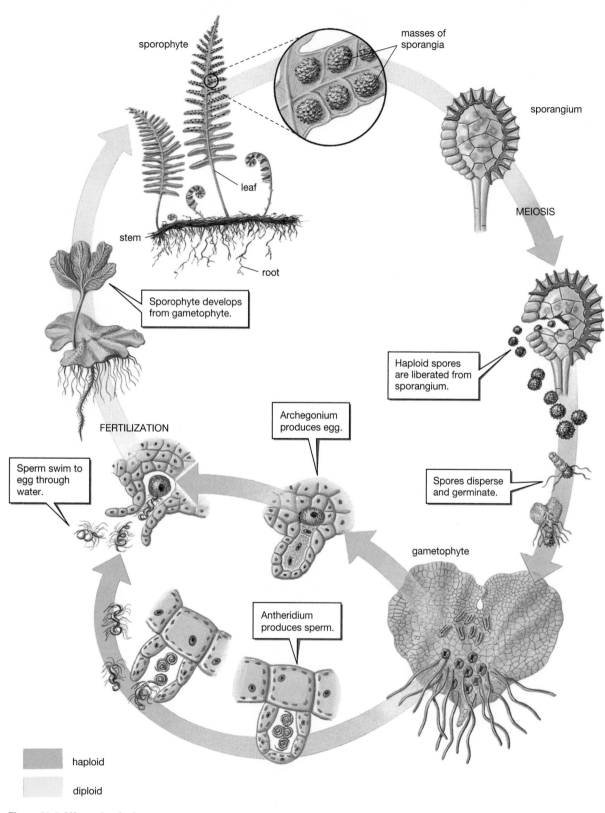

sporophyte

masses of sporangia

sporangium

leaf

MEIOSIS

stem

root

Sporophyte develops from gametophyte.

Haploid spores are liberated from sporangium.

FERTILIZATION

Archegonium produces egg.

Sperm swim to egg through water.

Spores disperse and germinate.

gametophyte

Antheridium produces sperm.

haploid

diploid

Figure 21-6 Life cycle of a fern

© 2003 Prentice Hall, Inc.

NOTES

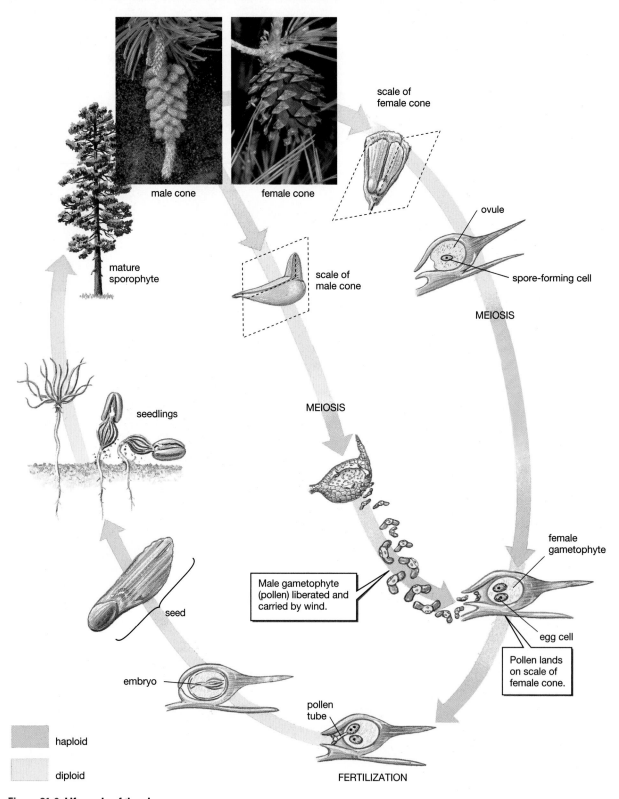

scale of
female cone

male cone

female cone

mature
sporophyte

scale of
male cone

ovule

spore-forming cell

MEIOSIS

seedlings

MEIOSIS

female
gametophyte

Male gametophyte
(pollen) liberated and
carried by wind.

egg cell

seed

Pollen lands
on scale of
female cone.

embryo

pollen
tube

haploid

diploid

FERTILIZATION

Figure 21-9 Life cycle of the pine

© 2003 Prentice Hall, Inc.

NOTES

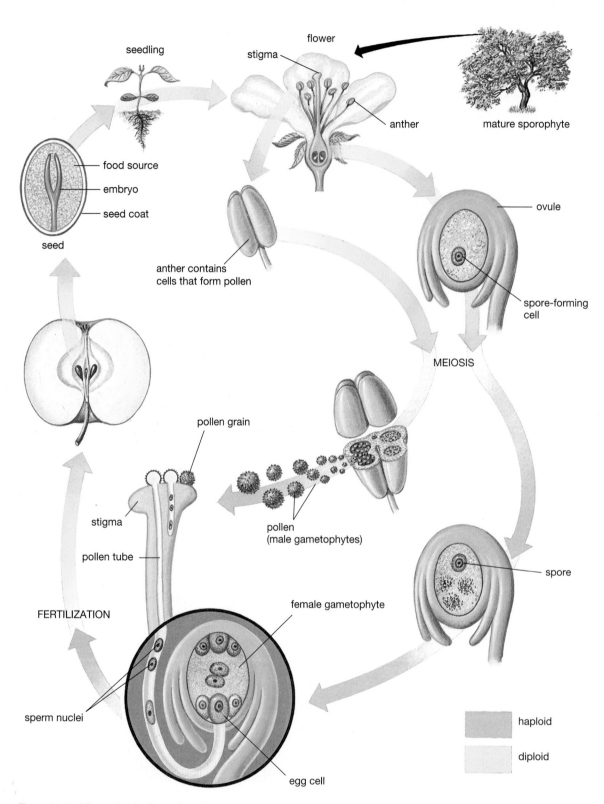

Figure 21-11 Life cycle of a flowering plant

© 2003 Prentice Hall, Inc.

NOTES

Thinking Through the Concepts

Multiple Choice

1. *Which of the following animals have radial symmetry?*
a. jellyfish   b. sea star
c. sea anemone   d. sea urchin
e. all of the above

2. *Animals in which of the following phyla have collar cells?*
a. Porifera   b. Cnidaria
c. Annelida   d. Gastropoda
e. Chordata

3. *What is a radula?*
a. a flexible supportive rod on the dorsal surface of chordates
b. a stinging cell used by sea anemones to capture prey
c. a gas-exchange structure in insects
d. a spiny ribbon of tissue used for feeding in snails
e. a locomotory structure of sea stars

4. *Which of the following groups of animals includes the first vertebrates to appear on Earth?*
a. the jawless fishes   b. the cartilaginous fishes
c. the bony fishes   d. the cephalopods
e. none of the above

5. *Which of the following animals molts its exoskeleton, allowing the animal to grow larger?*
a. the blue crab
b. the bat sea star
c. the scallop
d. the sea urchin
e. the Venus clam

6. *Which of the following has a digestive cavity with a single opening?*
a. sponges
b. sea stars
c. nematodes
d. flatworms
e. earthworms

? Review Questions

1. List the distinguishing characteristics of each of the phyla discussed in this chapter, and give an example of each.

2. Briefly describe each of the following adaptations, and explain the adaptive significance of each: amniote egg, bilateral symmetry, cephalization, closed circulatory system, coelom, placenta, radial symmetry, segmentation.

3. Describe and compare respiratory systems in the three major arthropod classes.

4. Describe the advantages and disadvantages of the arthropod exoskeleton.

5. State in which of the three major mollusk classes each of the following characteristics is found:
a. two hinged shells
b. a radula
c. tentacles
d. some sessile members
e. the best-developed brains
f. numerous eyes

6. Give three functions of the water-vascular system of echinoderms.

7. To what lifestyle is radial symmetry an adaptation? Bilateral symmetry?

8. List the vertebrate groups that have each of the following:
a. a skeleton of cartilage
b. a two-chambered heart
c. the amniote egg
d. warm-bloodedness
e. a four-chambered heart
f. a placenta
g. lungs supplemented by air sacs

9. Distinguish between vertebrates and invertebrates. List the major phyla found in each broad grouping.

10. List four distinguishing features of chordates.

11. Describe the ways in which amphibians are adapted to life on land. In what ways are amphibians still restricted to a watery or moist environment?

12. List the adaptations that distinguish reptiles from amphibians and help reptiles adapt to life in dry terrestrial environments.

13. List the adaptations of birds that contribute to their ability to fly.

14. How do mammals differ from birds, and what adaptations do they share?

15. How has the mammalian nervous system contributed to the success of mammals?

Applying the Concepts

1. The class Insecta is the largest taxon of animals on Earth. Its greatest diversity is in the Tropics, where habitat destruction and species extinction are occurring at an alarming rate. What biological, economic, and ethical arguments can you advance to persuade people and governments to preserve this biological diversity?

2. Animals, particularly laboratory rats, are used extensively in medical research. What advantages and disadvantages do lab rats have as research subjects in medicine? What are the advantages and disadvantages of using animals more closely related to humans?

3. Discuss at least three ways in which the ability to fly has contributed to the success and diversity of insects.

4. Discuss and defend what attributes you would use to define biological success among animals. Are humans a biological success by these standards? Why or why not?

(a) Radial symmetry

central axis

plane of symmetry

tentacle

(b) Bilateral symmetry

anterior

plane of symmetry

posterior

Figure 22-1 **Body symmetry and cephalization**

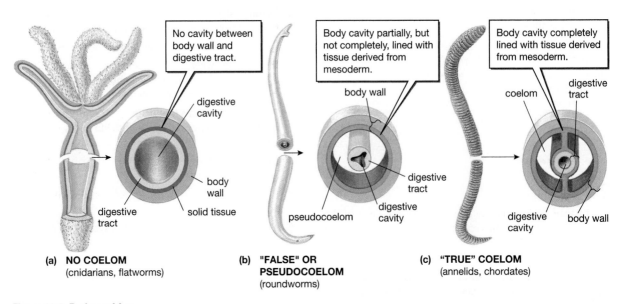

No cavity between body wall and digestive tract.

digestive cavity

body wall

digestive tract

solid tissue

(a) NO COELOM
(cnidarians, flatworms)

Body cavity partially, but not completely, lined with tissue derived from mesoderm.

body wall

digestive tract

digestive cavity

pseudocoelom

(b) "FALSE" OR PSEUDOCOELOM
(roundworms)

Body cavity completely lined with tissue derived from mesoderm.

coelom

digestive tract

digestive cavity

body wall

(c) "TRUE" COELOM
(annelids, chordates)

Figure 22-2 **Body cavities**

© 2003 Prentice Hall, Inc.

NOTES

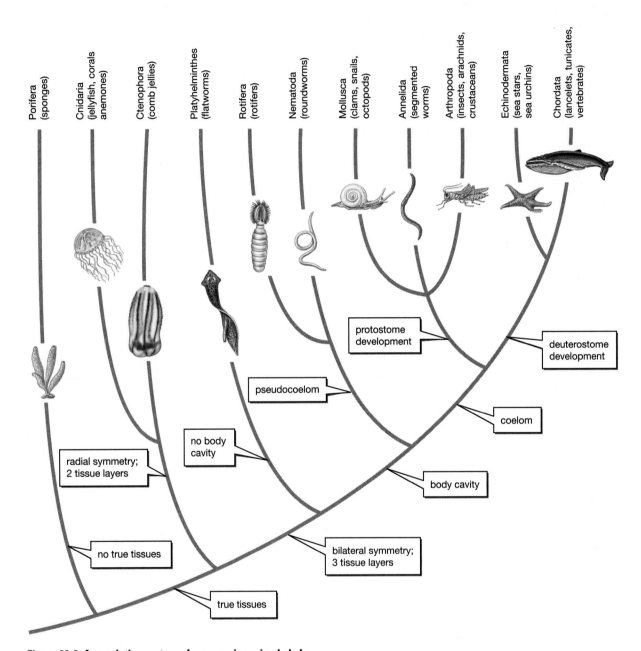

Figure 22-3 An evolutionary tree of some major animal phyla

© 2003 Prentice Hall, Inc.

NOTES

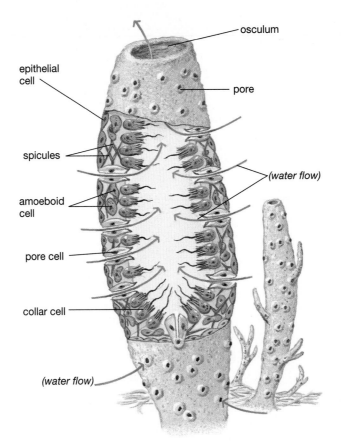

Figure 22-4 The body plan of sponges

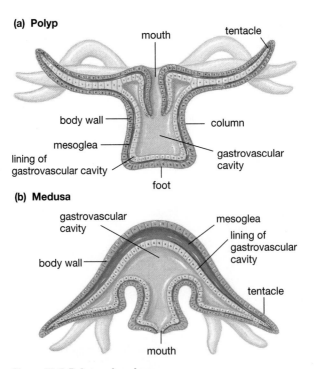

Figure 22-7 Polyp and medusa

© 2003 Prentice Hall, Inc.

NOTES

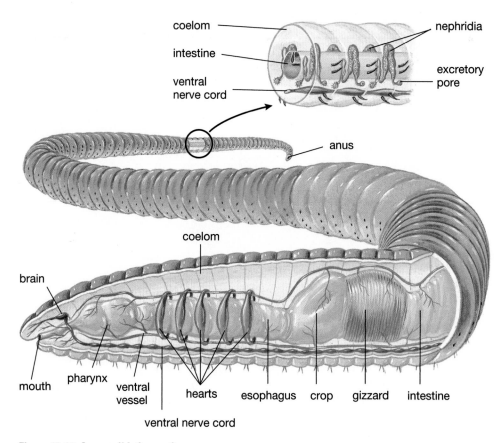

Figure 22-13 An annelid, the earthworm

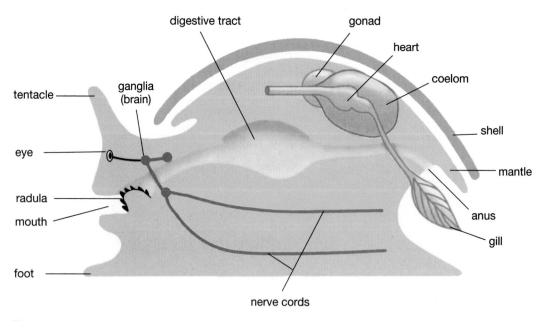

Figure 22-22 A generalized mollusk

© 2003 Prentice Hall, Inc.

NOTES

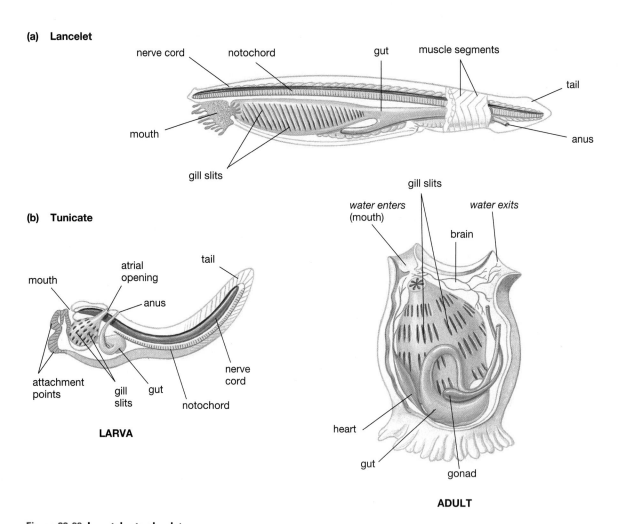

(a) Lancelet

nerve cord notochord gut muscle segments

tail

mouth

anus

gill slits

(b) Tunicate

mouth atrial opening tail

anus

attachment points gill slits gut nerve cord

notochord

LARVA

gill slits

water enters (mouth) water exits

brain

heart

gut

gonad

ADULT

Figure 22-29 **Invertebrate chordates**

© 2003 Prentice Hall, Inc.

NOTES

CHAPTER 23 Plant Form and Function

Thinking Through the Concepts

Multiple Choice

1. *In a mycorrhizal relationship, a plant root has a symbiotic relationship with*
a. a fungus that helps obtain minerals from the soil
b. a fungus that helps in the fixation of nitrogen from the air into a form usable by the plant
c. bacteria that help obtain minerals from the soil
d. bacteria that help in the fixation of nitrogen from the air into a form usable by the plant
e. an alga that helps the plant photosynthesize

2. *Which of the following is involved in the cohesion–tension theory of water movement in plants?*
a. the presence of hydrogen bonds that hold water molecules together
b. the attraction of water molecules to the walls of the xylem
c. the diffusion of water from cells in the root to cells in the shoot
d. the evaporation of water through the stomata
e. All of the above are involved in this theory.

3. *You and a friend carve your initials 5 feet above the ground on a tree on campus. The tree is now 40 feet tall. When you come back for your twenty-fifth reunion, the tree will be 100 feet tall. How high above the ground should you look for your initials?*
a. 5 feet
b. 40 feet
c. 60 feet
d. 95 feet
e. 100 feet

4. *If you wanted to show a friend how much you had learned in biology class, which of the following would you NOT use to identify a plant as a dicot?*
a. leaves with veins arranged like a net
b. hand-shaped leaves
c. six petals
d. a taproot
e. a seed with two cotyledons

5. *When water enters a plant root, it is forced to travel through the endodermal cells by the waxy*
a. cuticle
b. epidermis
c. periderm
d. xylem
e. Casparian strip

6. *Which of the following is NOT a special adaptation of certain roots, stems, or leaves?*
a. roots—photosynthesis
b. stems—water storage
c. leaves—defense
d. roots—prey capture
e. stems—producing new plants

? Review Questions

1. Describe the locations and functions of the three tissue systems in land plants.

2. Distinguish between primary growth and secondary growth, and describe the cell types involved in each.

3. Distinguish between meristem cells and differentiated cells. Which meristems cause primary growth? Which ones form secondary growth? Where is each type located?

4. Diagram the internal structure of a root after primary growth, labeling and describing the function of epidermis, cortex, endodermis, pericycle, xylem, and phloem. What tissues are located in the vascular cylinder?

5. How do xylem and phloem differ?

6. What are the main functions of roots, stems, and leaves?

7. What types of cells form root hairs? What is the function of root hairs?

8. Diagram the internal structure of leaves. What structures regulate water loss and CO_2 absorption by a leaf?

9. What role does abscisic acid play in controlling the opening and closing of stomata? Describe the daily cycle of the opening and closing of guard cells. How are various environmental conditions involved in this process?

Applying the Concepts

1. A mutant form of aphid, the klutzphid, inserts its stylet into the vessel elements of xylem. What materials are found in the fluids of xylem? Could an aphid live on xylem fluid? Would xylem fluid flow into the aphid? Explain your answer.

2. One of the foremost goals of molecular botanists is to insert the genes for nitrogen fixation, or the ability to enter into symbiotic relationships with nitrogen-fixing bacteria, into crop plants such as corn or wheat (see Chapter 13). Why would the insertion of such genes be useful? What changes in farming practices would this technique allow?

3. We learned in Chapter 2 about the peculiar characteristics of water. Discuss several ways in which the evolution of vascular plants has been greatly influenced by water's special characteristics.

4. A major environmental problem is desertification, in which overgrazing by cattle or other animals results in too few plants in an area. Show how what you know about the movement of water through plants enables you to understand this process, in which there is less water in the atmosphere, less rain, and thus dry, desertlike conditions.

5. The tropical rain forest contains a large number of as-yet unidentified plants, many of which may have uses as medicines or food. If you were given the job of searching a particular portion of the rain forest for useful products, how would you use the information you gained from this chapter to help you narrow your search? What kinds of plant tissues or organs would be most likely to contain such products?

6. The desert tends to have two types of plants with respect to their root systems—small grasses or herbs, and shrubs or small trees. The grasses and herbs typically form fibrous root systems. The shrubs and trees form taproot systems. What advantages can you think of for each system? How does each type of root allow for survival in a desert environment?

7. Grasses (monocots) form their primary meristem near the ground surface rather than at the tips of branches the way dicots do. How does this feature allow you to grow a lawn and mow it every week in the summer? What would happen if you had a dicot lawn and tried to mow it?

8. Discuss the structures and adaptations that might occur in the leaves of plants living in (a) dry, sunny habitats; (b) wet, sunny habitats; (c) dry, shady habitats; and (d) wet, shady habitats. Which of these habitats do you think would be most inhospitable (for example, in which habitat would it be most difficult to design a functioning leaf)?

© 2003 Prentice Hall, Inc.

NOTES

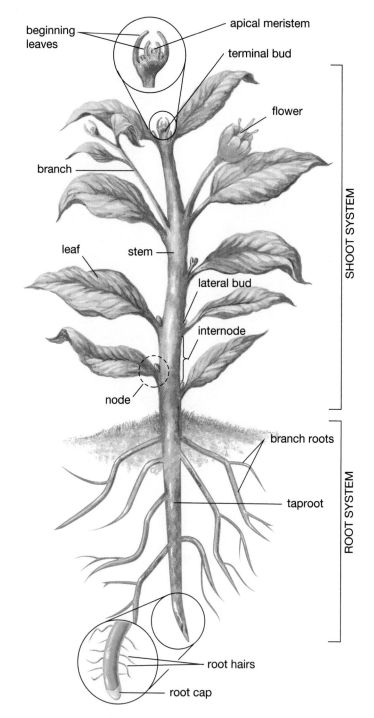

Figure 23-1 Flowering plant structure

© 2003 Prentice Hall, Inc.

NOTES

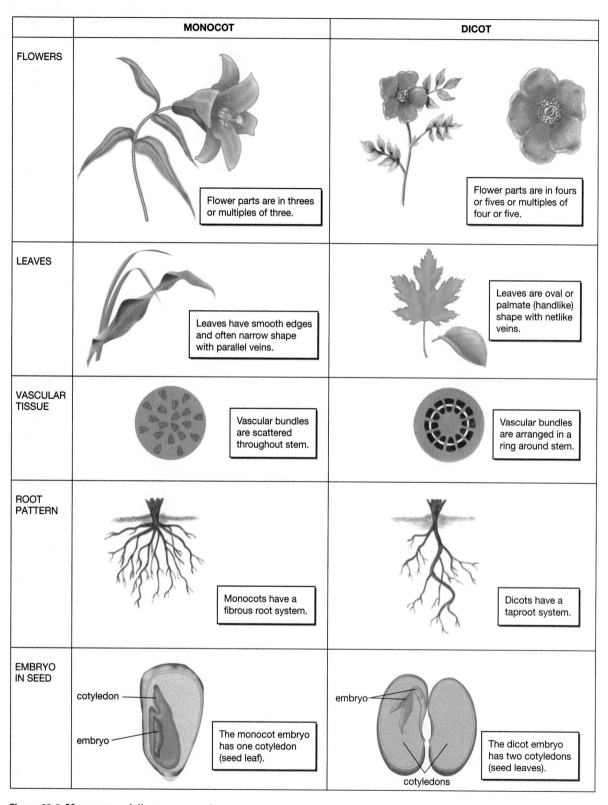

Figure 23-2 Monocots and dicots compared

© 2003 Prentice Hall, Inc.

NOTES

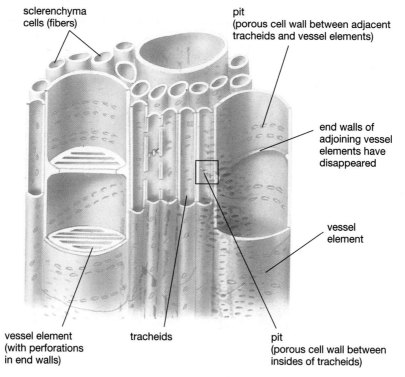

sclerenchyma
cells (fibers)

pit
(porous cell wall between adjacent
tracheids and vessel elements)

end walls of
adjoining vessel
elements have
disappeared

vessel
element

vessel element
(with perforations
in end walls)

tracheids

pit
(porous cell wall between
insides of tracheids)

Figure 23-6 **The structure of xylem**

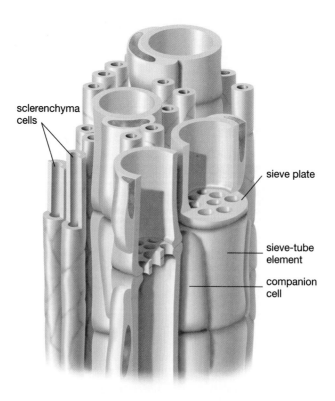

sclerenchyma
cells

sieve plate

sieve-tube
element

companion
cell

Figure 23-7 **The structure of phloem**

© 2003 Prentice Hall, Inc.

NOTES

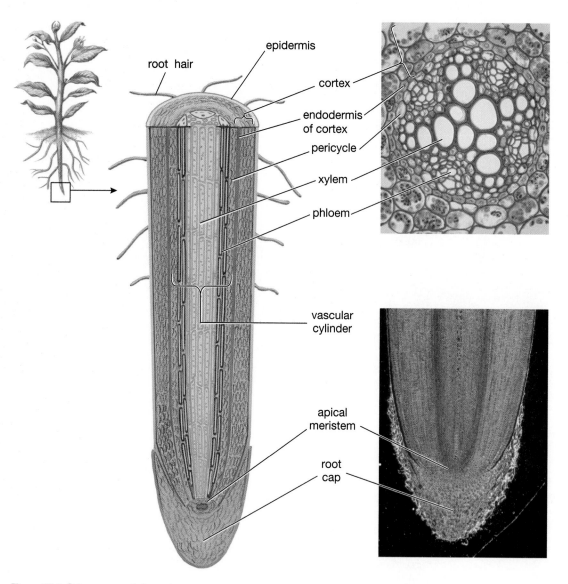

root hair

epidermis

cortex

endodermis
of cortex

pericycle

xylem

phloem

vascular
cylinder

apical
meristem

root
cap

Figure 23-9 Primary growth in roots

© 2003 Prentice Hall, Inc.

NOTES

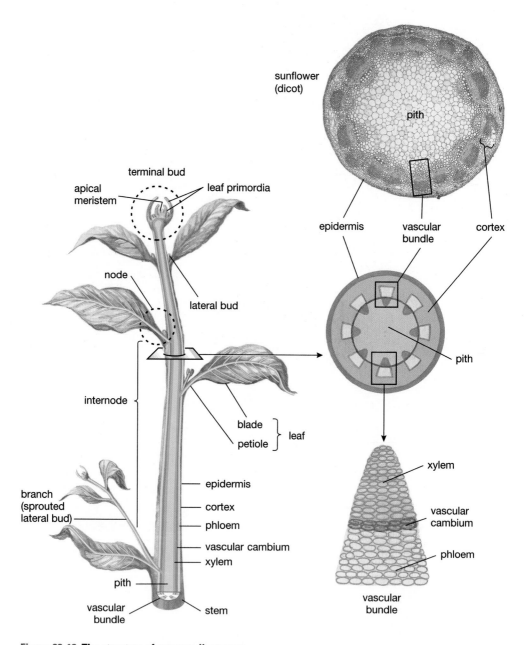

Figure 23-13 The structure of a young dicot stem

© 2003 Prentice Hall, Inc.

NOTES

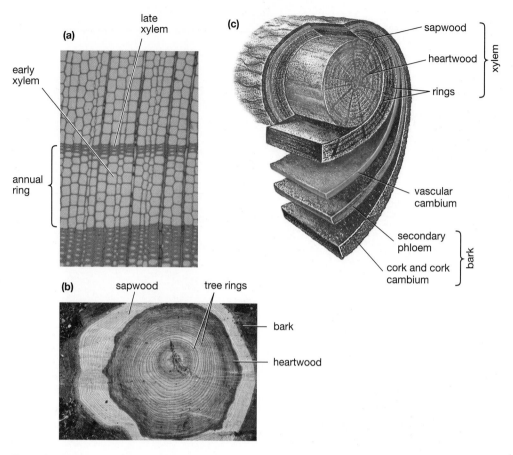

Figure 23-16 **How tree rings are formed**

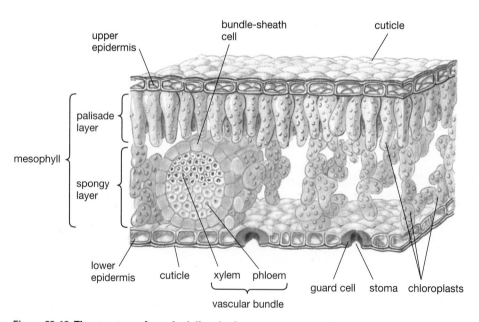

Figure 23-18 **The structure of a typical dicot leaf**

© 2003 Prentice Hall, Inc.

NOTES

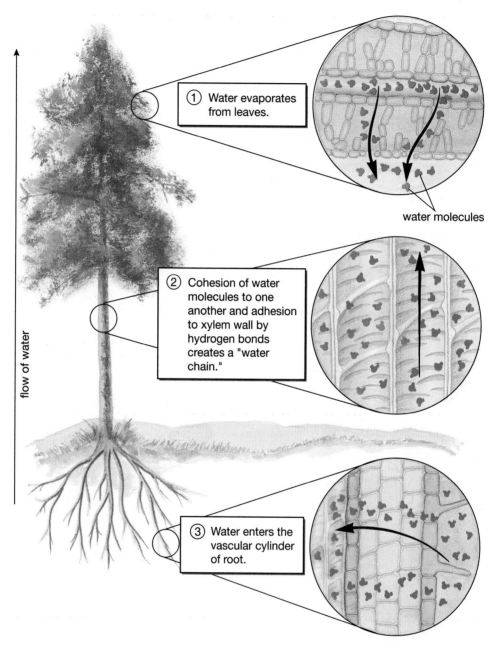

Figure 23-22 The cohesion–tension theory of water flow from root to leaf in xylem

© 2003 Prentice Hall, Inc.

NOTES

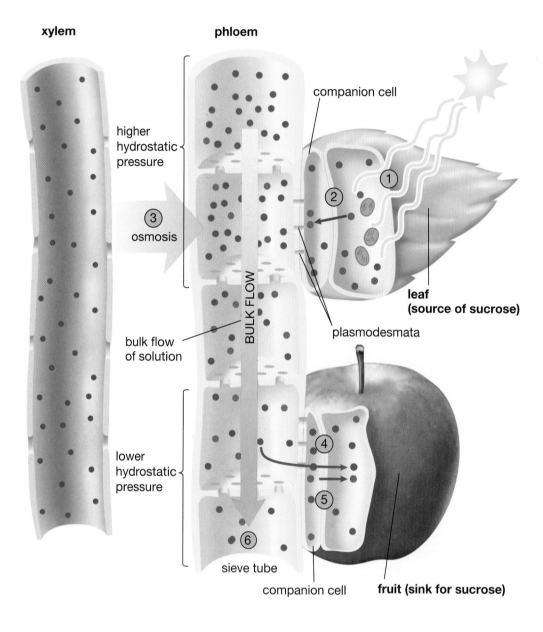

xylem

phloem

companion cell

higher
hydrostatic
pressure

③
osmosis

BULK FLOW

bulk flow
of solution

plasmodesmata

**leaf
(source of sucrose)**

lower
hydrostatic
pressure

sieve tube

companion cell

fruit (sink for sucrose)

• water ———→ osmosis

• sucrose ———→ active transport of sucrose

Figure 23-25 The pressure-flow theory

© 2003 Prentice Hall, Inc.

NOTES

CHAPTER 24 Plant Reproduction and Development

Thinking Through the Concepts

Multiple Choice

1. *When a bee gets nectar from a flower, the bee picks up pollen from the _____ and carries it to another flower.*
a. stigma
b. ovary
c. sepals
d. anthers
e. filament

2. *In plants, the gametophyte produces eggs and sperm by*
a. mitosis
b. meiosis
c. spore formation
d. fertilization
e. germination

3. *If you found a dark, rotten-smelling flower near the ground, it would most likely be pollinated by*
a. bats
b. bees
c. butterflies
d. moths
e. beetles

4. *Reproduction in flowering plants is known as double fertilization because*
a. one tube nucleus fuses with one egg, and one sperm nucleus fuses with another egg
b. two sperm nuclei fuse with one egg
c. one sperm fuses with two eggs
d. one sperm nucleus fuses with one egg, and another sperm nucleus fuses with the two haploid nuclei of the primary endosperm cell
e. two polar nuclei fuse with one egg nucleus

5. *In a peach, the fruit is derived from the*
a. wall of the ovary
b. endosperm
c. megaspores
d. sepals
e. petals

6. *The tassel on top of a corn plant is made up of male flowers that lack female structures. This flower is*
a. the sporophyte
b. the gametophyte
c. incomplete
d. complete
e. homologous

? Review Questions

1. Diagram the plant life cycle, comparing ferns with flowering plants. Which stages are haploid, and which are diploid? At which stage are gametes formed?

2. What are the advantages of the reduced gametophyte stages in flowering plants, compared with the more substantial gametophytes of ferns?

3. Diagram a complete flower. Where are the male and female gametophytes formed? What are these gametophytes called?

4. How does an egg develop within an embryo sac? How does this structure allow double fertilization to occur?

5. What does it mean when we say that pollen is the male gametophyte? How is pollen formed?

6. What are the parts of a seed, and how does each part help in the development of a seedling?

7. Describe the characteristics you would expect to find in flowers that are pollinated by the wind, beetles, bees, and hummingbirds, respectively. In each case, explain why.

8. What is the endosperm? From which cell of the embryo sac is it derived? Is endosperm more abundant in the mature seed of a dicot or of a monocot?

9. Describe three mechanisms whereby seed dormancy is broken in different types of seeds. How are these mechanisms related to the normal environment of the plant?

10. How do monocot and dicot seedlings protect the delicate shoot tip during seed germination?

11. Describe three types of fruits and the mechanisms whereby these fruit structures help disperse their seeds.

Applying the Concepts

1. A friend gives you some seeds for you to grow in your yard. When you plant some, nothing happens. What might you try to get the seed to germinate?

2. In areas where farms have been left uncultivated for several years, it is often possible to see certain kinds of trees growing in straight lines, which mark old fences where birds sat and deposited seeds they had eaten. Why are such seeds more likely to germinate than are those of the same species that have not passed through a bird's digestive tract? How might an anthropologist use such lines of trees to study past inhabitants of an area?

3. Charles Darwin once described a flower that produced nectar at the bottom of a tube 25 centimeters (10.5 inches) deep. He predicted that there must be a moth or other animal with a 25-centimeter-long tongue to match; he was right. Such specialization almost certainly means that this particular flower could be pollinated only by that specific moth. What are the advantages and disadvantages of such specialization?

4. Many plants that we call *weeds* were brought from another continent either accidentally or purposefully. In a new environment they have few competitors or animal predators, so they tend to grow in such large amounts that they come to be considered weeds. Think of all the ways you can in which humans become involved in plant dispersal. To what degree do you think humans have changed the distributions of plants? In what ways is this change helpful to humans? In what ways is it a disadvantage?

5. In the Tropics there are a number of plant–animal coevolutionary relationships in which both are dependent on the relationship. In light of the rapid rate of destruction of tropical ecosystems, how does this type of relationship leave both organisms particularly vulnerable to extinction? What political and economic problems might this rapid rate of extinction create?

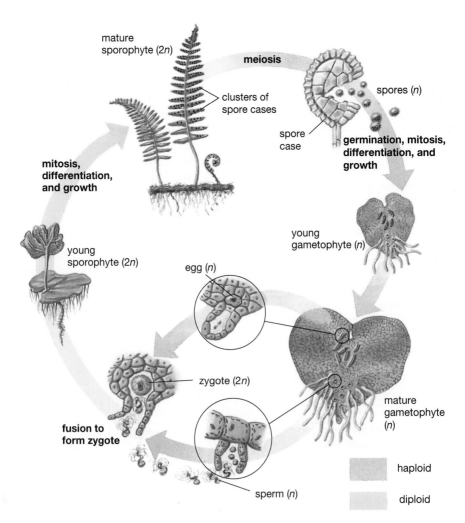

Figure 24-1 The life cycle of a fern—a nonflowering plant

© 2003 Prentice Hall, Inc.

NOTES

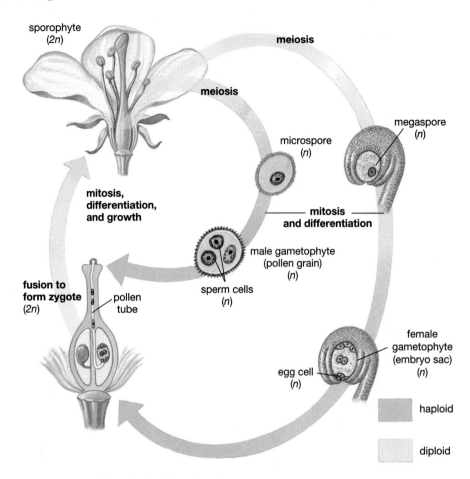

Figure 24-2 **The life cycle of a flowering plant**

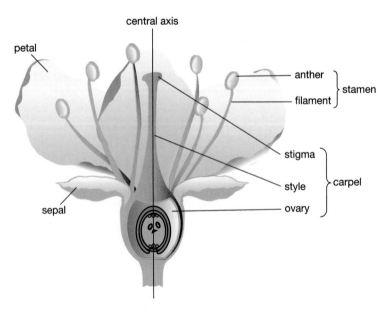

Figure 24-4 **A complete flower**

© 2003 Prentice Hall, Inc.

NOTES

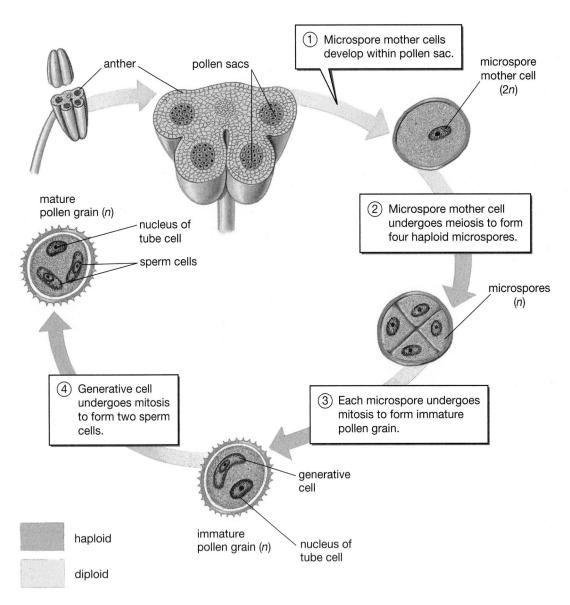

anther   pollen sacs

① Microspore mother cells develop within pollen sac.

microspore mother cell (2n)

② Microspore mother cell undergoes meiosis to form four haploid microspores.

microspores (n)

mature pollen grain (n)

nucleus of tube cell

sperm cells

④ Generative cell undergoes mitosis to form two sperm cells.

③ Each microspore undergoes mitosis to form immature pollen grain.

generative cell

immature pollen grain (n)

nucleus of tube cell

haploid

diploid

Figure 24-6 Pollen development in flowering plants

© 2003 Prentice Hall, Inc.

NOTES

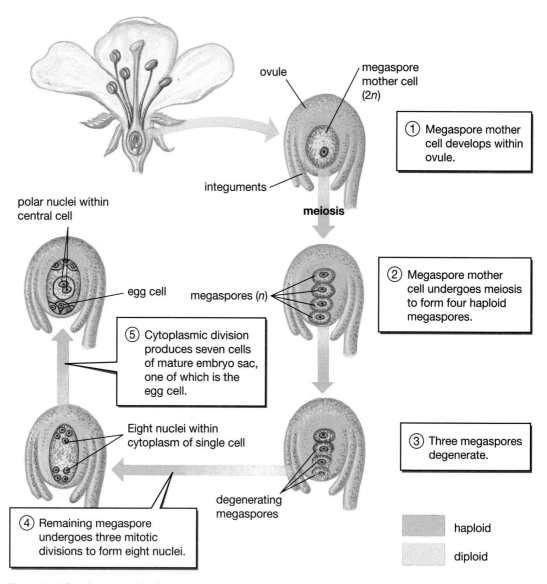

ovule

megaspore mother cell (2*n*)

① Megaspore mother cell develops within ovule.

integuments

meiosis

polar nuclei within central cell

egg cell

megaspores (*n*)

② Megaspore mother cell undergoes meiosis to form four haploid megaspores.

⑤ Cytoplasmic division produces seven cells of mature embryo sac, one of which is the egg cell.

Eight nuclei within cytoplasm of single cell

③ Three megaspores degenerate.

degenerating megaspores

④ Remaining megaspore undergoes three mitotic divisions to form eight nuclei.

haploid

diploid

Figure 24-8 Development of the female gametophyte

© 2003 Prentice Hall, Inc.

NOTES

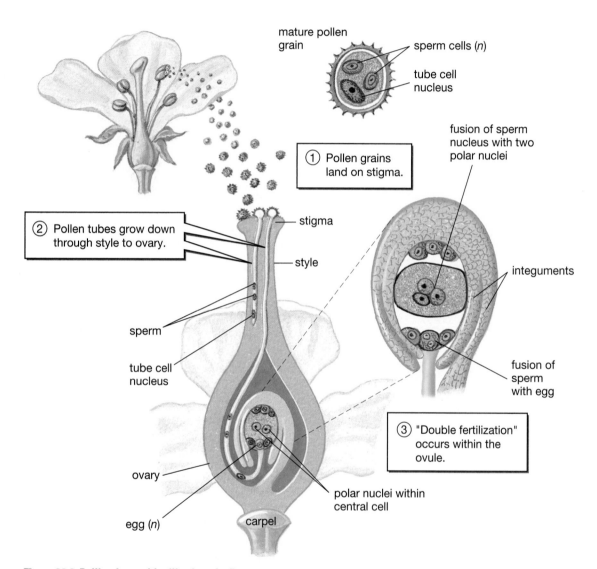

mature pollen grain

sperm cells (*n*)

tube cell nucleus

① Pollen grains land on stigma.

② Pollen tubes grow down through style to ovary.

stigma

style

sperm

tube cell nucleus

ovary

egg (*n*)

carpel

polar nuclei within central cell

fusion of sperm nucleus with two polar nuclei

integuments

fusion of sperm with egg

③ "Double fertilization" occurs within the ovule.

Figure 24-9 Pollination and fertilization of a flower

© 2003 Prentice Hall, Inc.

NOTES

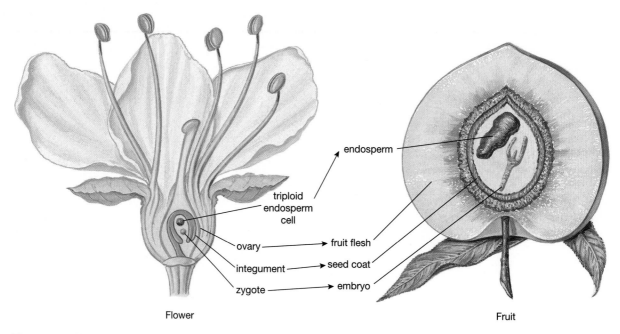

Figure 24-10 Development of fruit and seeds from flower parts

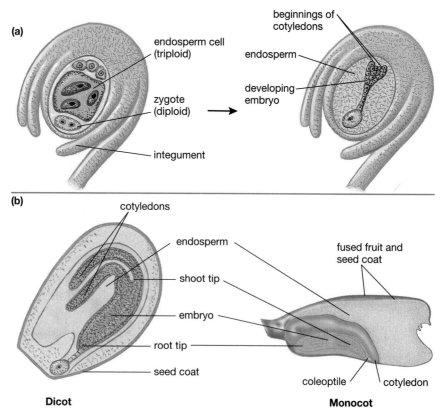

Figure 24-11 Seed development

© 2003 Prentice Hall, Inc.

NOTES

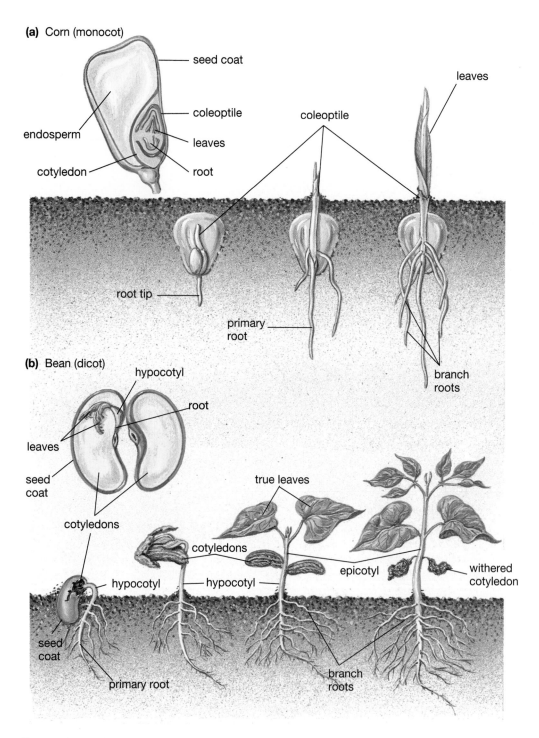

(a) Corn (monocot)

seed coat

coleoptile

endosperm

leaves

cotyledon

root

coleoptile

leaves

root tip

primary root

branch roots

(b) Bean (dicot)

hypocotyl

root

leaves

seed coat

cotyledons

hypocotyl

hypocotyl

true leaves

cotyledons

epicotyl

withered cotyledon

seed coat

primary root

branch roots

Figure 24-12 Seed germination

© 2003 Prentice Hall, Inc.

NOTES

CHAPTER 25

Plant Responses
to the Environment

Thinking Through the Concepts

Multiple Choice

1. *If you put an underripe banana in a bag with an apple, the banana will quickly ripen because of the hormone _____ produced by the apple.*
a. auxin
b. cytokinin
c. gibberellin
d. abscisic acid
e. ethylene

2. *Roots turn downward in a process known as*
a. phototropism
b. abscission
c. apical dominance
d. gravitropism
e. dormancy

3. *If you grow coleus plants, you will need to cut or pinch off the top bud frequently to keep the plant from becoming tall and spindly. Pinching off this bud will slow the production of _____ by the apical bud and allow the plant to become bushy.*
a. auxin
b. cytokinin
c. gibberellin
d. abscisic acid
e. ethylene

4. *In your warm house, poinsettias act as short-day plants that turn red when the daylength is less than 12 hours. If you want to get a poinsettia ready for Christmas, which of the following would work best?*
a. Give it continuous light.
b. Give it continuous darkness.
c. Keep it in the dark, but shine a light on it for an hour every 13 hours.
d. Keep it in the light except for turning off the light once a day for 1 hour.
e. None of these would get it to turn red.

5. *When a seed is first formed in the fall, it typically will not germinate because _____ must first be washed from the seed by a hard rain or broken down by cycles of freezing and thawing.*
a. auxin
b. cytokinin
c. gibberellin
d. abscisic acid
e. ethylene

6. *The seed of Question 5 germinates as levels of _____ increase.*
a. auxin
b. cytokinin
c. gibberellin
d. abscisic acid
e. ethylene

? Review Questions

1. What did the Darwins, Boysen-Jensen, and Went each contribute to our understanding of phototropism? Do their experiments truly prove that auxin is the hormone controlling phototropism? What other experiments would you like to see?

2. How do hormones interact to cause apical dominance? To control seed dormancy?

3. How can one hormone, an auxin, cause shoots to grow up and roots to grow down?

4. What is the phytochrome system? Why does this chemical exist in two forms? How do the two forms interact to help control the plant life cycle?

5. Which hormones cause fruit development? From where do these hormones come? Which hormone causes fruit ripening?

6. What is a biological clock?

7. Describe the role of phytochrome in stem elongation in seedlings that grow in the shade of other plants. What is the likely adaptive significance of this response?

8. What is apical dominance? How do auxin and cytokinin interact in determining the growth of lateral buds?

9. Which hormone(s) is (are) involved in leaf and fruit drop? In bud dormancy?

Applying the Concepts

1. Suppose you got a job in a greenhouse in which the owner was trying to start the flowering of chrysanthemums (a short-day plant) for Mother's Day. You accidentally turned on the light in the middle of the night. Would you be likely to lose your job? Why or why not? What would happen if you turned on the lights in the day?

2. A student reporting on a project said that one of her seeds did not grow properly because it was planted upside down so that it got confused and tried to grow down. Do you think the teacher accepted this explanation? Why or why not? Which plant hormone or hormones would be involved?

3. Agent Orange, a combination of two synthetic auxins, was used in Vietnam to defoliate the rain forest during the Vietnam War. When they are similar to natural growth hormones, how can synthetic auxins be used to harm or kill plants? What do you think would happen if natural auxins were used in excess quantities on plants?

4. Bean sprouts such as those you might eat in a salad have to be grown in the dark for them to form the long, yellowish stems that you see. We call such stems *etiolated*. If they are grown in the light, they will be short and green. Why do seedlings grow etiolated in the dark? Under what conditions does etiolation occur in nature? How do plant hormones enable these seedlings to form this shape?

5. Suppose that on July 4, you discover that both a short-day plant and a long-day plant have bloomed in your garden. Discuss how it is possible for both to bloom.

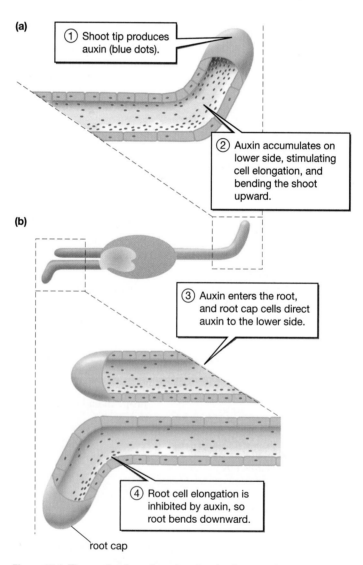

(a)

① Shoot tip produces auxin (blue dots).

② Auxin accumulates on lower side, stimulating cell elongation, and bending the shoot upward.

(b)

③ Auxin enters the root, and root cap cells direct auxin to the lower side.

④ Root cell elongation is inhibited by auxin, so root bends downward.

root cap

Figure 25-1 The mechanism of gravitropism in shoots and roots

© 2003 Prentice Hall, Inc.

NOTES

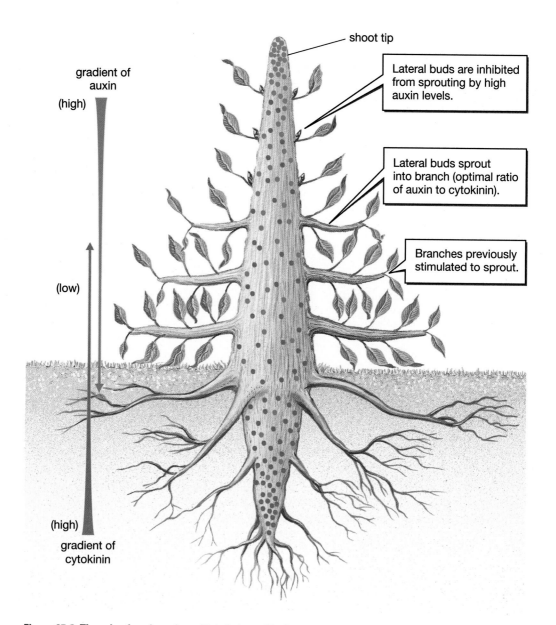

shoot tip

Lateral buds are inhibited from sprouting by high auxin levels.

Lateral buds sprout into branch (optimal ratio of auxin to cytokinin).

Branches previously stimulated to sprout.

gradient of auxin

(high)

(low)

(high)

gradient of cytokinin

Figure 25-3 **The role of auxin and cytokinin in lateral bud sprouting**

© 2003 Prentice Hall, Inc.

NOTES

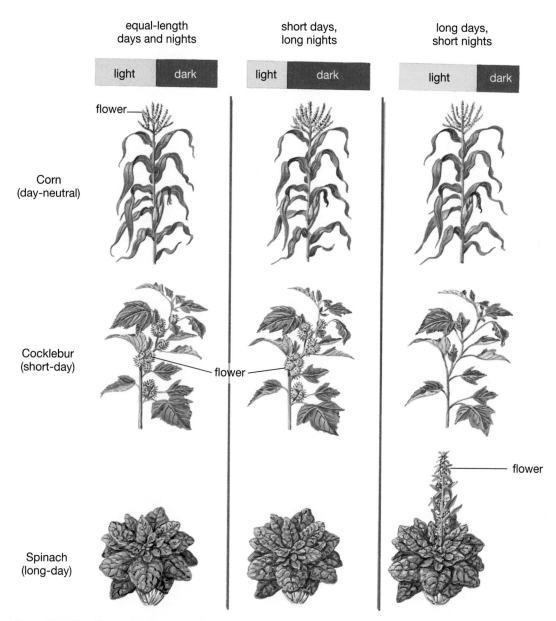

Figure 25-4 The effects of daylength on flowering

© 2003 Prentice Hall, Inc.

NOTES

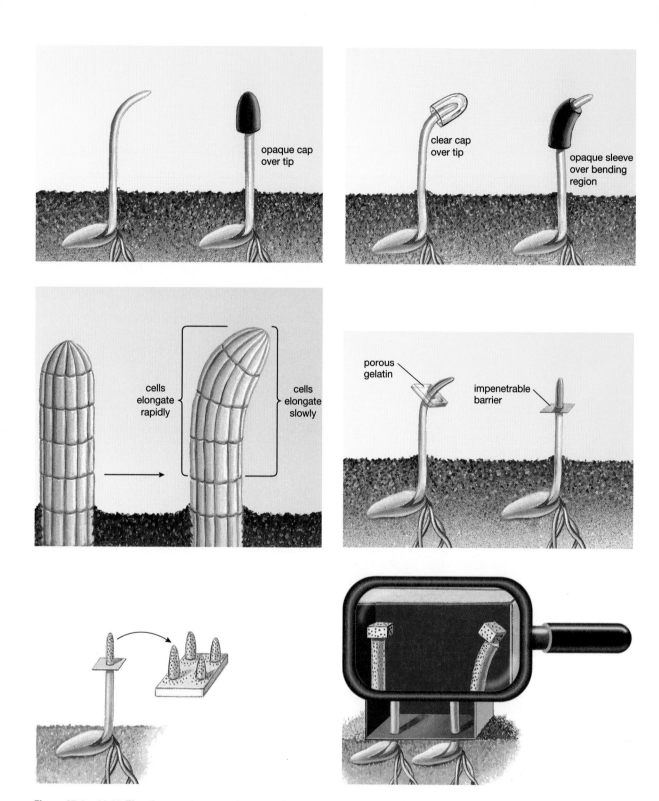

Figure 25-1un01-06 The phototropism experiments of Charles and Francis Darwin

© 2003 Prentice Hall, Inc.

NOTES

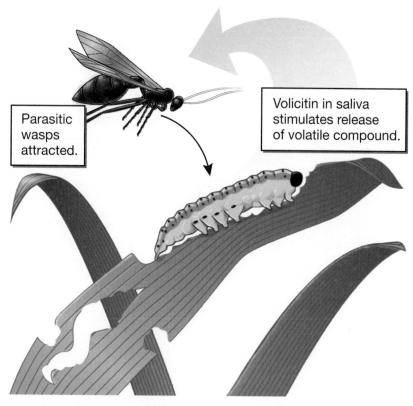

Figure 25-9 A chemical cry for help

© 2003 Prentice Hall, Inc.

NOTES

CHAPTER 26 Homeostasis and the Organization of the Animal Body

Thinking Through the Concepts

Multiple Choice

1. *The skin contains*
   a. epithelial tissue
   b. connective tissue
   c. nerve tissue
   d. muscle tissue
   e. all of the above

2. *Glands that become separated from the epithelium that produced them are called _____ glands.*
   a. sebaceous
   b. sweat
   c. exocrine
   d. endocrine
   e. saliva

3. *Epithelial membranes*
   a. cover the body
   b. line body cavities
   c. may create barriers that alter the movement of certain substances
   d. are continuously replaced by cell division
   e. all of the above

4. *All of the following are examples of connective tissue EXCEPT*
   a. tendons
   b. ligaments
   c. blood
   d. muscle
   e. adipose tissue

5. *Which of the following statements about muscle is true?*
   a. Smooth muscle is important in locomotion.
   b. Skeletal muscle is not under conscious control.
   c. Cardiac muscle utilizes gap junctions.
   d. Smooth muscle is called voluntary muscle.
   e. Smooth muscle moves the skeleton.

6. *All of the following are found in the dermis EXCEPT*
   a. arteries
   b. sensory nerve endings
   c. hair follicles
   d. sebaceous glands
   e. cells packed with keratin

? Review Questions

1. Define *homeostasis*, and explain how negative feedback helps maintain it. Explain one example of homeostasis in the human body.

2. Explain positive feedback, and provide one physiological example. Explain why this type of feedback is relatively rare in physiological processes.

3. Explain why body temperature in humans cannot be maintained at *exactly* 37 °C (98.6 °F) at all times.

4. Describe the structure and functions of epithelial tissue.

5. What property distinguishes connective tissue from all other tissue types? List five types of connective tissue, and briefly describe the function of each type.

6. Describe the skin, a representative organ. Include the various tissues that compose it and the role of each tissue.

Applying the Concepts

1. Why does life on land present more difficulties in maintaining homeostasis than does life in water? What made it evolutionarily advantageous for organisms to colonize dry land?

2. The majority of homeostatic regulatory mechanisms in animals are "autonomic"—that is, not requiring conscious control. Discuss several reasons why this type of regulation is more advantageous to the animal than is conscious regulation of homeostatic controls.

3. Third-degree burns are usually painless. Skin regenerates only from the edges of these wounds. Second-degree burns regenerate from cells located at the burn edges, in hair follicles and in sweat glands. First-degree burns are painful but heal rapidly from undamaged epidermal cells. From this information, draw the depth of first-, second-, and third-degree burns on Figure 26-10.

4. A coroner dictates the following description during an autopsy: "The tissue I am looking at forms part of the fetal skeleton. The extracellular matrix appears transparent. Fibers of collagen are present but are small and evenly dispersed in the extracellular matrix. Chondrocytes appear in tiny spaces, *lacunae,* within the matrix. Blood vessels have not yet penetrated the matrix." What tissue is the coroner describing?

5. Imagine you are a health-care professional teaching a prenatal class for fathers. Design a real-world analogy with sensors, electrical currents, motors, and so on to illustrate feedback relationships involved in the initiation of labor that a layperson could understand.

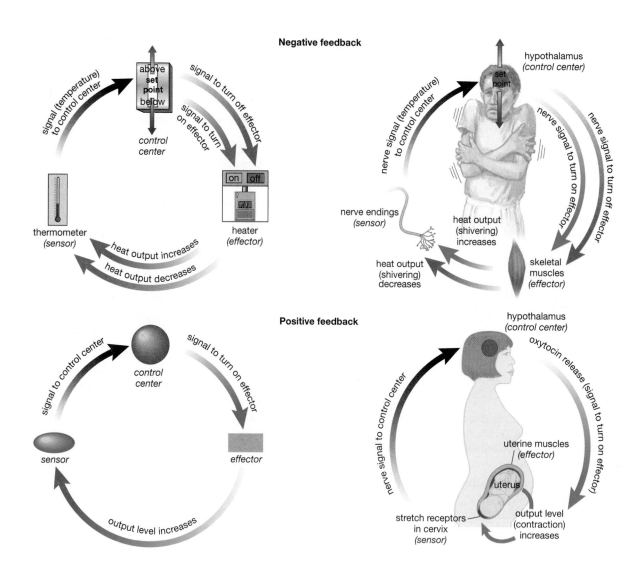

Figure 26-1 Negative and positive feedbacks

© 2003 Prentice Hall, Inc.

NOTES

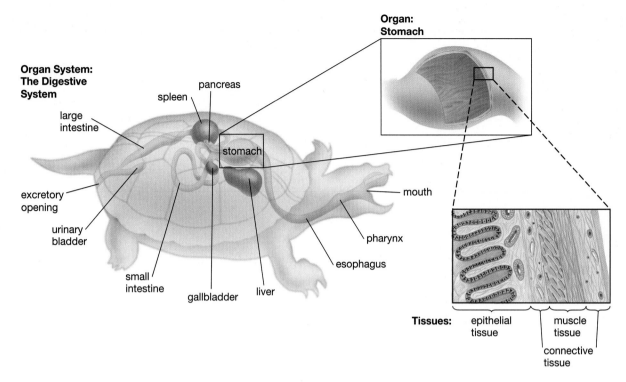

**Organ:
Stomach**

**Organ System:
The Digestive
System**

pancreas

spleen

large
intestine

stomach

excretory
opening

mouth

urinary
bladder

pharynx

esophagus

small
intestine

gallbladder   liver

Tissues: epithelial   muscle
              tissue   tissue

connective
tissue

Figure 26-2 Organ systems, organs, and tissues

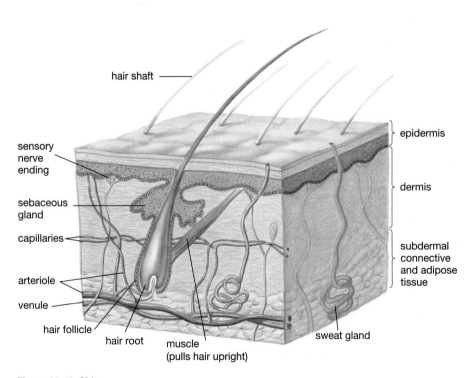

hair shaft

epidermis

sensory
nerve
ending

dermis

sebaceous
gland

capillaries

subdermal
connective
and adipose
tissue

arteriole

venule

hair follicle

hair root   muscle
              (pulls hair upright)

sweat gland

Figure 26-10 Skin

© 2003 Prentice Hall, Inc.

NOTES

CHAPTER 27 Circulation

Thinking Through the Concepts

Multiple Choice

1. *Which of the following is NOT an important function of the vertebrate circulatory system?*
   a. transport of nutrients and respiratory gases
   b. regulation of body temperature
   c. protection of the body by circulating antibodies
   d. removal of waste products for excretion from the body
   e. defense against blood loss, through clotting

2. *Which event initiates blood clotting?*
   a. contact with an irregular surface by platelets and other factors in plasma
   b. production of the enzyme thrombin
   c. conversion of fibrinogen into fibrin
   d. conversion of fibrin into fibrinogen
   e. excess flow of blood through a capillary

3. *The sites of exchange of wastes, nutrients, gases, and hormones between the blood and body cells are the*
   a. arteries
   b. arterioles
   c. capillaries
   d. veins
   e. all blood vessels

4. *What produces systolic blood pressure?*
   a. contraction of the right atrium
   b. contraction of the right ventricle
   c. contraction of the left atrium
   d. contraction of the left ventricle
   e. the pause between heartbeats

5. *Which of the following is NOT a component of plasma?*
   a. water
   b. globulins
   c. fibrinogen
   d. albumins
   e. platelets

6. *Lymph most closely resembles which of the following?*
   a. blood
   b. urine
   c. plasma
   d. interstitial fluid
   e. water

? Review Questions

1. Trace the flow of blood through the circulatory system, starting and ending with the right atrium.

2. List three types of blood cells, and describe their principal functions.

3. What are five functions of the vertebrate circulatory system?

4. In what way do veins and lymph vessels resemble one another? Describe how fluid is transported in each of these vessels.

5. Describe three important functions of the lymphatic system.

6. Distinguish among plasma, interstitial fluid, and lymph.

7. Describe veins, capillaries, and arteries, noting their similarities and differences.

8. Trace the evolution of the vertebrate heart from two chambers to four chambers.

9. Explain in detail what causes the vertebrate heart to beat.

10. Describe the cardiac cycle, and relate the contractions of the atria and ventricles to the two readings taken during the measurement of blood pressure.

11. Describe how the number of red blood cells is regulated by a negative feedback system.

12. Describe the formation of an atherosclerotic plaque. What are the risks associated with atherosclerosis?

Applying the Concepts

1. Discuss the steps you can take now and in the future to reduce your risks of developing heart disease.

2. Discuss why a four-chambered heart is much more efficient than a two-chambered heart in delivering oxygenated blood to the various body parts. What evolutionary changes in the lifestyles of organisms selected for the evolution of the four-chambered heart?

3. Heart surgeons have attempted to transplant baboon hearts into humans whose hearts were failing. Discuss the implications of this operation from as many angles as you can think of.

4. Considering the prevalence of cardiovascular disease and the high, increasing costs of treating it, certain treatments may not be available to all who might benefit from them. What factors would you take into account in rationing cardiovascular procedures, such as heart transplants?

5. Joe, a 45-year-old executive of a major corporation, has been diagnosed with mild hypertension. What treatments or lifestyle changes might Joe's physician recommend? If Joe's hypertension becomes more severe, what treatments might Joe's physician use? Should Joe be concerned about mild hypertension? Explain your answer.

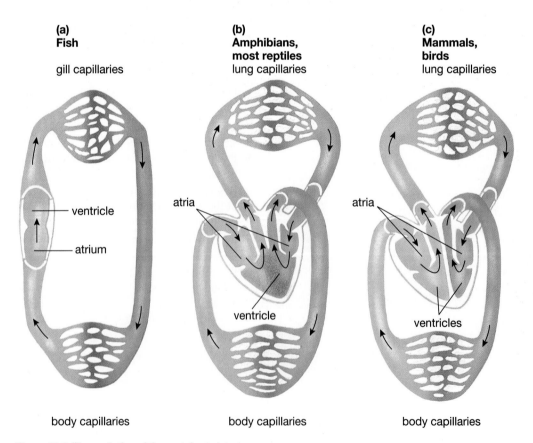

(a)
Fish

gill capillaries

ventricle

atrium

body capillaries

(b)
**Amphibians,
most reptiles**

lung capillaries

atria

ventricle

body capillaries

(c)
**Mammals,
birds**

lung capillaries

atria

ventricles

body capillaries

Figure 27-2 The evolution of the vertebrate heart

© 2003 Prentice Hall, Inc.

NOTES

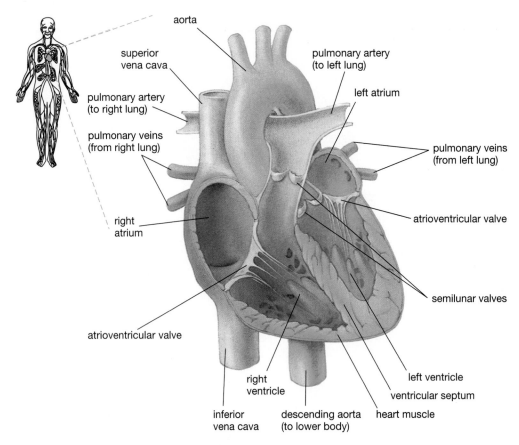

Figure 27-3 The human heart and its valves and vessels

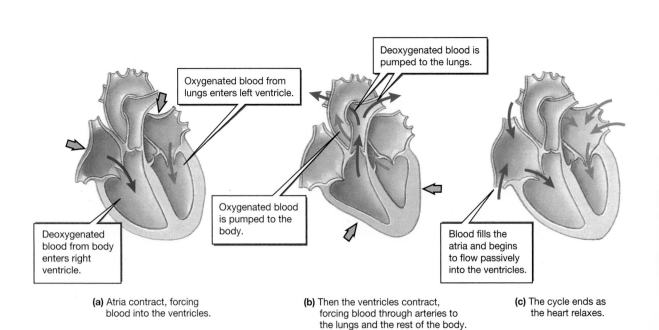

(a) Atria contract, forcing
blood into the ventricles.

(b) Then the ventricles contract,
forcing blood through arteries to
the lungs and the rest of the body.

(c) The cycle ends as
the heart relaxes.

Figure 27-4 The cardiac cycle

© 2003 Prentice Hall, Inc.

NOTES

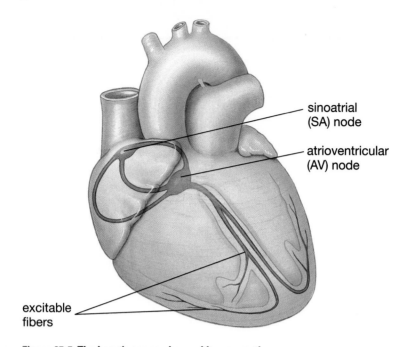

sinoatrial
(SA) node

atrioventricular
(AV) node

excitable
fibers

Figure 27-7 The heart's pacemaker and its connections

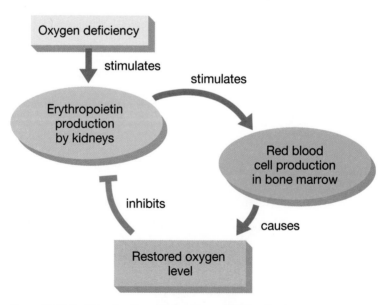

Figure 27-10 Red blood cell regulation by negative feedback

© 2003 Prentice Hall, Inc.

NOTES

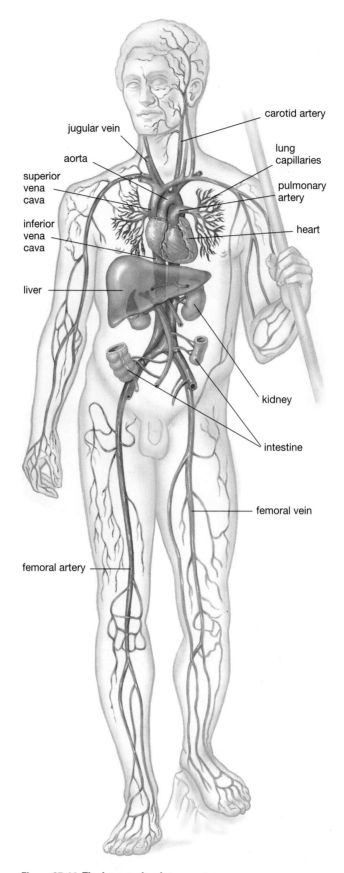

Figure 27-14 The human circulatory system

© 2003 Prentice Hall, Inc.

NOTES

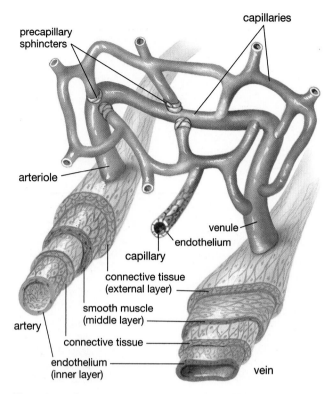

Figure 27-15 Structures and interconnections of blood vessels

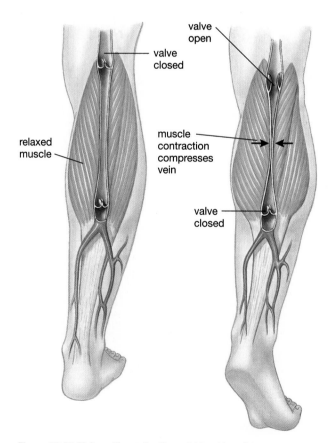

Figure 27-17 Valves direct the flow of blood in veins

© 2003 Prentice Hall, Inc.

NOTES

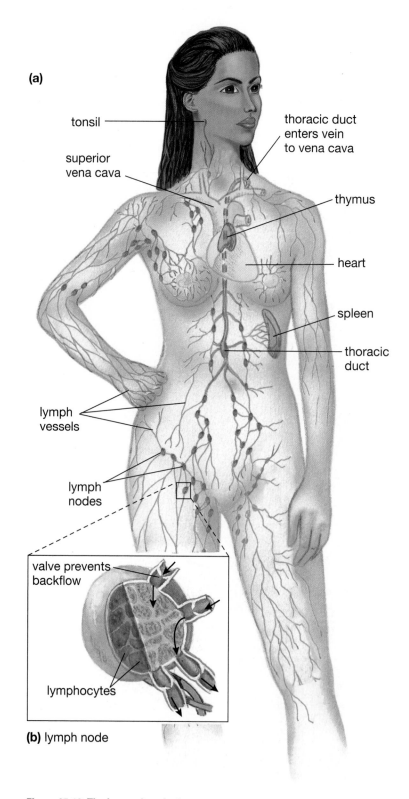

(a)

tonsil

superior
vena cava

thoracic duct
enters vein
to vena cava

thymus

heart

spleen

thoracic
duct

lymph
vessels

lymph
nodes

valve prevents
backflow

lymphocytes

(b) lymph node

Figure 27-18 The human lymphatic system

© 2003 Prentice Hall, Inc.

NOTES

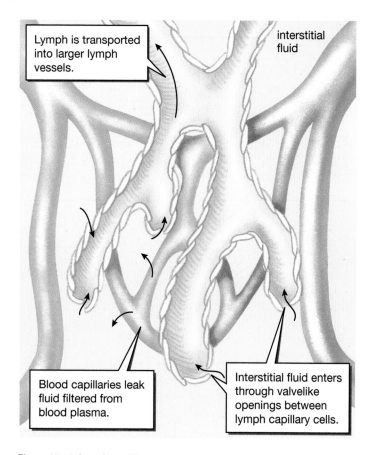

Figure 27-19 Lymph capillary structure

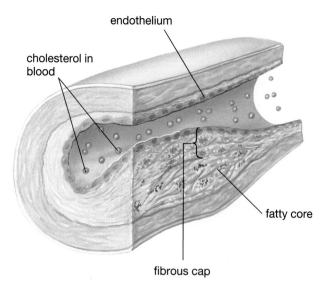

Figure E27-2 Plaques clog arteries

© 2003 Prentice Hall, Inc.

NOTES

CHAPTER 28 Respiration

Thinking Through the Concepts

Multiple Choice

1. *With which other system do specialized respiratory systems most closely interface in exchanging gases between the cells and the environment?*
   a. the skin
   b. the excretory system
   c. the circulatory system
   d. the muscular system
   e. the nervous system

2. *The gas-exchange portion of the human respiratory system is the*
   a. larynx
   b. trachea
   c. bronchi
   d. pharynx
   e. alveoli

3. *Which of the following types of animal use tracheae for respiration?*
   a. mollusks
   b. snails
   c. insects
   d. fish
   e. bookworms

4. *How is most of the oxygen transported in the blood?*
   a. dissolved in plasma
   b. bound to hemoglobin
   c. in the form of CO_2
   d. as bicarbonate
   e. dissolved in water

5. *Which of the following statements regarding cigarette smoking is true?*
   a. Cigarette smoke damages the alveoli.
   b. Cigarette smoke decreases the amount of oxygen in the blood.
   c. Cigarette smoke causes many types of cancer.
   d. Cigarette smoke can lead to heart damage.
   e. all of the above

6. *Which of the following pairs of respiratory adaptations and animals are NOT correct?*
   a. gills: fish
   b. parabronchi: birds
   c. lungs: mammals
   d. moist skin: snakes
   e. spiracles: insects

? Review Questions

1. Describe three arthropod respiratory systems and two vertebrate respiratory systems.

2. Trace the route taken by air in the vertebrate respiratory system, listing the structures through which it flows and the point at which gas exchange occurs.

3. Explain some characteristics of animals in moist environments that may supplement respiratory systems or make them unnecessary.

4. How are human respiratory movements initiated? How are they modified, and why are these controls adaptive?

5. What events occur during human inhalation? Exhalation? Which of these is always an active process?

6. Trace the pathway of an oxygen molecule in the human body, starting with the nose and ending with a body cell.

7. Describe the effects of smoking on the human respiratory system.

8. Explain how bulk flow and diffusion interact to promote gas exchange between air and blood and between blood and tissues.

9. Compare carbon dioxide and oxygen transport in the blood. Include the source and destination of each.

10. Explain how the structure and arrangement of alveoli make them well suited for their role in gas exchange.

Applying the Concepts

1. Heart–lung transplants are performed in some cases, but donors are scarce. On the basis of your knowledge of the respiratory and circulatory systems and of lifestyle factors that might damage them, what criteria would you use in selecting a recipient for such a transplant?

2. Nicotine is a drug in tobacco that is responsible for several of the effects that smokers crave. Discuss the advantages and disadvantages of low-nicotine cigarettes.

3. Discuss why a brief exposure to carbon monoxide is much more dangerous than a brief exposure to carbon dioxide.

4. Describe several adaptations that might evolve to help members of a species of mammal respire better if the population began living continuously for many generations at very high altitudes.

5. Mary, a strong-willed 3-year-old, threatens to hold her breath until she dies if she doesn't get her way. Can she carry out her threat? Explain.

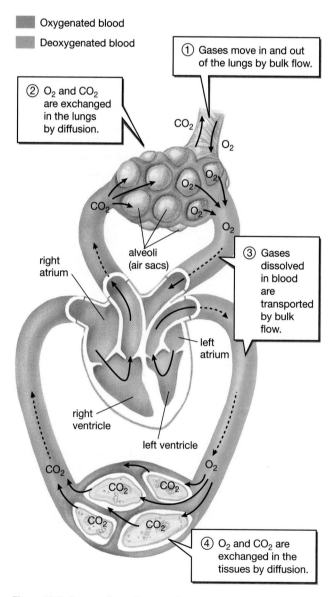

Figure 28-2 An overview of gas exchange

© 2003 Prentice Hall, Inc.

NOTES

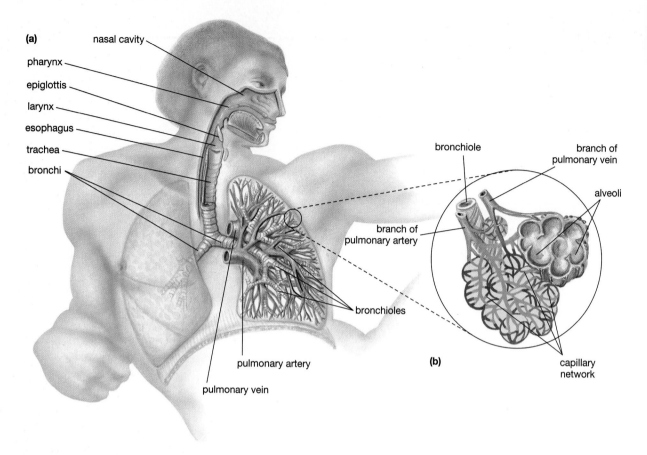

(a)

nasal cavity
pharynx
epiglottis
larynx
esophagus
trachea
bronchi

bronchiole
branch of pulmonary vein
alveoli

branch of pulmonary artery

bronchioles

pulmonary artery

pulmonary vein

(b)

capillary network

Figure 28-7 The human respiratory system

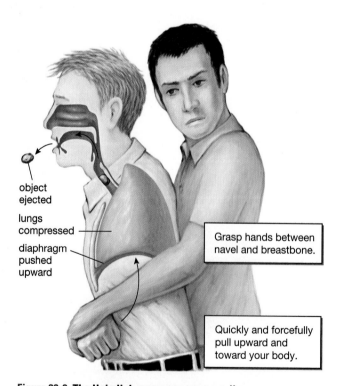

object ejected

lungs compressed

diaphragm pushed upward

Grasp hands between navel and breastbone.

Quickly and forcefully pull upward and toward your body.

Figure 28-8 The Heimlich maneuver can save lives

© 2003 Prentice Hall, Inc.

NOTES

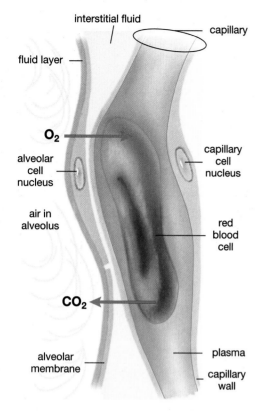

Figure 28-9 Gas exchange between alveoli and capillaries

(a) Transport of oxygen ( )

① O_2 diffuses through lung capillary wall.

③ O_2 diffuses through tissue capillary walls.

② O_2 is carried to tissues bound to hemoglobin.

lung

body cells

(b) Transport of carbon dioxide ( )

dissolved in plasma

HCO_3^- as bicarbonate

bound to hemoglobin

lung

body cells

② CO_2 is carried to lungs.

③ CO_2 diffuses through lung capillary wall.

① CO_2 diffuses through tissue capillary walls.

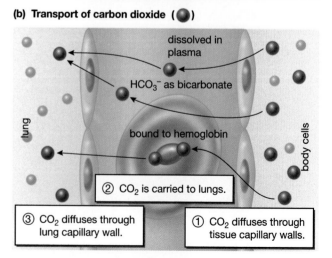

Figure 28-10 The chemistry and mechanism of gas exchange

© 2003 Prentice Hall, Inc.

NOTES

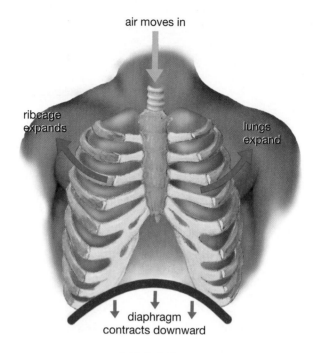

(a) Inhalation

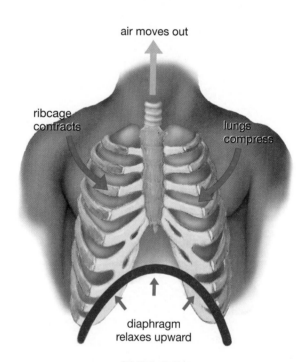

(b) Exhalation

Figure 28-11 **The mechanics of breathing**

© 2003 Prentice Hall, Inc.

NOTES

CHAPTER 29 Nutrition and Digestion

Thinking Through the Concepts

Multiple Choice

1. An acidic mixture of partially digested food that moves from the stomach into the small intestine is called
a. cholecystokinin
b. bile
c. lymph
d. secretin
e. chyme

2. The hormone responsible for stimulating the secretion of hydrochloric acid by stomach cells is
a. pepsin
b. gastrin
c. cholecystokinin
d. insulin
e. secretin

3. A sudden increase in the amount of secretin circulating in the blood is an indication that food has recently been introduced to the
a. mouth
b. pharynx
c. stomach
d. small intestine
e. large intestine

4. Humans lack digestive enzymes to attack chitin, a complex polysaccharide in the exoskeleton of lobster and crayfish. We also lack enzymes that degrade
a. peptides
b. plant starch
c. cellulose
d. sucrose
e. lipids

5. Which of the following is NOT characteristic of bile?
a. It is produced in the gallbladder.
b. It is a mixture of special salts, water, and cholesterol.
c. It acts as a detergent or emulsifying agent.
d. It helps expose a large surface area of lipid for attack by lipases.
e. It works in the small intestine.

6. "Water-soluble compound that works primarily as an enzyme helper" would be a good definition of
a. vitamin C
b. vitamin A
c. vitamin B
d. vitamin E
e. vitamin D

? Review Questions

1. List four general types of nutrients, and describe the role of each in nutrition.

2. List and describe the function of the three principal secretions of the stomach.

3. List the substances secreted into the small intestine, and describe the origin and function of each.

4. Name and describe the muscular movements that usher food through the human digestive tract.

5. Vitamin C is a vitamin for humans but not for dogs. Certain amino acids are essential for humans but not for plants. Explain.

6. Name four structural or functional adaptations of the human small intestine that ensure good digestion and absorption.

7. Describe protein digestion in the stomach and small intestine.

Applying the Concepts

1. The food label on a soup can shows that the product contains 10 grams of protein, 4 grams of carbohydrate, and 3 grams of fat. How many Calories are in this soup?

2. Stomach ulcers that resist antibiotic therapy are treated with several kinds of drugs. Anticholinergic drugs decrease nerve signals to the stomach walls that are produced by the sight, smell, and taste of food. Antacids neutralize stomach acid. Why would it be inadvisable to take anticholinergics and antacids together?

3. Small birds have high metabolic rates, efficient digestive tracts, and high-calorie diets. Some birds consume an amount of food equivalent to 30% of their body weight every day. They rarely eat leaves or grass but often eat small stones. The bird's small intestine has an attached pancreas and liver. Using this information and Figure 29-7a, explain how a bird's digestive tract is adapted to its lifestyle (foods consumed, flight, habitat, and so on).

4. Control of the human digestive tract involves several feedback loops and messages that coordinate activity in one chamber with those taking place in subsequent chambers. List the coordinating events you discovered in this chapter, in order, beginning with tasting, chewing, and swallowing a piece of meat and ending with residue that enters the large intestine. What turns on and what shuts off each process?

5. Symbiotic protozoa in the digestive tracts of termites produce cellulase that the hosts use. In return, termites provide protozoa with food and shelter. Imagine that the human species is gradually invaded, over many generations, by symbiotic protozoa capable of producing cellulase. What evolutionary adaptive changes in body structure and function might occur simultaneously?

6. Trace a ham and cheese with lettuce sandwich through the human digestive system, discussing what happens to each part of the sandwich as it passes through each region of the digestive tract.

7. One of the common remedies for constipation (difficulty eliminating feces) is a laxative solution that contains magnesium salts. In the large intestine, magnesium salts are absorbed very slowly by the intestinal wall, remaining in the intestinal tract for long periods of time. Thus, the salts affect water movement in the large intestine. On the basis of this information, explain the laxative action of magnesium salts.

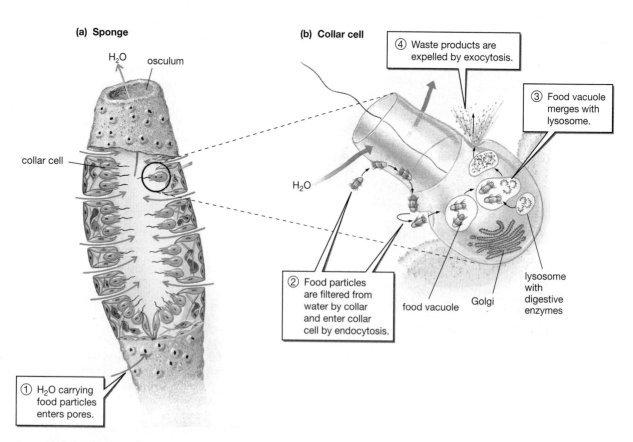

Figure 29-4 Intracellular digestion in a sponge

© 2003 Prentice Hall, Inc.

NOTES

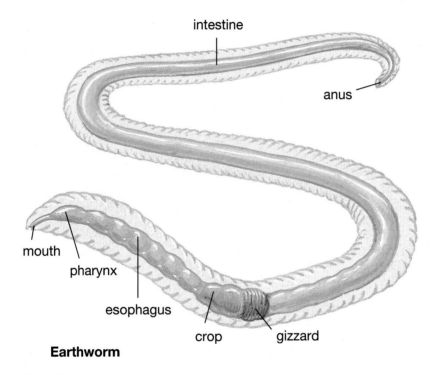

Earthworm

Figure 29-6 Tubular digestive tracts

© 2003 Prentice Hall, Inc.

NOTES

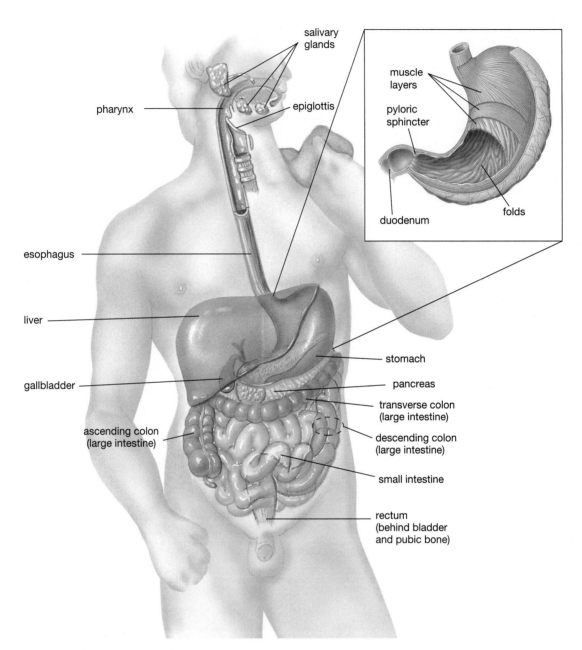

salivary glands

muscle layers

pyloric sphincter

pharynx

epiglottis

duodenum

folds

esophagus

liver

stomach

gallbladder

pancreas

transverse colon (large intestine)

ascending colon (large intestine)

descending colon (large intestine)

small intestine

rectum (behind bladder and pubic bone)

Figure 29-8 The human digestive tract

© 2003 Prentice Hall, Inc.

NOTES

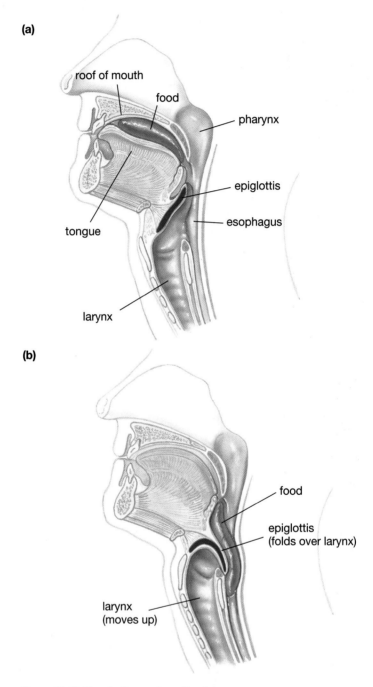

Figure 29-10 The challenge of swallowing

© 2003 Prentice Hall, Inc.

NOTES

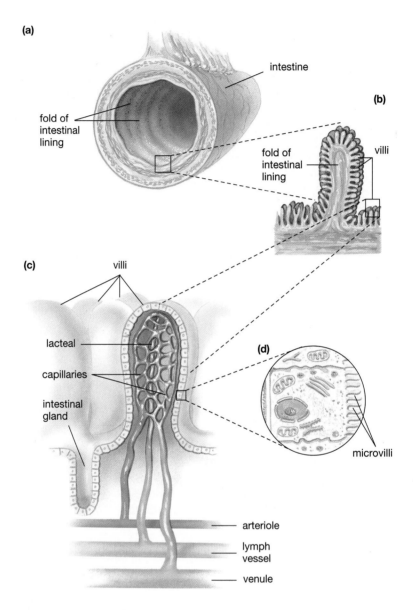

Figure 29-12 The small intestine

© 2003 Prentice Hall, Inc.

NOTES

CHAPTER 30 The Urinary System

Multiple Choice

1. *Which of the following is false?*
   a. Urea is more toxic than ammonia.
   b. Ammonia is converted to urea in the liver.
   c. Ammonia is produced in body cells.
   d. The fluid collected in Bowman's capsule is called the *filtrate.*
   e. *Tubule* means "little tube."

2. *The walls of the _____ are made more or less permeable to water, depending on the need to conserve water.*
   a. ureter
   b. urethra
   c. proximal tubule
   d. collecting duct
   e. glomerulus

3. *Which of the following conditions will cause a decrease in ADH production?*
   a. dehydration
   b. drinking beer
   c. an increase in osmotic pressure of blood
   d. abnormally high blood sugar
   e. strenuous exercise

4. *The function of the glomerulus and Bowman's capsule of the nephron is to*
   a. reabsorb water into the blood
   b. eliminate ammonia from the body
   c. reabsorb salts and amino acids
   d. filter the blood and capture the filtrate
   e. concentrate the urine

5. *What determines the ability of a mammal to concentrate its urine?*
   a. the number of nephrons
   b. the length of the tubules
   c. the length of the collecting duct
   d. the size of the glomerulus
   e. the length of the loop of Henle

6. *Which of the following processes does NOT occur in the nephron and collecting duct?*
   a. filtration
   b. elimination of urea from the body
   c. reabsorption of nutrients
   d. tubular secretion
   e. concentration of urine

? Review Questions

1. Explain the two major functions of excretory systems.
2. Trace a urea molecule from the bloodstream to the external environment.
3. What is the function of the loop of Henle? The collecting duct? Antidiuretic hormone?
4. Describe and compare the processes of filtration, tubular reabsorption, and tubular secretion.
5. Describe the role of the kidneys as organs of homeostasis.
6. Compare and contrast the excretory systems of humans, earthworms, and flatworms. In what general ways are they similar? Different?

Applying the Concepts

1. Discuss the differences in function of the two major capillary beds in the kidneys: the glomerular capillaries and those surrounding the tubules.

2. Desert animals need to conserve water. These animals have larger kidneys than do animals that live in moist environments and thus need not conserve water. The larger kidneys allow for a greater distance between the glomerulus and the bottom of the loop of Henle. Discuss why this anatomical difference assists water conservation in the desert animals.

3. Some "quick weight loss" diets require the ingestion of much protein-rich food and the elimination of carbo-hydrates. Two side effects of such diets are increased thirst and increased urination. Explain the connections between the diets and the side effects.

4. Some employers require their employees to submit to urine tests before they can be employed and at random intervals during their employment. Refusal to take the test or failure to "pass" the test could be grounds for termination. What is the purpose of the urine test? What types of employers might find such tests necessary? How do you feel about urine tests for obtaining or keeping a job? Explain your answers.

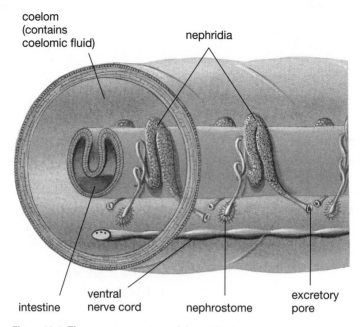

Figure 30-2 The excretory system of the earthworm

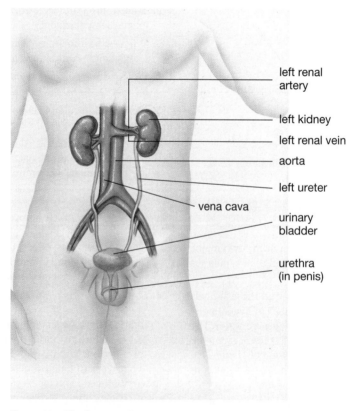

Figure 30-4 The human urinary system

© 2003 Prentice Hall, Inc.

NOTES

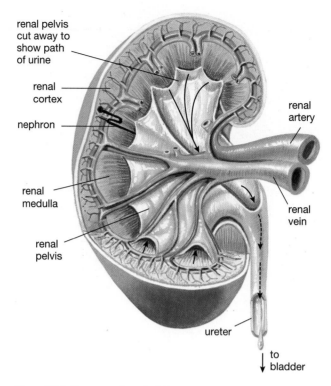

renal pelvis cut away to show path of urine

renal cortex

nephron

renal medulla

renal pelvis

renal artery

renal vein

ureter

to bladder

Figure 30-5 Cross section of a kidney

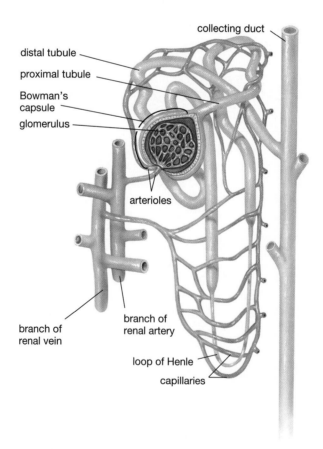

collecting duct

distal tubule

proximal tubule

Bowman's capsule

glomerulus

arterioles

branch of renal vein

branch of renal artery

loop of Henle

capillaries

Figure 30-6 An individual nephron and its blood supply

© 2003 Prentice Hall, Inc.

NOTES

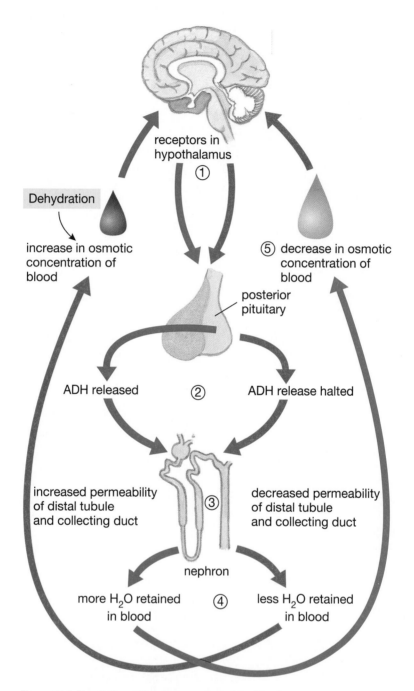

Figure 30-8 Regulation of the water content of the blood

© 2003 Prentice Hall, Inc.

NOTES

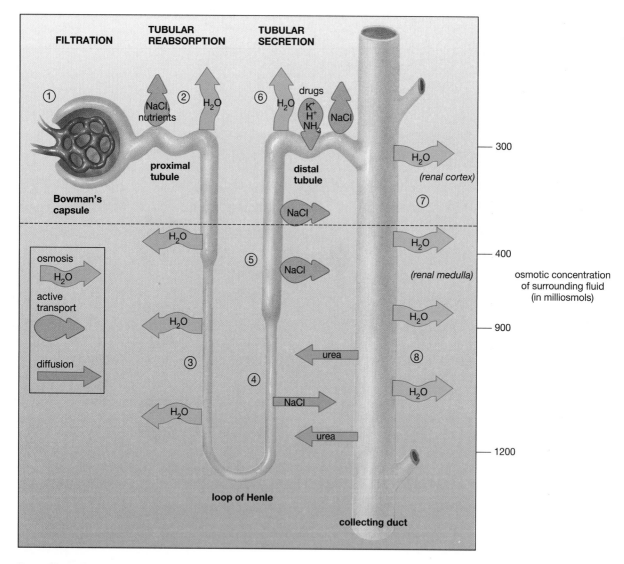

Figure E30-1 Details of urine formation

© 2003 Prentice Hall, Inc.

NOTES

CHAPTER 31 Defenses Against Disease: The Immune Response

Multiple Choice

1. *In addition to the immune system, we are protected from disease by*
   a. the skin
   b. mucous membranes
   c. natural secretions such as acids, protein-digesting enzymes, and antibiotics
   d. cilia
   e. all of the above

2. *The first line of defense against body cells infected by viruses is produced by*
   a. antibodies
   b. phagocytes
   c. natural killer cells
   d. histamines
   e. natural antibiotics

3. *Fevers*
   a. decrease interferon production
   b. decrease the concentration of iron in the blood
   c. decrease the activity of phagocytes
   d. increase the reproduction rate of invading bacteria
   e. do all of the above

4. *T cells and B cells are*
   a. lymphocytes
   b. macrophages
   c. natural killer cells
   d. red blood cells
   e. phagocytes

5. *During allergic responses*
   a. the foreign substance binds to antibodies on B cells
   b. B cells produce antibodies to the foreign substance
   c. antibodies to the foreign substance bind to that substance and to mast cells
   d. stimulation of mast cells causes them to release histamine
   e. all of the above

6. *What shuts off the immune response in T cells and B cells after an infection has been conquered?*
   a. cytotoxic T cells
   b. histamine
   c. pyrogens
   d. natural killer cells
   e. suppressor T cells

? Review Questions

1. List the human body's three lines of defense against invading microbes. Which are nonspecific (that is, act against all types of invaders), and which are specific (act only against a particular type of invader)? Explain your answer.

2. How do natural killer cells and cytotoxic T cells destroy their targets?

3. Describe humoral immunity and cell-mediated immunity. Include in your answer the types of immune cells involved in each, the location of antibodies and receptors that bind foreign antigens, and the mechanisms by which invading cells are destroyed.

4. How does the immune system construct so many different antibodies?

5. How does the body distinguish "self" from "non-self"?

6. Diagram the structure of an antibody. What parts bind to antigens? Why does each antibody bind only to a specific antigen?

7. What are memory cells? How do they contribute to long-lasting immunity to specific diseases?

8. What is a vaccine? How does it confer immunity to a disease?

9. Compare and contrast an inflammatory response with an allergic reaction from the standpoint of cells involved, substances produced, and symptoms experienced.

10. Distinguish between autoimmune diseases and immune deficiency diseases, and give one example of each.

11. Describe the causes and eventual outcome of AIDS. How do AIDS treatments work? How is the HIV virus spread?

12. Why is cancer sometimes fatal?

Applying the Concepts

1. Why is it essential that antibodies and T-cell receptors bind only relatively large molecules (such as proteins) and not relatively small molecules (such as amino acids)?

2. There are smallpox virus stocks in two laboratories—one in the U.S. and one in Russia. A debate is raging about whether these stocks should be destroyed. In brief, one side argues that having smallpox around is too dangerous. The other side argues that we may be able to learn things from smallpox, answers to questions we don't know enough to ask yet, that may help us conquer future diseases. Do you believe the smallpox stocks should be destroyed? Why or why not?

3. The essay "Health Watch: Can We Beat the Flu Bug?" states that the flu virus is different each year. If that is true, what good is it to get a "flu shot" each winter?

4. Organ transplant patients typically receive the drug cyclosporine. This drug inhibits the production of interleukin-2, a regulatory molecule that stimulates helper T cells to proliferate. How does cyclosporine prevent the rejection of transplanted organs? Some patients who received successful transplants many years ago are now developing various kinds of cancers. Propose a hypothesis to explain this phenomenon.

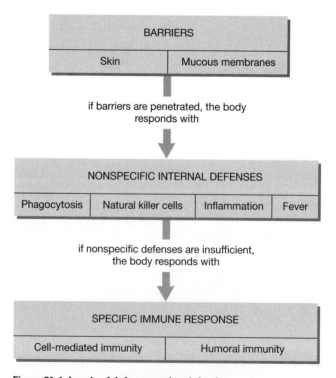

Figure 31-1 Levels of defense against infection

© 2003 Prentice Hall, Inc.

NOTES

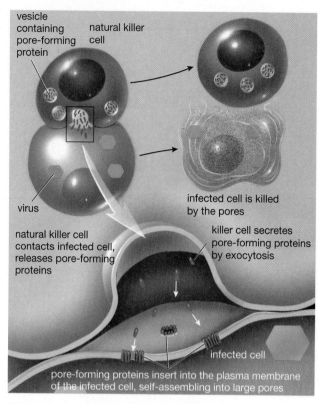

Figure 31-4 **How natural killer cells kill their targets**

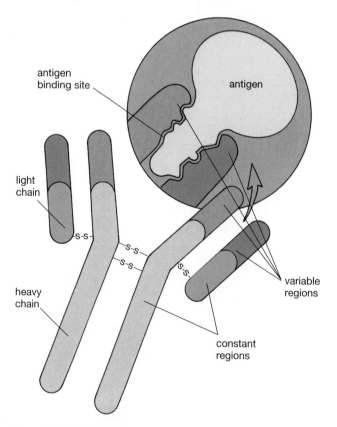

Figure 31-5 **Antibody structure**

© 2003 Prentice Hall, Inc.

NOTES

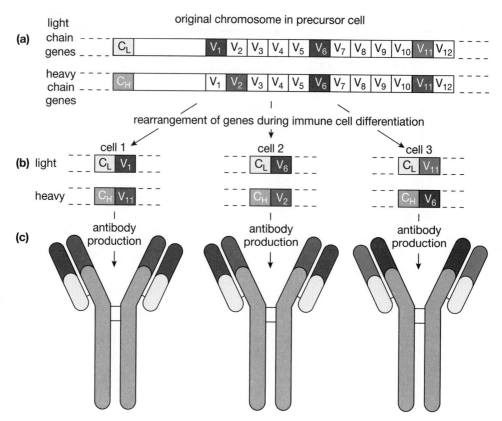

Figure 31-7 Recombination during the construction of antibody genes

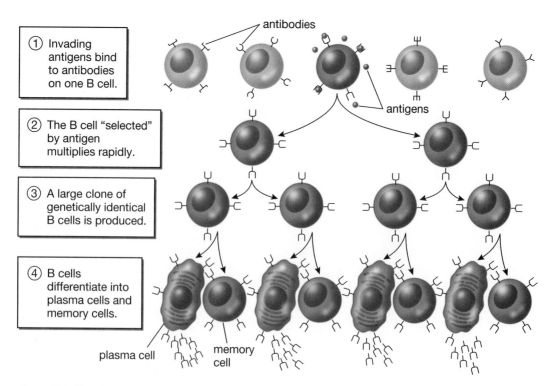

Figure 31-8 Clonal selection among B cells by invading antigens

© 2003 Prentice Hall, Inc.

NOTES

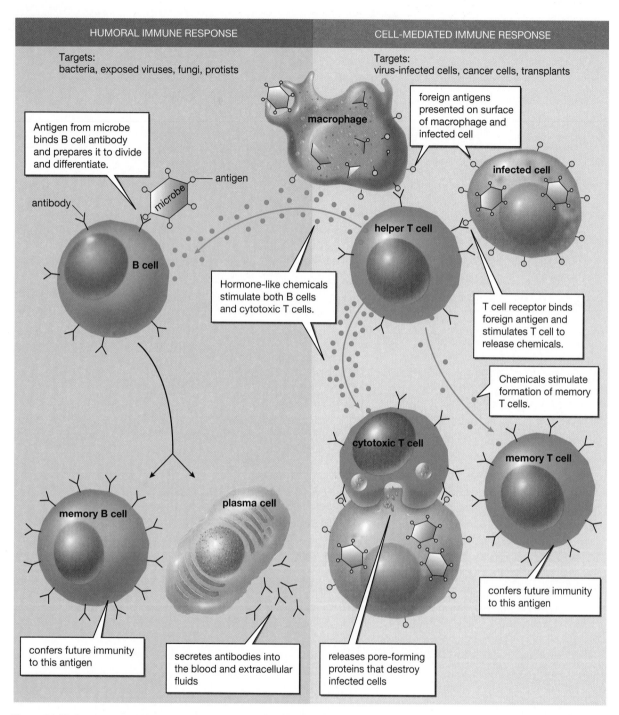

Figure 31-11 A summary of humoral and cell-mediated immune responses

© 2003 Prentice Hall, Inc.

NOTES

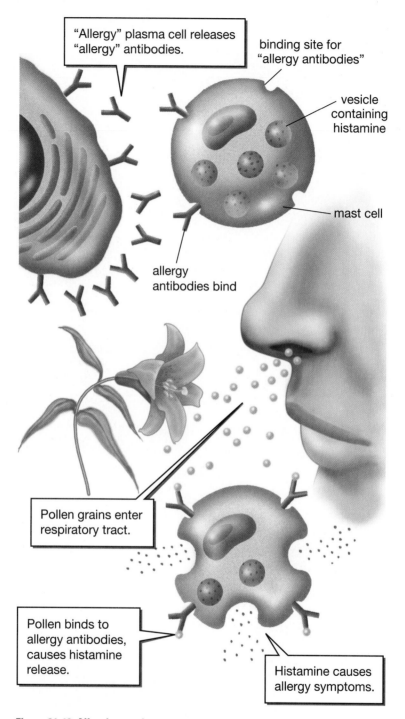

Figure 31-13 Allergic reactions

© 2003 Prentice Hall, Inc.

NOTES

CHAPTER 32 Chemical Control of the Animal Body: The Endocrine System

Thinking Through the Concepts

Multiple Choice

1. *Steroid hormones*
   a. alter the activity of genes
   b. trigger rapid, short-term responses in cells
   c. work via second messengers
   d. initiate open channels in plasma membranes
   e. bind to cell-surface receptors

2. *Examples of posterior pituitary hormones are*
   a. FSH and LH
   b. prolactin and parathormone
   c. secretin and cholecystokinin
   d. melatonin and prostaglandin
   e. ADH and oxytocin

3. *Negative feedback to the hypothalamus controls the level of _____ in the blood.*
   a. thyroxine   b. estrogen
   c. glucocorticoids   d. insulin
   e. all of the above

4. *The primary targets for FSH are cells in the*
   a. hypothalamus   b. ovary
   c. thyroid gland   d. adrenal medulla
   e. pituitary gland

5. *The kidney is a source of*
   a. thyroxine and parathormone
   b. calcitonin and oxytocin
   c. renin and erythropoietin
   d. ANP and epinephrine
   e. glucagon and glucocorticoids

6. *Hormones that are produced by many different types of body cells and cause a variety of localized effects are known as*
   a. peptide hormones   b. parathormones
   c. releasing hormones d. prostaglandins
   e. exocrine hormones

? Review Questions

1. What are the four types of molecules used as hormones in vertebrates? Give an example of each.

2. What is the difference between an endocrine gland and an exocrine gland? Which type releases hormones?

3. When peptide hormones attach to target cell receptors, what cellular events follow? How do steroid hormones behave?

4. Diagram the process of negative feedback, and give an example of it in the control of hormone action.

5. What are the major endocrine glands in the human body, and where are they located?

6. Describe the structure of the hypothalamus–pituitary complex. Which pituitary hormones are neurosecretory? What are their functions?

7. Describe how releasing hormones regulate the secretion of hormones by cells of the anterior pituitary. Name the hormones of the anterior pituitary, and give one function of each.

8. Describe how the hormones of the pancreas act together to regulate the concentration of glucose in the blood.

9. Compare the adrenal cortex and adrenal medulla by answering the following questions: Where are they located within the adrenal gland? What are their embryological origins? Which hormones do they produce? Which organs do their hormones target? What homeostatic processes regulate blood levels of the respective hormones?

Applying the Concepts

1. A student decides to do a science project on the effect of the thyroid gland on frog metamorphosis. She sets up three aquaria with tadpoles. She adds thyroxine to the water of one, the drug thiouracil to a second, and noth-ing to the third. Thiouracil reacts with thyroxine in tadpoles to produce an ineffective compound. Assuming that the student uses appropriate physiological con-centrations, predict what will happen.

2. If you were obese, would you consider injections of leptin? What pros and cons can you think of? Defend your decision.

3. Suggest a hypothesis about the endocrine system to explain why many birds lay their eggs in the spring and why poultry farmers keep lights on at night in their egg-laying operations.

4. Anabolic steroids, used by risk-taking athletes and body-builders, are chemically related to testosterone. They increase bone mass and muscle mass and seem to improve athletic performance. But anabolic steroids can cause liver problems, heart attacks, strokes, testicular atrophy, and personality changes in males. Females on anabolic steroids also have liver and circulatory problems. In addition, their voices deepen, their bodies develop more hair, and their menstrual cycles are dis-

turbed. Explain how the same compound can produce different effects in males and females.

5. Some parents who are interested in college sports scholarships for their children are asking physicians to prescribe growth hormone treatments. Farmers also have an economic incentive to treat cows with growth hormone, which can now be produced in large quantities by genetic-engineering techniques. What biological and ethical problems do you foresee for parents, children, physicians, coaches, college scholarship boards, food consumers, farmers, the U.S. Food and Drug Administration, and biotechnology companies?

6. Argue for and against banning or restricting the use of common endocrine disruptors, such as plasticizers and certain pesticides. What compromises can you suggest?

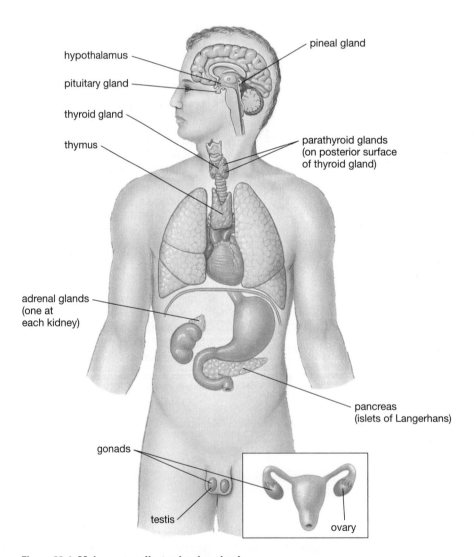

Figure 32-1 Major mammalian endocrine glands

© 2003 Prentice Hall, Inc.

NOTES

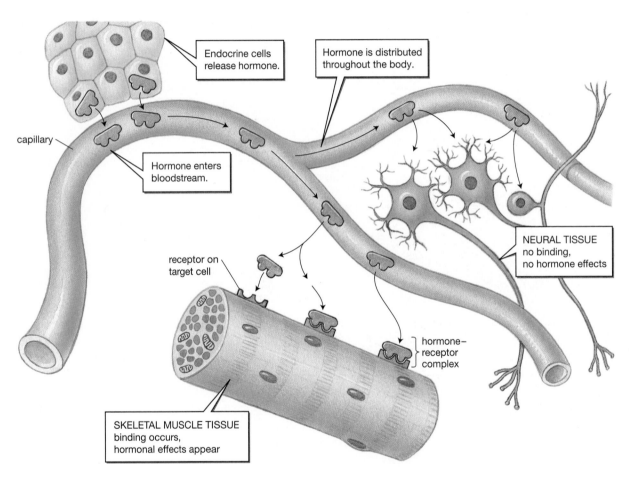

Figure 32-2 Endocrine glands, hormones, and target cells

Endocrine cells release hormone.

Hormone is distributed throughout the body.

capillary

Hormone enters bloodstream.

NEURAL TISSUE no binding, no hormone effects

receptor on target cell

hormone–receptor complex

SKELETAL MUSCLE TISSUE binding occurs, hormonal effects appear

© 2003 Prentice Hall, Inc.

NOTES

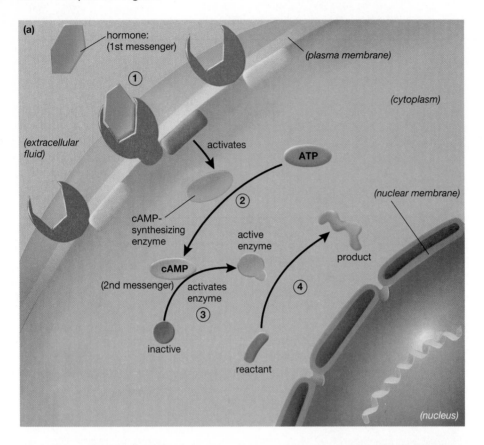

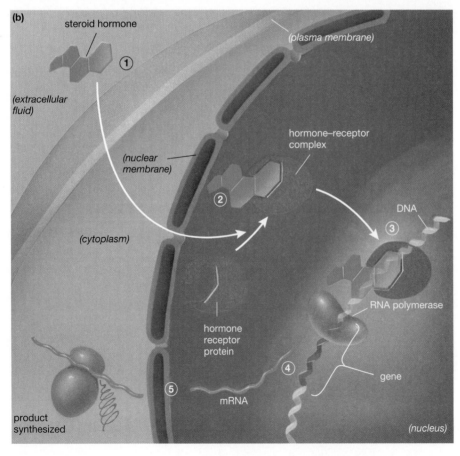

Figure 32-3 Modes of action of hormones

© 2003 Prentice Hall, Inc.

NOTES

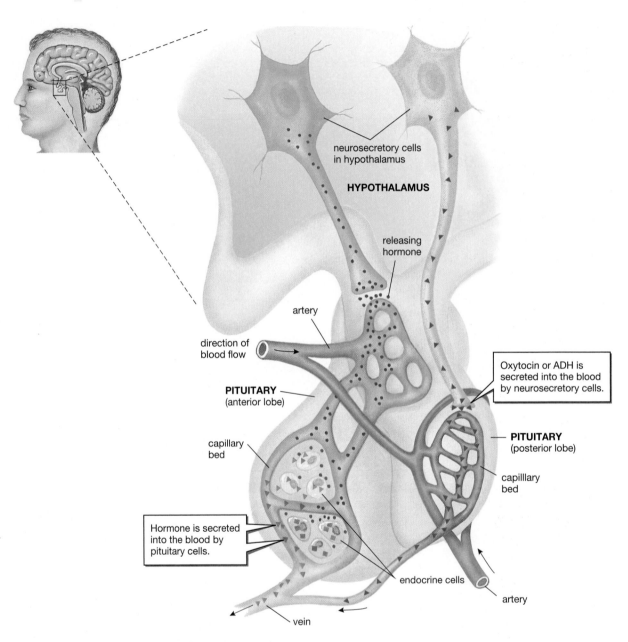

neurosecretory cells
in hypothalamus

HYPOTHALAMUS

releasing
hormone

artery

direction of
blood flow

Oxytocin or ADH is
secreted into the blood
by neurosecretory cells.

PITUITARY
(anterior lobe)

PITUITARY
(posterior lobe)

capillary
bed

capilllary
bed

Hormone is secreted
into the blood by
pituitary cells.

endocrine cells

artery

vein

Figure 32-4 The hypothalamus controls the pituitary

© 2003 Prentice Hall, Inc.

NOTES

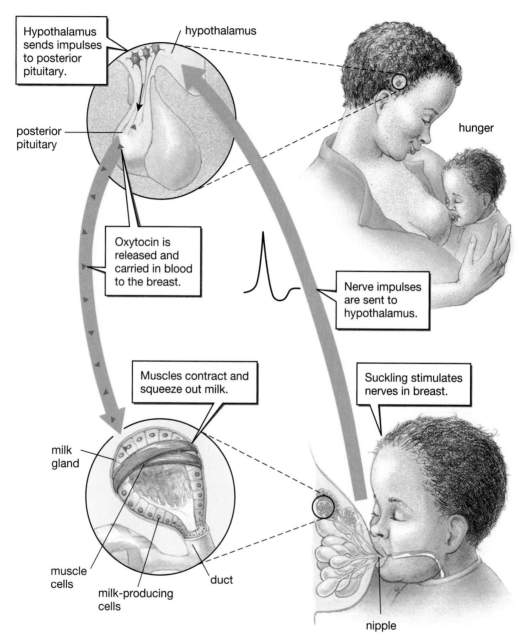

Hypothalamus sends impulses to posterior pituitary.

hypothalamus

posterior pituitary

Oxytocin is released and carried in blood to the breast.

hunger

Nerve impulses are sent to hypothalamus.

Muscles contract and squeeze out milk.

Suckling stimulates nerves in breast.

milk gland

muscle cells

milk-producing cells

duct

nipple

Figure 32-6 **Hormones and breastfeeding**

© 2003 Prentice Hall, Inc.

NOTES

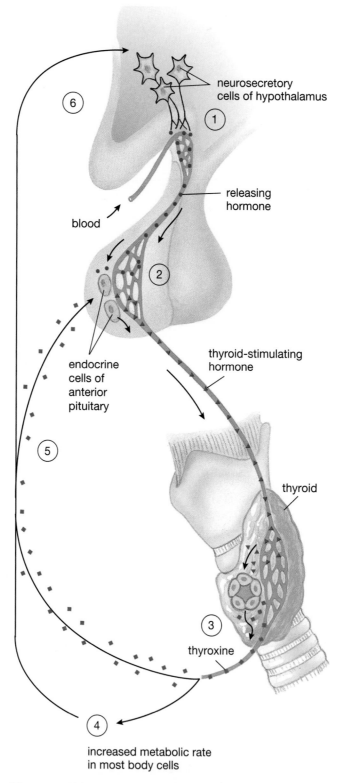

neurosecretory
cells of hypothalamus

releasing
hormone

blood

endocrine
cells of
anterior
pituitary

thyroid-stimulating
hormone

thyroid

thyroxine

increased metabolic rate
in most body cells

Figure 32-8 **Negative feedback in thyroid gland function**

© 2003 Prentice Hall, Inc.

NOTES

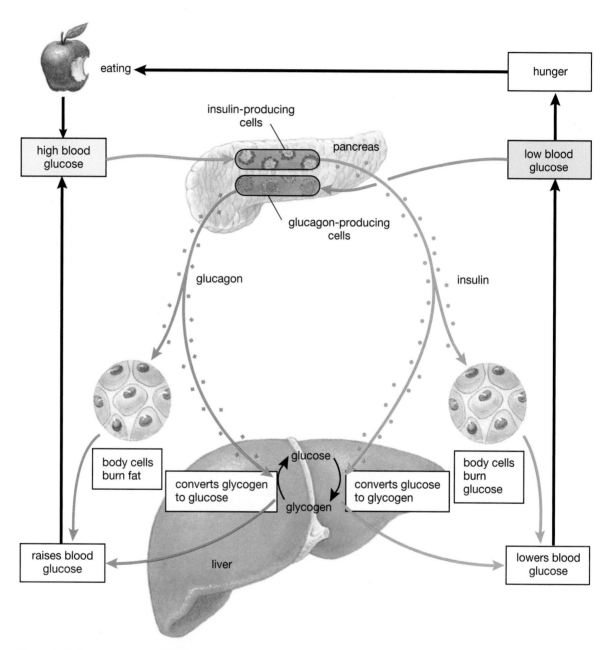

Figure 32-9 The pancreas controls blood glucose levels

© 2003 Prentice Hall, Inc.

NOTES

CHAPTER 33   The Nervous System and the Senses

Thinking Through the Concepts

Multiple Choice

1. _____ are integration centers in neurons.
   a. dendrites   b. axons
   c. cell bodies   d. ion channels
   e. synapses

2. *The role of the axon is to*
   a. integrate signals from the dendrites
   b. release neurotransmitter
   c. conduct the action potential to the synaptic terminal
   d. synthesize cellular components
   e. stimulate a muscle, gland, or another neuron

3. *Which of the following statements is FALSE?*
   a. The hindbrain contains the medulla, pons, and cerebellum.
   b. The thalamus is an important sensory relay structure.
   c. The cerebral cortex in humans is folded into convolutions.
   d. The hippocampus has an important role in recognizing and experiencing fear.
   e. The hypothalamus coordinates the activities of the autonomic nervous system.

4. *The fovea is*
   a. the blind spot
   b. a clear area in front of the pupil and iris
   c. the tough outer covering of the eyeball
   d. the substance that gives the eyeball its shape
   e. the central focal region of the vertebrate retina

5. *Light entering the eye and striking the choroid would travel first, in order, through the*
   a. lens, vitreous humor, cornea, aqueous humor, and retina
   b. retina, aqueous humor, lens, vitreous humor, and cornea
   c. cornea, aqueous humor, retina, vitreous humor, and lens
   d. cornea, aqueous humor, lens, vitreous humor, and retina
   e. lens, aqueous humor, cornea, vitreous humor, and retina

6. *Sound reception is carried out by hair cells, which are a special type of*
   a. chemoreceptor   b. photoreceptor
   c. mechanoreceptor   d. magnetoreceptor
   e. thermoreceptor

? Review Questions

1. List four major parts of a neuron, and explain the specialized function of each part.

2. Diagram a synapse. How are signals transmitted from one neuron to another at a synapse?

3. How does the brain perceive the intensity of a stimulus? The type of stimulus?

4. What are the four elements of a simple nervous pathway? Describe how these elements function in the human pain-withdrawal reflex.

5. Draw a cross section of the spinal cord. What types of neurons are located in the spinal cord? Explain why severing the cord paralyzes the body below the level where it is severed.

6. Describe the functions of the following parts of the human brain: medulla, cerebellum, reticular formation, thalamus, limbic system, and cerebrum.

7. What structure connects the two cerebral hemispheres? Describe the evidence that the two hemispheres are specialized for distinct intellectual functions.

8. Distinguish between long-term memory and working memory.

9. What are the names of the specific receptors used for taste, vision, hearing, smell, and touch?

10. Why are we apparently able to distinguish hundreds of different flavors if we have only five types of taste receptors? How are we able to distinguish so many different odors?

11. Describe the structure and function of the various parts of the human ear by tracing a sound wave from the air outside the ear to the cells that cause action potentials in the auditory nerve.

12. How does the structure of the inner ear allow for the perception of pitch? Of sound intensity?

13. Diagram the overall structure of the human eye. Label the cornea, iris, lens, sclera, retina, and choroid. Describe the function of each structure.

14. How does the lens change shape to allow focusing of distant objects? What defect makes focusing on distant objects impossible, and what is this condition called? What type of lens can be used to correct it, and how does it do so?

15. List the similarities and differences between rods and cones.

16. Distinguish between taste and olfaction.

17. Describe how pain is signaled by tissue damage.

Applying the Concepts

1. Argue for or against the statement "Consciousness by its nature is incomprehensible; the brain will never understand the mind."

2. In Parkinson's disease, which afflicts several million Americans, the cells that produce the neurotransmitter dopamine degenerate in a small part of the brain that is important in the control of movement. Some physicians have reported improvement after injecting cells taken from the same general brain region of an aborted fetus into appropriate parts of the brain of a Parkinson's patient. Discuss this type of surgery from as many viewpoints as possible: ethical, financial, practical, and so on. On the basis of your responses, is fetal transplant surgery the answer to curing Parkinson's disease?

3. If the axons of human spinal cord neurons were un-myelinated, would the spinal cord be larger or smaller? Would you move faster or slower? Explain your answer.

4. What is the adaptive value of reflexes? If Christopher Reeve was accidentally pricked on the toe by a thumbtack, would he withdraw his leg? Explain your answer.

5. Explain the statement "Your sensory perceptions are purely a creation of your brain." Discuss the implications for communicating with other humans, with other animals, and with intelligent life from another universe.

6. Corneal transplants can help restore vision and greatly improve the recipient's quality of life. What properties of the cornea make it an excellent candidate for transplantation? Suggest some ways in which society could improve the availability of corneal and other tissues for transplantation.

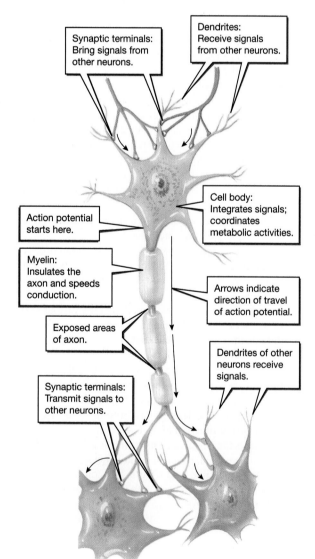

Figure 33-1 A nerve cell, showing its specialized parts and their functions

© 2003 Prentice Hall, Inc.

NOTES

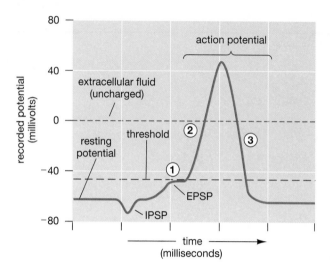

Figure 33-3 The electrical events during an action potential

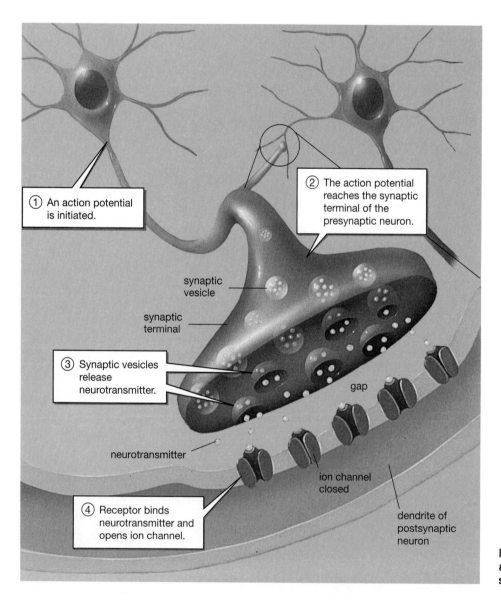

Figure 33-4 The structure and operation of the synapse

© 2003 Prentice Hall, Inc.

NOTES

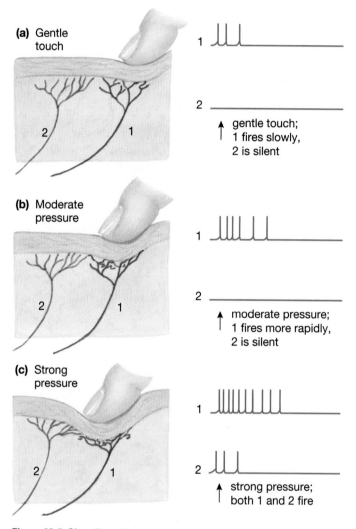

(a) Gentle touch

1

2

gentle touch; 1 fires slowly, 2 is silent

(b) Moderate pressure

1

2

moderate pressure; 1 fires more rapidly, 2 is silent

(c) Strong pressure

1

2

strong pressure; both 1 and 2 fire

Figure 33-5 Signaling stimulus intensity

© 2003 Prentice Hall, Inc.

NOTES

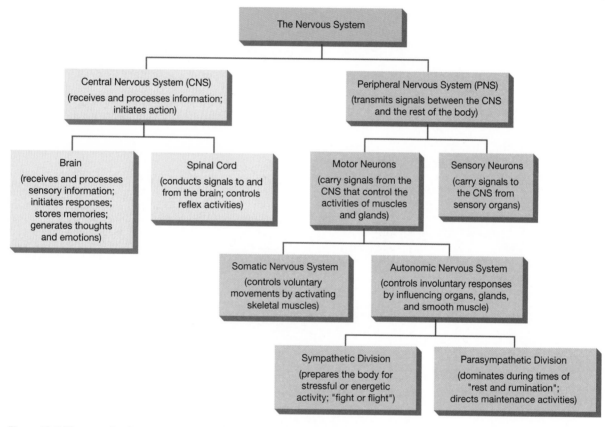

Figure 33-7 The organization and functions of the vertebrate nervous system

© 2003 Prentice Hall, Inc.

NOTES

PARASYMPATHETIC

SYMPATHETIC

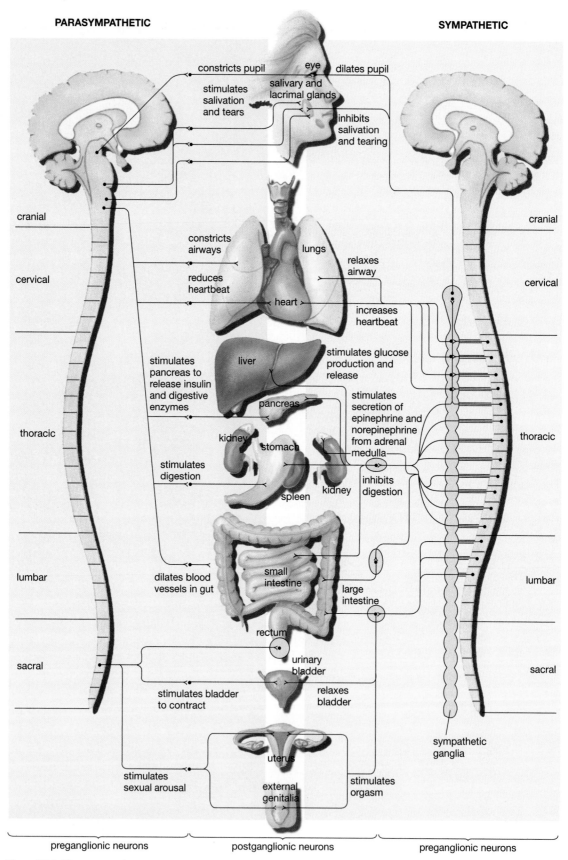

Figure 33-8 The autonomic nervous system

© 2003 Prentice Hall, Inc.

NOTES

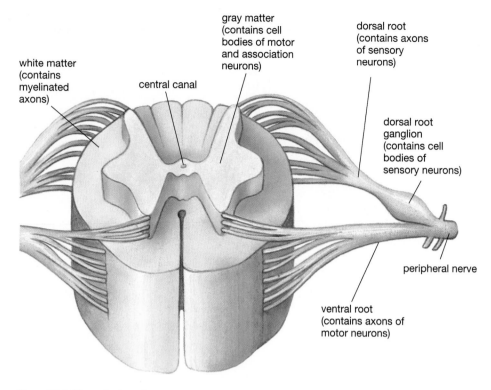

white matter (contains myelinated axons)

central canal

gray matter (contains cell bodies of motor and association neurons)

dorsal root (contains axons of sensory neurons)

dorsal root ganglion (contains cell bodies of sensory neurons)

peripheral nerve

ventral root (contains axons of motor neurons)

Figure 33-9 The spinal cord

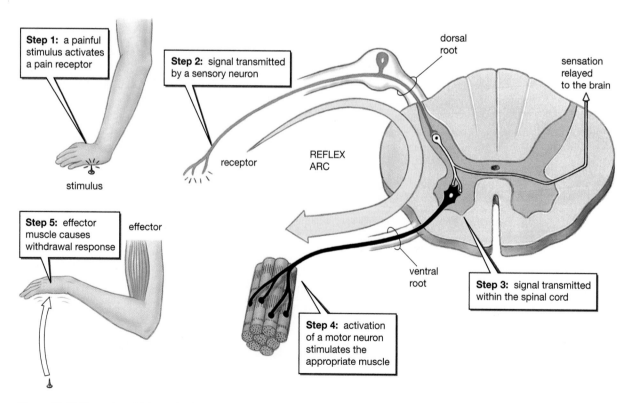

Step 1: a painful stimulus activates a pain receptor

Step 2: signal transmitted by a sensory neuron

dorsal root

sensation relayed to the brain

receptor

REFLEX ARC

stimulus

Step 5: effector muscle causes withdrawal response

effector

ventral root

Step 3: signal transmitted within the spinal cord

Step 4: activation of a motor neuron stimulates the appropriate muscle

Figure 33-10 The pain-withdrawal reflex

© 2003 Prentice Hall, Inc.

NOTES

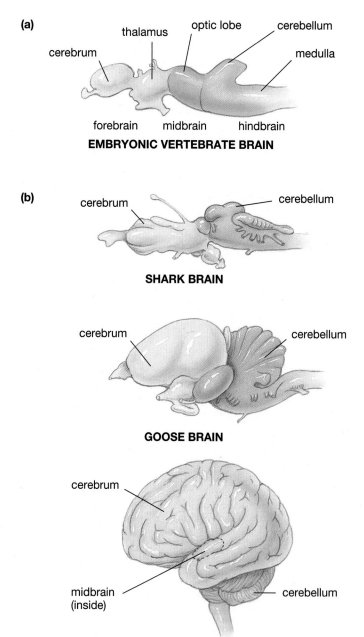

(a)

cerebrum thalamus optic lobe cerebellum medulla

forebrain midbrain hindbrain

EMBRYONIC VERTEBRATE BRAIN

(b)

cerebrum cerebellum

SHARK BRAIN

cerebrum cerebellum

GOOSE BRAIN

cerebrum

midbrain (inside) cerebellum

HUMAN BRAIN

Figure 33-11 A comparison of vertebrate brains

© 2003 Prentice Hall, Inc.

NOTES

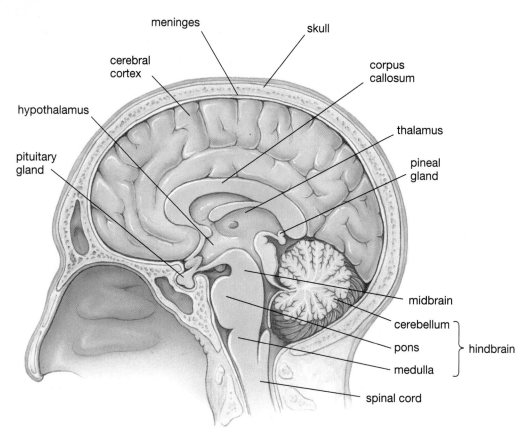

Figure 33-12 The human brain

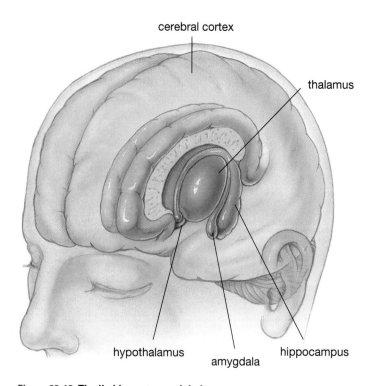

Figure 33-13 The limbic system and thalamus

© 2003 Prentice Hall, Inc.

NOTES

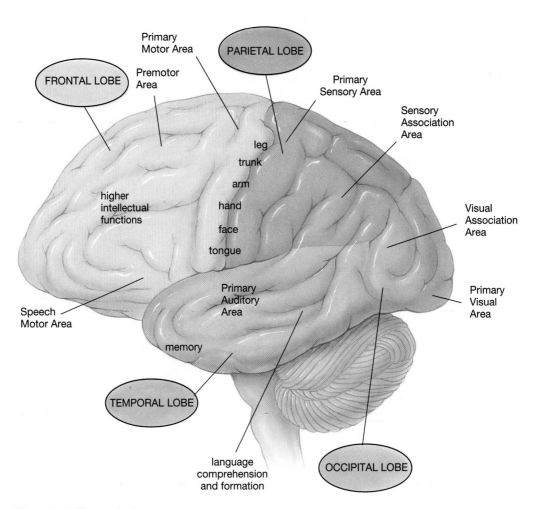

Figure 33-14 The cerebral cortex

© 2003 Prentice Hall, Inc.

NOTES

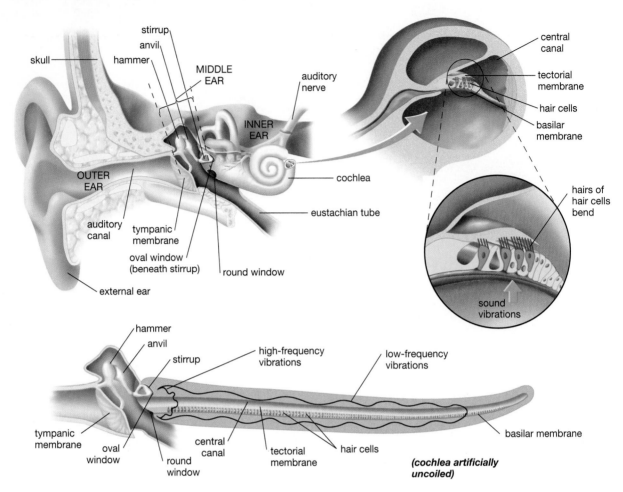

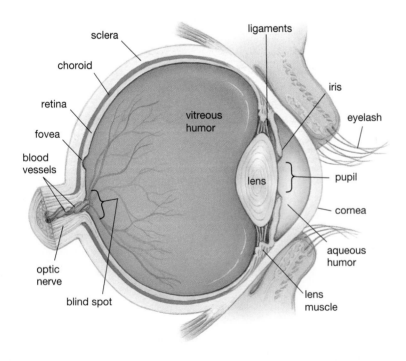

Figure 33-16 The human ear

Figure 33-19 The human eye

© 2003 Prentice Hall, Inc.

NOTES

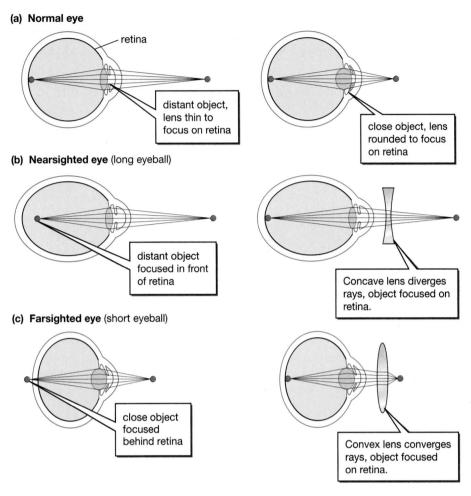

Figure 33-20 Focusing in the human eye

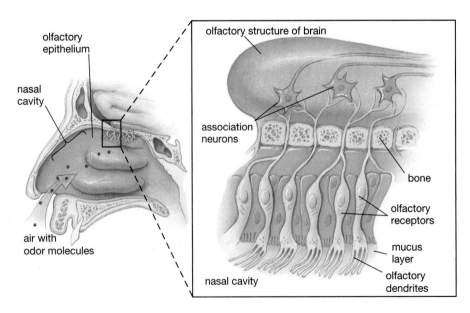

Figure 33-23 Human olfactory receptors

© 2003 Prentice Hall, Inc.

NOTES

(a) The human tongue

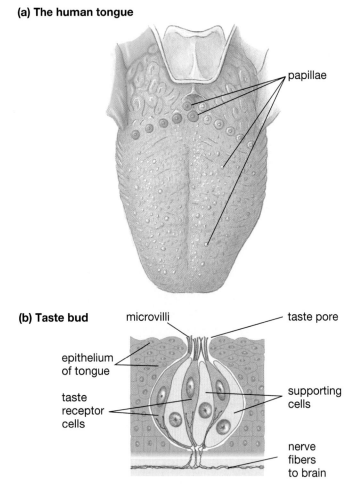

Figure 33-24 **Human taste receptors**

© 2003 Prentice Hall, Inc.

NOTES

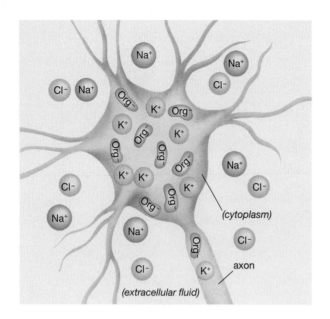

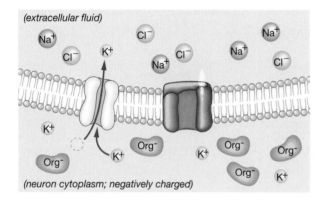

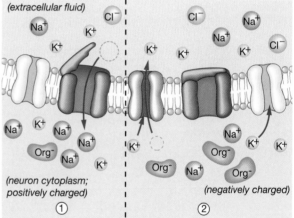

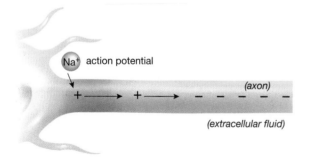

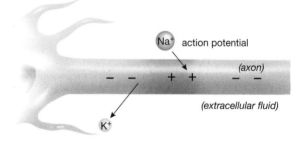

Figure 33-27 **The neuron maintains ionic gradients**

© 2003 Prentice Hall, Inc.

NOTES

CHAPTER 34 Action and Support: The Muscles and Skeleton

Thinking Through the Concepts

Multiple Choice

1. *Thin filaments in myofibrils consist of*
   a. actin and accessory proteins
   b. sarcomeres
   c. cross-bridges
   d. Z lines
   e. myosin

2. *The deep infoldings of muscle fiber membranes that conduct action potentials are called*
   a. sarcoplasmic reticula b. Z lines
   c. myofilaments d. T tubules
   e. sarcomeres

3. *The force of muscle contraction depends on the*
   a. number of muscle fibers stimulated
   b. number of motor units stimulated
   c. frequency of action potentials in each motor unit
   d. frequency of action potentials in each muscle fiber
   e. all of the above

4. *Smooth muscle fibers can be distinguished from striated ones because smooth fibers*
   a. contract more rapidly
   b. lack regular arrangements of sarcomeres
   c. lack gap junctions
   d. contain only actin filaments
   e. contain sarcoplasmic reticulum

5. *Bone-dissolving cells are called*
   a. chondrocytes b. osteoblasts
   c. osteoclasts d. osteocytes
   e. erythroblasts

6. *Osteons contain all of the following EXCEPT*
   a. blood vessels b. intervertebral discs
   c. osteocytes
   d. calcium phosphate crystals
   e. concentric layers of bone

? Review Questions

1. Sketch a relaxed muscle fiber containing a myofibril, sarcomeres, and thick and thin filaments. How would a contracted muscle fiber look by comparison?

2. Describe the process of skeletal muscle contraction, beginning with an action potential in a motor neuron and ending with the relaxation of the muscle. Your answer should include the following words: *neuromuscular junction, T tubule, sarcoplasmic reticulum, calcium, thin filaments, binding sites, thick filaments, sarcomere, Z line,* and *active transport.*

3. Explain the following two statements: Muscles can only actively contract; muscle fibers lengthen passively.

4. What are the three types of skeletons found in animals? For one of these, describe how the muscles are arranged around the skeleton and how contractions of the muscles result in movement of the skeleton.

5. Compare the structure and function of the following pairs: spongy and compact bone, smooth and striated muscle, and cartilage and bone.

6. Explain the functions of osteoblasts, osteoclasts, and osteocytes.

7. How is cartilage converted to bone during embryonic development? Where is cartilage located in the body, and what functions does it serve?

8. Describe a hinge joint and how it is moved by antagonistic muscles.

Applying the Concepts

1. Discuss some of the problems that would result if the human heart were made of skeletal muscle instead of cardiac muscle.

2. Muscle fibers in individuals with Duchenne muscular dystrophy (DMD) lack a protein called *dystrophin,* which normally helps control calcium release from sarcoplasmic reticulum. Lack of dystrophin leads to a constant leaking of calcium ions, which activates an enzyme that dissolves muscle fibers. The gene that causes DMD is inherited as a sex-linked recessive gene. Women with this gene have a 50% chance of passing the disease to their male children and a 50% chance of passing the gene to their female children. Afflicted children gradually become unable to walk and die of respiratory problems as young adults. Recently tests have been developed that allow a woman to determine if she is a carrier and if her fetus has inherited the gene. What factors would make a woman a candidate for this test? If a woman discovers she carries this gene, what are her options with regard to having children? Discuss the ethical implications of these various options.

3. Myasthenia gravis is caused by the abnormal production of antibodies that bind to acetylcholine receptors on muscle cells and that eventually destroy the receptors. The disease causes muscles to become flaccid, weak, or paralyzed. Drugs, such as neostigmine, that inhibit the action of acetylcholinesterase (an enzyme that breaks down acetylcholine) are used to treat myasthenia gravis. How does neostigmine restore muscle activity?

4. Some insects would have a tough time flying if one nerve impulse was required for each muscle contraction. Gnats, for example, may beat their wings 1000 times a second. At such high frequencies, contraction is "myogenic," originating from the stretching caused by the contraction of antagonistic muscles. Also, insect flight muscle cells are filled with giant mitochondria. Suggest a mechanism to explain how myogenic contraction works inside cells. Explain the significance of giant mitochondria.

5. Human muscle cells contain a mixture of three types of muscle fibers: slow-twitch oxidative, fast-twitch oxidative, and fast-twitch glycolytic. Slow-twitch muscle cells break down ATP slowly; they contain many mitochondria and large amounts of myoglobin, a dark pigment that acts as a reservoir for oxygen. All fast-twitch muscle cells break down ATP rapidly. Fast-twitch oxidative fibers have moderate amounts of myoglobin and glycogen. Fast-twitch glycolytic fibers have little myoglobin and lots of glycogen. The relative numbers of these fibers in different muscles is under genetic control. Use this information to explain the location of dark and white meat in birds. Predict the relative numbers of slow-twitch and fast-twitch fibers in muscle samples from the thighs of world-class marathon runners and world-class sprinters.

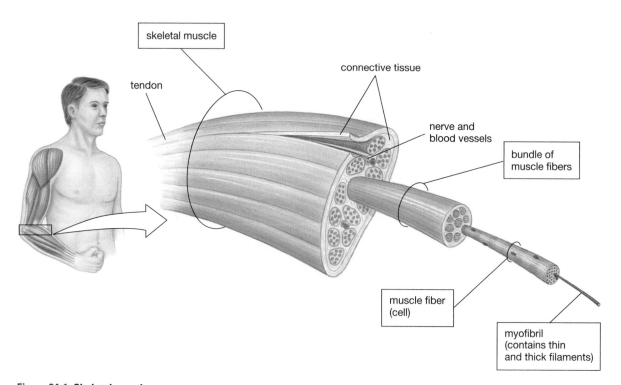

Figure 34-1 Skeletal muscle structure

© 2003 Prentice Hall, Inc.

NOTES

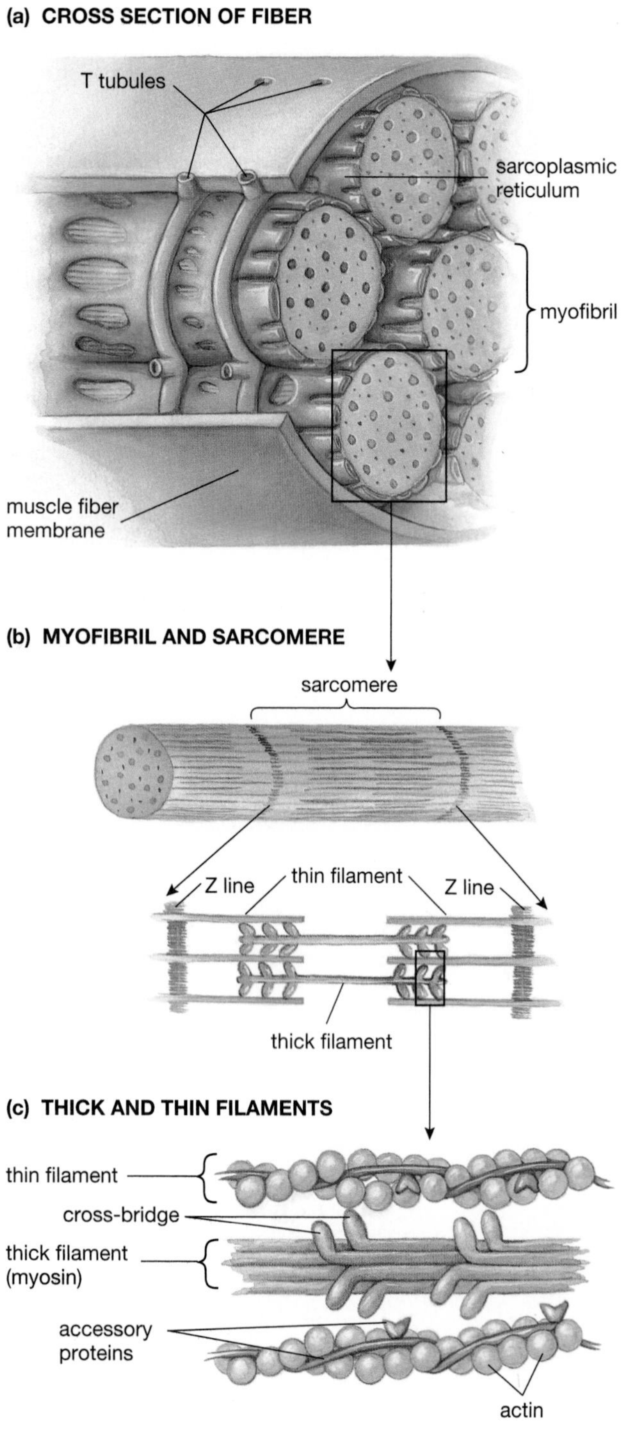

(a) CROSS SECTION OF FIBER

T tubules

sarcoplasmic
reticulum

myofibril

muscle fiber
membrane

HYDROSTATIC SKELETONS

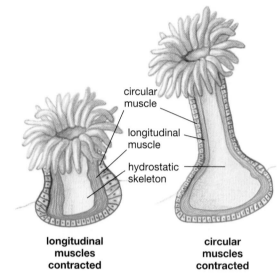

circular
muscle

longitudinal
muscle

hydrostatic
skeleton

**longitudinal
muscles
contracted**

**circular
muscles
contracted**

Figure 34-5 Not all skeletons are made of bone

(b) MYOFIBRIL AND SARCOMERE

sarcomere

Z line   thin filament   Z line

thick filament

(c) THICK AND THIN FILAMENTS

thin filament

cross-bridge

thick filament
(myosin)

accessory
proteins

actin

Figure 34-2 A skeletal muscle fiber

© 2003 Prentice Hall, Inc.

NOTES

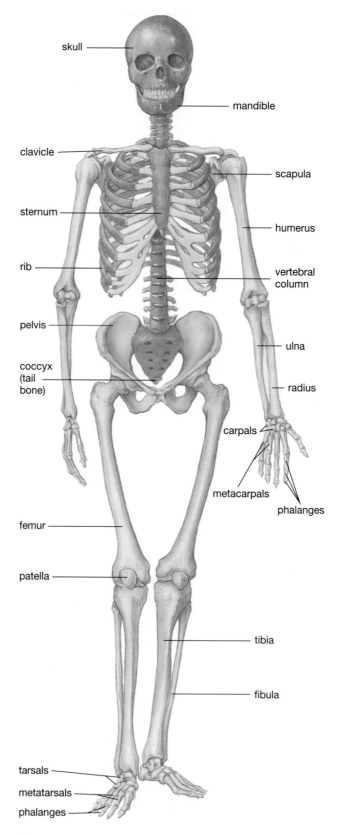

skull

mandible

clavicle

scapula

sternum

humerus

rib

vertebral column

pelvis

ulna

coccyx (tail bone)

radius

carpals

metacarpals

phalanges

femur

patella

tibia

fibula

tarsals

metatarsals

phalanges

Figure 34-6 The human skeleton

© 2003 Prentice Hall, Inc.

NOTES

(a)

(b)

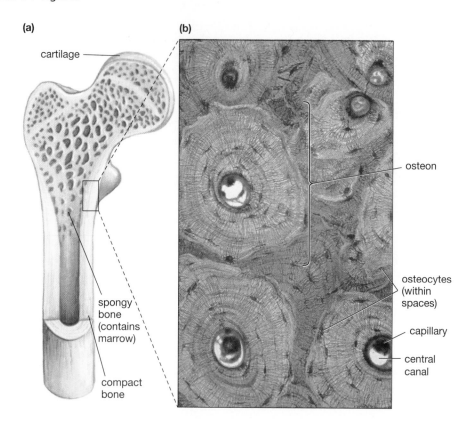

cartilage

osteon

osteocytes (within spaces)

capillary

central canal

spongy bone (contains marrow)

compact bone

Figure 34-9 **The structure of bone**

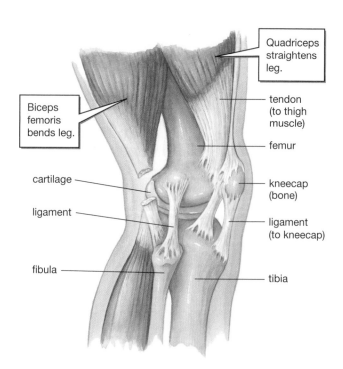

Quadriceps straightens leg.

Biceps femoris bends leg.

tendon (to thigh muscle)

femur

cartilage

kneecap (bone)

ligament

ligament (to kneecap)

fibula

tibia

Figure 34-10 **A hinge joint**

© 2003 Prentice Hall, Inc.

NOTES

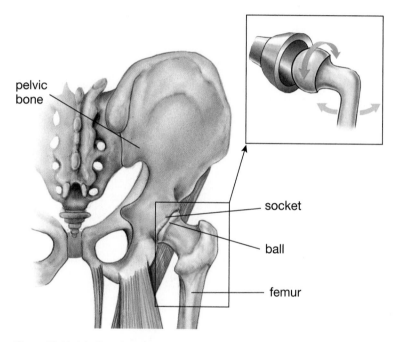

Figure 34-11 A ball-and-socket joint

© 2003 Prentice Hall, Inc.

NOTES

CHAPTER 35 Animal Reproduction

Thinking Through the Concepts

Multiple Choice

1. *Budding and fission are processes used by*
   a. dioecious species
   b. hermaphroditic organisms
   c. organisms requiring new gene combinations for each generation
   d. sexually reproducing species
   e. asexually reproducing species

2. *All of the following are barrier contraceptive devices EXCEPT the*
   a. IUD
   b. female condom
   c. cervical cap
   d. diaphragm
   e. male condom

3. *In humans, spermatogenesis yields _____ sperm for each diploid sex cell, and oogenesis yields _____ secondary oocyte(s) for each sex cell.*
   a. one, four
   b. two, one
   c. one, two
   d. four, one
   e. four, two

4. *Which structure adds the final secretions to semen as it moves out of the male reproductive tract?*
   a. epididymis
   b. bulbourethral gland
   c. seminal vesicle
   d. prostate gland
   e. interstitial cells

5. *The corpus luteum*
   a. accompanies the egg as it enters the oviduct
   b. is the fertilized egg
   c. secretes prostaglandin
   d. forms in the uterus
   e. secretes both estrogen and progesterone

6. *The primary hormone that inhibits GnRH is*
   a. FSH
   b. LH
   c. progesterone
   d. estrogen
   e. a hypothalamic releasing factor

? Review Questions

1. List the advantages and disadvantages of asexual reproduction, sexual reproduction, external fertilization, and internal fertilization, including an example of an animal that uses each type.

2. Compare the structures of the egg and sperm. What structural modifications do sperm have that facilitate movement, energy use, and digestion?

3. What is the role of the corpus luteum in a menstrual cycle? In early pregnancy? What determines its survival after ovulation?

4. Construct a chart of common sexually transmitted diseases. List the disease's name, the cause (organism), symptoms, and treatment.

5. List the structures, in order, through which a sperm passes on its way from the seminiferous tubules of the testis to the uterine tube of the female.

6. Name the three accessory glands of the male reproductive tract. What are the functions of the secretions they produce?

7. Diagram the menstrual cycle, and describe the interactions among hormones secreted by the pituitary gland and ovaries that produce the cycle.

Applying the Concepts

1. Discuss the most effective or appropriate method of birth control for each of the following couples: Couple A, which has intercourse three times a week but never wants to have children; Couple B, which has intercourse once a month and may want to have children someday; and couple C, which has intercourse three times a week and wants to have children someday.

2. *Pelvic endometriosis* is a relatively common disease of women in which bits of the endometrial lining find their way onto abdominal organs and respond in typical ways to hormones during a menstrual cycle. When the uterine lining bleeds during menstruation, so do these implants. Common treatments are oral contraceptives, Danazol™ (a compound that inhibits gonadotropins), and synthetic GnRH analogues that are, paradoxically, powerful inhibitors of FSH and LH. How does each of these compounds provide relief?

3. Would contraceptive drugs that block cell receptors for FSH be useful in males and/or females? Explain. What side effects would such drugs have?

4. Think of all the choices a couple has to obtain a child, including *in vitro* fertilization using the couple's eggs and sperm, *in vitro* fertilization using a donor's sperm or egg, and insemination of a surrogate mother with sperm from the couple's husband. Think of some more. What ethical issues do these various options present?

5. Fertility drugs have greatly increased the incidence of multiple births. When more than two embryos share the uterus, the incidence of premature birth and developmental problems increases substantially. The costs of caring for multiple premature infants is staggering. When fertility drugs produce multiple embryos, the physician can selectively eliminate some of these embryos early in development, so the remaining few have a better chance to develop fully and normally. Given these facts, discuss the ethical implications of taking fertility drugs.

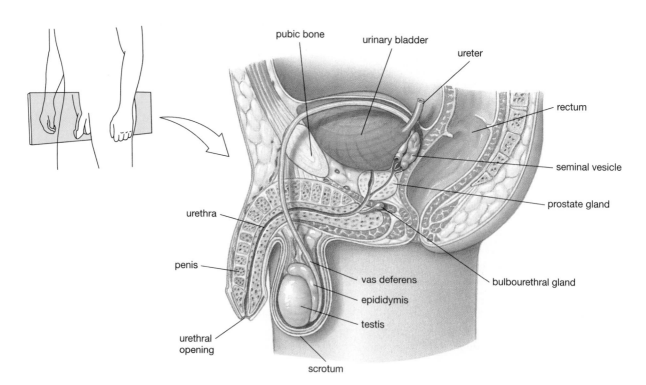

Figure 35-8 The human male reproductive tract

© 2003 Prentice Hall, Inc.

NOTES

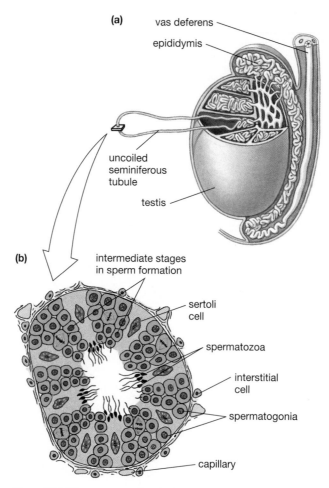

(a)

vas deferens

epididymis

uncoiled
seminiferous
tubule

testis

(b)

intermediate stages
in sperm formation

sertoli
cell

spermatozoa

interstitial
cell

spermatogonia

capillary

Figure 35-9 **The structures involved in spermatogenesis**

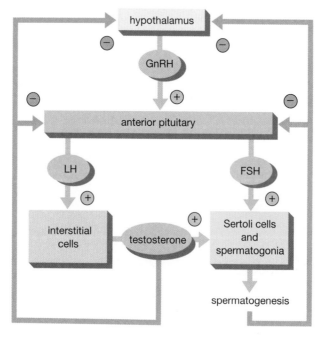

hypothalamus

GnRH

anterior pituitary

LH

FSH

interstitial
cells

testosterone

Sertoli cells
and
spermatogonia

spermatogenesis

Figure 35-12 **Hormonal control of spermatogenesis**

© 2003 Prentice Hall, Inc.

NOTES

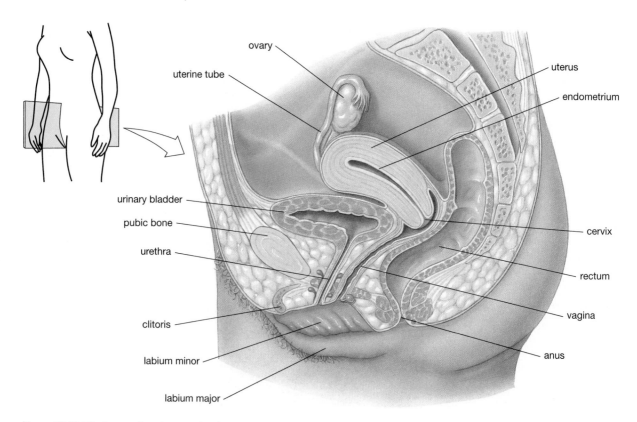

Figure 35-13 The human female reproductive tract

© 2003 Prentice Hall, Inc.

NOTES

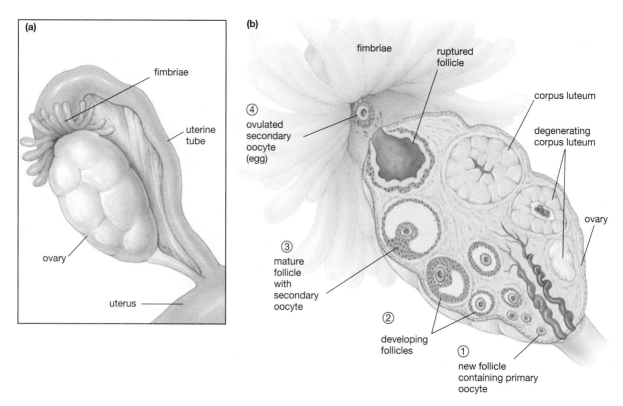

(a)

fimbriae

uterine tube

ovary

uterus

(b)

fimbriae

ruptured follicle

corpus luteum

degenerating corpus luteum

④ ovulated secondary oocyte (egg)

③ mature follicle with secondary oocyte

ovary

② developing follicles

① new follicle containing primary oocyte

Figure 35-14 **The structures involved in oogenesis**

© 2003 Prentice Hall, Inc.

NOTES

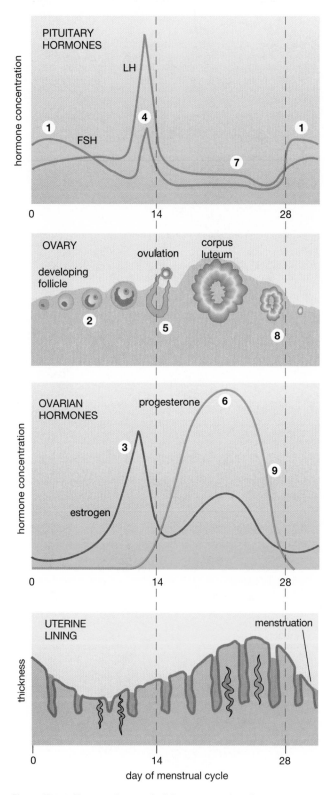

Figure E35-1 Hormonal control of the menstrual cycle

© 2003 Prentice Hall, Inc.

NOTES

Thinking Through the Concepts

Multiple Choice

1. *Cells become differentiated through all of the following events EXCEPT*
   a. binding of regulatory molecules to chromosomes
   b. chemical messages received from other cells
   c. unequal distribution of gene-regulating substances during cleavage
   d. transcription of different genes
   e. progressive loss of genes as cells divide

2. *Indirect development is characteristic of animals that normally produce*
   a. few eggs
   b. eggs with large amounts of yolk
   c. young that are sexually immature versions of adults
   d. all of the above
   e. none of the above

3. *In bird eggs, the allantois*
   a. exchanges oxygen and carbon dioxide
   b. produces the shell
   c. stores wastes
   d. encloses the embryo in a watery environment
   e. contains stored food

4. *The endoderm gives rise to the*
   a. lining of the digestive tract
   b. epidermis of skin
   c. skeletal system
   d. muscles
   e. nervous system

5. *In human development, ectoderm cells migrate through the primitive streak to form*
   a. endoderm
   b. mesoderm
   c. the chorion
   d. the yolk sac
   e. the amnion

6. *The process by which a tissue causes another tissue to differentiate is called*
   a. gastrulation
   b. metamorphosis
   c. cleavage
   d. induction
   e. indirect development

? Review Questions

1. Distinguish between indirect and direct development, and give examples of each.

2. Describe the structure and function of four extraembryonic membranes found in reptiles and birds. Are these four present in placental mammals? In what ways are their roles similar in reptiles and birds *vs.* mammals? How do they differ?

3. What is yolk? How does it influence cleavage?

4. What is gastrulation? Describe gastrulation in frogs and in humans.

5. Name two structures derived from each of the three embryonic tissue layers—endoderm, ectoderm, and mesoderm.

6. How does cell death contribute to development?

7. Describe the process of induction, and give two examples.

8. Define *differentiation*. How do cells differentiate; that is, how is it that adult cells express some but not all the genes of the fertilized egg?

9. What role do gradients of morphogens play in animal development?

10. In humans, where does fertilization occur, and what stages of development occur before the fertilized egg reaches the uterus?

11. Describe how the human blastocyst gives rise to the embryo and its extraembryonic membranes.

12. Explain how the structure of the placenta prevents mixing of fetal and maternal blood while allowing the exchange of substances between the mother and the fetus.

13. Is the placenta an effective barrier against substances that can harm the fetus? Describe two types of harmful agents that can cross the placenta and their effects on the fetus.

14. How do changes in the breast prepare a mother to nurse her newborn? How do hormones influence these changes and stimulate milk production?

15. Describe the events that lead to the expulsion of the baby and the placenta from the uterus. Explain why this is an example of positive feedback.

Applying the Concepts

1. When fetal ectoderm tissue from the mouth of an embryo is transplanted into a region of mesoderm of another embryo of a different species, the mesoderm induces the ectoderm to form mouth structures of the type of organism from which the ectoderm tissue was taken. When ectoderm from a chick is implanted into a mouse embryo, the chicken tissue produces teeth. What does this experiment tell us about why the adage "scarce as hen's teeth" is true? Also, what does this experiment tell us about the evolutionary origin of chickens?

2. On the basis of your knowledge of genetics (Unit II) and evolution (Unit III), explain why the human embryo passes through a developmental stage in which it has gill grooves and a tail.

3. Embryologists have used embryo fusion to produce *tetraparental* (four-parent) mice and have also produced "geeps" from goat and sheep embryos. The resulting bodies are patchworks of cells from both animals. Why does fusion succeed with very early embryos (four-cell to eight-cell stages) and fail when much older embryos are used?

4. If the nuclei of adult cells can be transplanted into eggs from which the nucleus has been removed to produce clones of the parent, is it theoretically possible to produce human clones? Would such clones yield offspring that are *exactly* identical to the parents who supplied the nuclei? Explain.

5. Estimates of the number of women in the U.S. who self-medicate with over-the-counter (OTC) drugs during pregnancy range from 65% to 95%. Evidently, the public doesn't perceive nonprescription substances as drugs. Many subtle disorders, especially of the nervous system, will probably be connected to over-the-counter use in coming years. If you were engaged in pharmaceutical research, which OTC drugs would you focus on as possible culprits? Which months of pregnancy would you study closely? Who would you choose as your study population?

© 2003 Prentice Hall, Inc.

NOTES

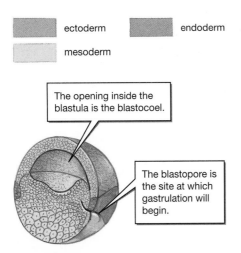

ectoderm   endoderm

mesoderm

The opening inside the blastula is the blastocoel.

The blastopore is the site at which gastrulation will begin.

(a) The blastula just before gastrulation.

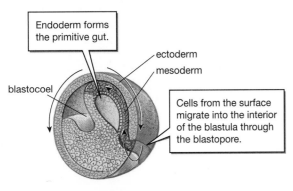

Endoderm forms the primitive gut.

ectoderm

mesoderm

blastocoel

Cells from the surface migrate into the interior of the blastula through the blastopore.

(b) Cells migrate at the start of gastrulation. These cells will form the endoderm and mesoderm layers of the gastrula; the cells remaining on the surface will form ectoderm.

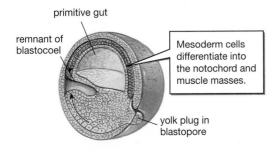

primitive gut

remnant of blastocoel

Mesoderm cells differentiate into the notochord and muscle masses.

yolk plug in blastopore

(c) Mesoderm differentiates.

Figure 36-3 Gastrulation in the frog

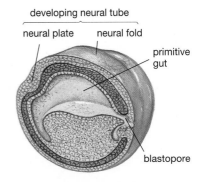

developing neural tube

neural plate   neural fold

primitive gut

blastopore

(d) The notochord induces ectoderm cells lying directly above it to form the neural tube.

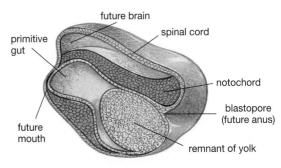

future brain

primitive gut

spinal cord

future mouth

notochord

blastopore (future anus)

remnant of yolk

(e) Further development. The neural tube differentiates into brain and spinal cord. A future mouth is produced when the opening formed by the primitive gut breaks through at the end of the embryo opposite the blastopore. The blastopore is the future anus.

© 2003 Prentice Hall, Inc.

NOTES

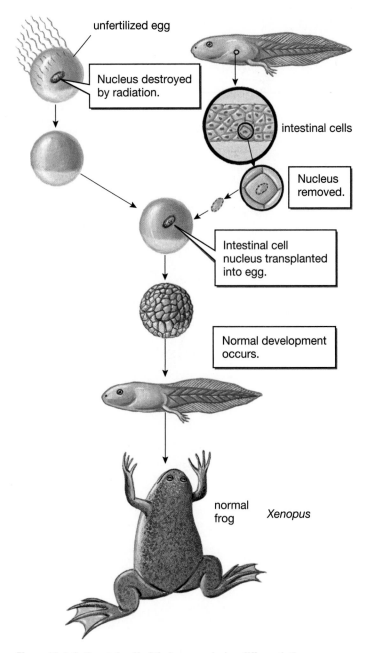

unfertilized egg

Nucleus destroyed by radiation.

intestinal cells

Nucleus removed.

Intestinal cell nucleus transplanted into egg.

Normal development occurs.

normal frog   *Xenopus*

Figure 36-4 Cells retain all of their genes during differentiation

© 2003 Prentice Hall, Inc.

NOTES

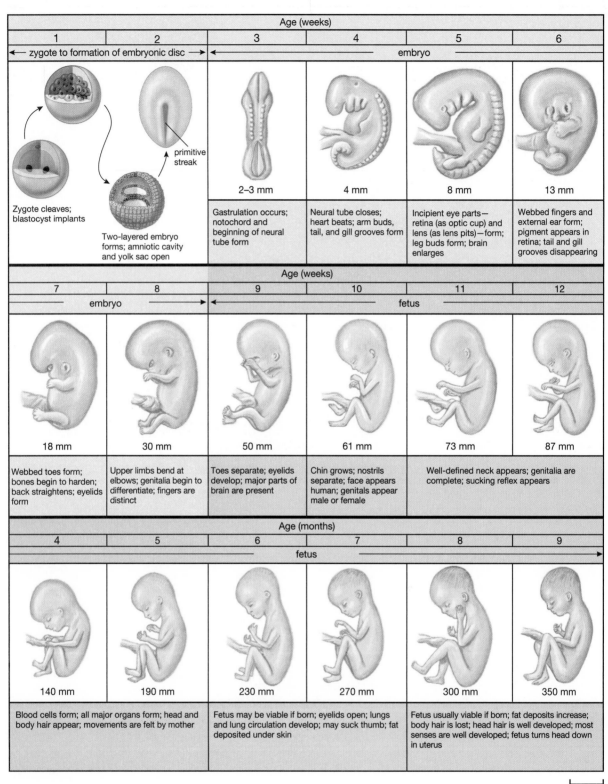

for reference: 10 mm

Figure 36-7 Human embryonic development

© 2003 Prentice Hall, Inc.

NOTES

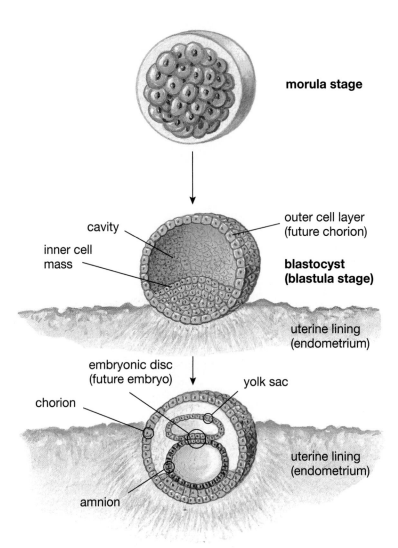

morula stage

cavity

inner cell mass

outer cell layer (future chorion)

blastocyst (blastula stage)

uterine lining (endometrium)

embryonic disc (future embryo)

yolk sac

chorion

uterine lining (endometrium)

amnion

Figure 36-9 **Human development during the first and second weeks**

© 2003 Prentice Hall, Inc.

NOTES

(a)

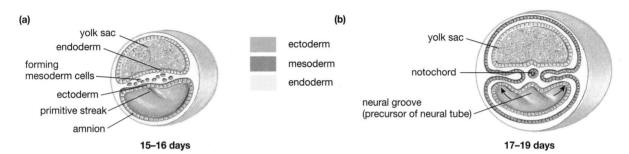

yolk sac
endoderm
forming
mesoderm cells
ectoderm
primitive streak
amnion

ectoderm
mesoderm
endoderm

15–16 days

Shortly after implantation, gastrulation occurs. The two-layered embryonic disc soon splits open, and the primitive streak develops in the ectoderm. Ectoderm cells migrate in, forming mesoderm.

(b)

yolk sac

notochord

neural groove
(precursor of neural tube)

17–19 days

Some mesoderm cells form the notochord, which induces development of the neural tube, forerunner of the brain and spinal cord.

(c)

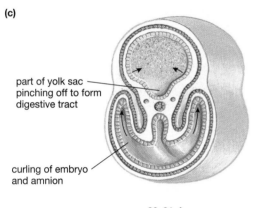

part of yolk sac
pinching off to form
digestive tract

curling of embryo
and amnion

20–21 days

During the third and fourth weeks of development, the embryo curls toward the yolk sac, forming a tubelike embryo typical of vertebrates.

(d)

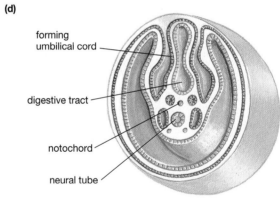

forming
umbilical cord

digestive tract

notochord

neural tube

22–25 days

As the embryo curls, part of the (empty) yolk sac pinches to form the digestive tract. The amnion curls with the embryo, eventually completely enclosing it, except where the umbilical cord extends through.

Figure 36-10 Human development during the third and fourth weeks

© 2003 Prentice Hall, Inc.

NOTES

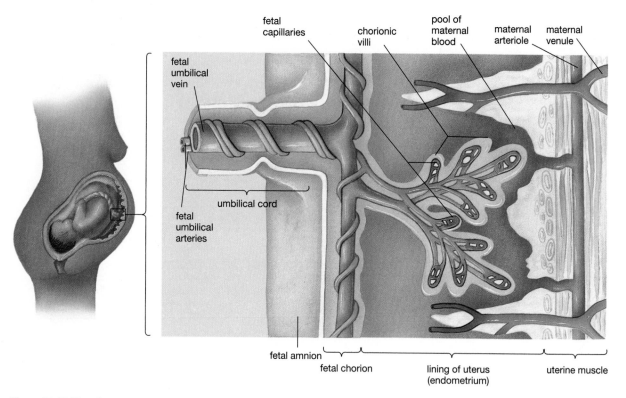

Figure 36-12 The placenta

© 2003 Prentice Hall, Inc.

NOTES

CHAPTER 37 Animal Behavior

Thinking Through the Concepts

Multiple Choice

1. *In general, animal behaviors*
   a. are determined mainly by genetic factors
   b. are determined mainly by environmental factors
   c. arise from an interaction between genes and the environment
   d. do not affect an individual's chances of survival

2. *Which of the following is NOT a feature of play?*
   a. Young animals play more often than adults.
   b. It may borrow movements from other behaviors.
   c. It uses considerable energy.
   d. It always has a clear, immediate function.
   e. It is potentially dangerous.

3. *Naked mole rats are unique among mammals, in that*
   a. they live in colonies
   b. most of their life is spent underground
   c. even adults have little body hair
   d. most individuals never reproduce
   e. they use pheromones to communicate

4. *In which of the following ways does an individual benefit from a social grouping with other animals?*
   a. increased ability to detect, repel, or confuse predators
   b. increased hunting efficiency
   c. increased likelihood of finding mates
   d. increased efficiency due to division of labor
   e. all of the above

5. *Which of the following pairs of communication forms and advantages is NOT accurate?*
   a. pheromones, long-lasting
   b. visual displays, instantaneous
   c. sound communication, effective at night
   d. pheromones, convey rapidly changing information
   e. touch, maintains social bonds

6. *In an insect society, such as the honeybee society,*
   a. the division of labor is based on biologically determined castes
   b. all adult members share labor equally
   c. all adult members have the opportunity to reproduce
   d. reproduction is altered seasonally among the adults
   e. the organization of the society is flexible and adaptable

? Review Questions

1. Explain why neither "innate" nor "learned" adequately describes the behavior of any given organism.

2. Explain why animals play. Include the features of play in your answer.

3. List four senses through which animals communicate, and give one example of each form of communication. After each, present both advantages and disadvantages of that form of communication.

4. A bird will ignore a squirrel in its territory but will act aggressively toward a member of its own species. Explain why.

5. Why are most aggressive encounters among members of the same species relatively harmless?

6. Discuss advantages and disadvantages of group living.

7. In what ways do naked mole rat societies resemble those of the honeybee?

Applying the Concepts

1. Male mosquitoes orient toward the high-pitched whine of the female, and female mosquitoes (only females suck blood) are attracted to the warmth, humidity, and carbon dioxide exuded by their prey. Using this information, design a mosquito trap or killer that exploits a mosquito's innate behaviors. Now design one for moths.

2. You raise honeybees but are new at the job. Trying to increase honey production, you introduce several queens into the hive. What is the likely outcome? What different things could you do to increase production?

3. Describe and give an example of a dominance hierarchy. What role does it play in social behavior? Give a human parallel, and describe its role in human society. Are the two roles similar? Why or why not? Repeat this exercise for territorial behavior in humans and in another animal.

4. You are manager of an airport. Planes are being endangered by large numbers of flying birds, which can be sucked into engines, disabling the engines. Without harming the birds, what might you do to discourage them from nesting and flying near the airport and its planes?

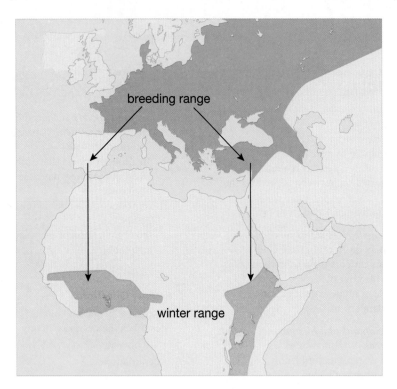

Figure 37-8 Genes influence migratory behavior

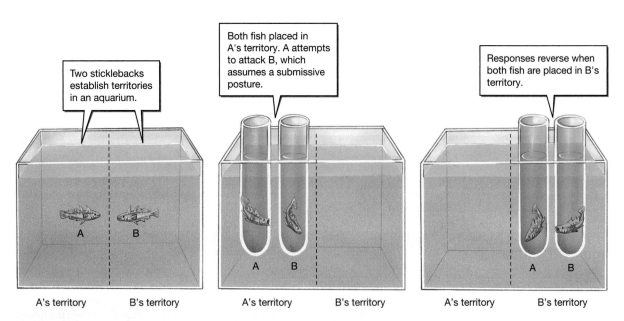

Figure 37-20 Territory ownership and aggression

© 2003 Prentice Hall, Inc.

NOTES

(a) A male, inconspicuously colored, leaves the school of males and females to establish a breeding territory.

(b) As his belly takes on the red color of the breeding male, he displays aggressively at other red-bellied males, exposing his red underside.

(c) Having established a territory, the male begins nest construction by digging a shallow pit that he will fill with bits of algae cemented together by a sticky secretion from his kidneys.

(d) After he tunnels through the nest to make a hole, his back begins to take on the blue courting color that makes him attractive to females.

(e) An egg-carrying female displays her enlarged belly to him by assuming a head-up posture. Her swollen belly and his courting colors are passive visual displays.

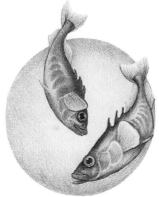

(f) Using a zigzag dance, he leads her to the nest.

(g) After she enters, he stimulates her to release eggs by prodding at the base of her tail.

(h) He enters the nest as she leaves and deposits sperm, which fertilize the eggs.

Figure 37-24 Courtship of the three-spined stickleback

© 2003 Prentice Hall, Inc.

NOTES

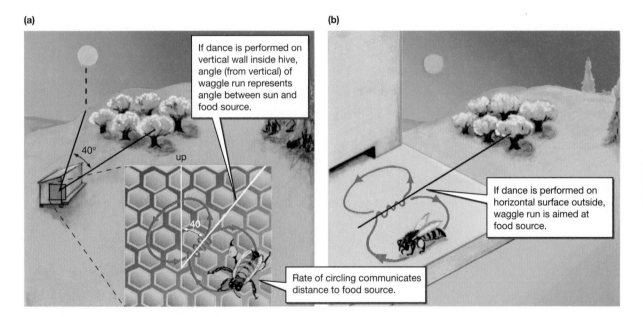

Figure 37-27 **Bee language: the waggle dance**

NOTES

CHAPTER 38 Population Growth and Regulation

Thinking Through the Concepts

Multiple Choice

1. *Which of the following factors is NOT an example of density-dependent environmental resistance?*
   a. weather
   b. competition
   c. predation
   d. parasitism
   e. lack of food

2. *For exponential growth to occur, it is necessary that*
   a. there is no mortality
   b. there are no density-independent limits
   c. the birth rate consistently exceed the death rate
   d. a species is very fast reproducing
   e. the species is an exotic invader in an ecosystem

3. *Which of the following currently contributes most to human population growth within the U.S.?*
   a. the consequences of the baby boom
   b. immigration
   c. a birth rate above RLF
   d. both a and b
   e. all of the above

4. *Which is the most common type of spatial distribution?*
   a. logistic
   b. uniform
   c. random
   d. exponential
   e. clumped

5. *Which continent has the highest rate of natural increase in the human population?*
   a. North America
   b. Africa
   c. Asia
   d. Australia
   e. South America

6. *If a population exceeds its carrying capacity,*
   a. it must immediately crash
   b. it can remain stable at this level indefinitely
   c. it will continue to increase for the indefinite future
   d. it must decline sooner or later
   e. the food supply will increase to support it

? Review Questions

1. Define *biotic potential* and *environmental resistance*.

2. Draw the growth curve of a population before it encounters significant environmental resistance. What is the name of this type of growth, and what is its distinguishing characteristic?

3. Distinguish between density-independent and density-dependent forms of environmental resistance.

4. Describe (or draw a graph illustrating) what is likely to happen to a population that far exceeds the carrying capacity of its ecosystem. Explain your answer.

5. List three density-dependent forms of environmental resistance, and explain why each is density-dependent.

6. Distinguish between populations showing concave and convex survivorship curves. Which is characteristic of people living in the U.S., and why?

7. Given that the U.S. birth rate is currently at replacement-level fertility, why is our population growing?

8. Discuss some reasons why making the transition from a growing to a stable population can be economically difficult.

Applying the Concepts

1. Explain natural selection in terms of biotic potential and environmental resistance.

2. The U.S. has a long history of accepting large numbers of immigrants. Discuss the implications of immigration for population stabilization.

3. What factors encourage rapid population growth in developing countries? What will it take to change this growth?

4. Contrast age structure in rapidly growing versus stable human populations. Why is there a momentum in population growth built into a population that is above RLF?

5. Why is the concept of carrying capacity difficult to apply to human populations? In reference to human population, should the concept be modified to include quality of life?

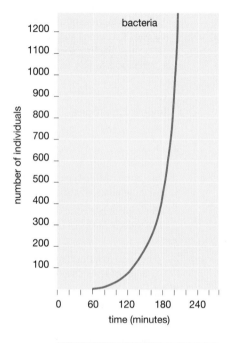

time (minutes)	number of bacteria
0	1
20	2
40	4
60	8
80	16
100	32
120	64
140	128
160	256
180	512
200	1024
220	2048

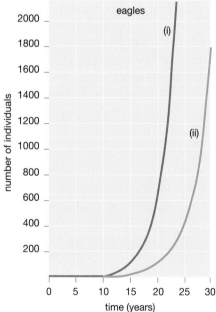

time (years)	number of eagles (i)	number of eagles (ii)
0	2	2
2	2	2
4	4	2
6	8	4
8	14	8
10	28	12
12	52	18
14	100	32
16	190	54
18	362	86
20	630	142
22	1314	238
24	2504	392
26	4770	644
28	9088	1066
30	17314	1764

Figure 38-1 Exponential growth curves

© 2003 Prentice Hall, Inc.

NOTES

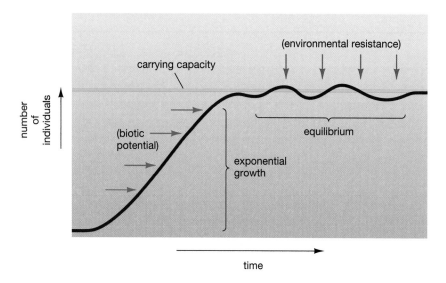

Figure 38-5 The S-curve of population growth

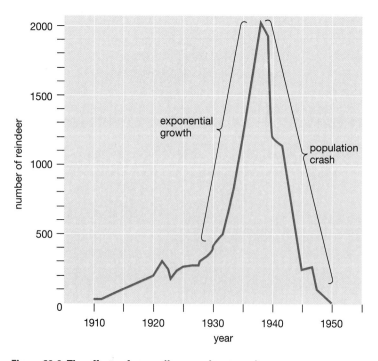

Figure 38-6 The effects of exceeding carrying capacity

© 2003 Prentice Hall, Inc.

NOTES

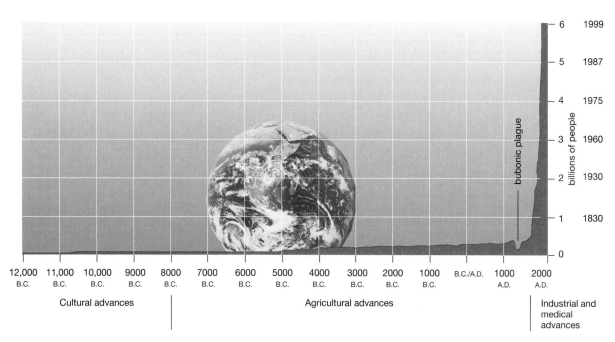

Figure 38-11 Human population growth

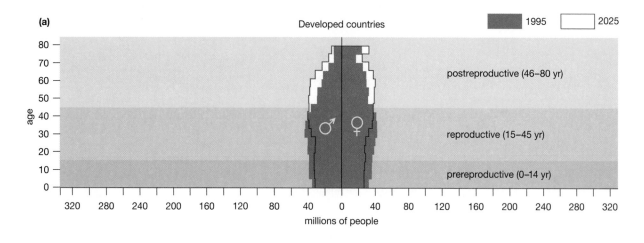

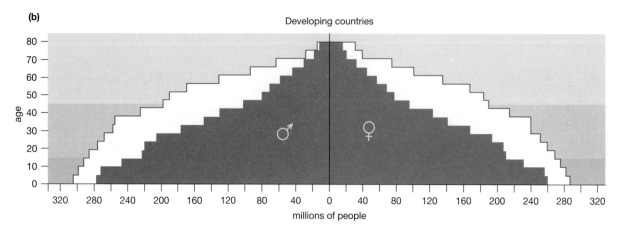

Figure 38-12 Age structures compared

© 2003 Prentice Hall, Inc.

NOTES

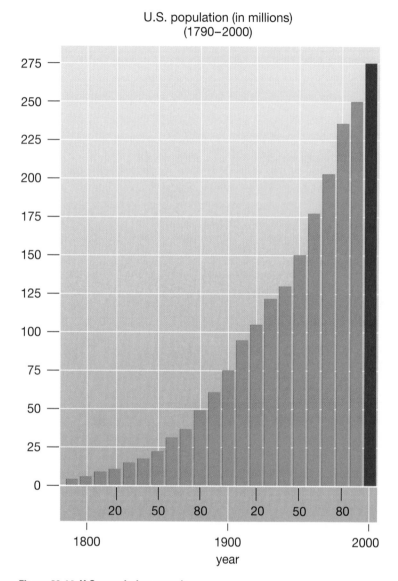

Figure 38-14 U.S. population growth

© 2003 Prentice Hall, Inc.

NOTES

CHAPTER 39   Community Interactions

Multiple Choice

1. *Which of the following is usually NOT true of climax communities?*
   a. They have more species than do pioneer communities.
   b. They have longer-lived species than do early successional stages.
   c. Climax communities are relatively stable.
   d. Some climax communities are maintained by fire.
   e. Climax communities vary with the location of the ecosystem.

2. *What were the differences in the niches of the* Paramecium *in Gause's second experiment that allowed them to coexist?*
   a. food eaten
   b. body size
   c. feeding area
   d. preferred water temperature
   e. preferred pH

3. *Which of the following is a mutualistic relationship?*
   a. flowering plants and their pollinators
   b. a caterpillar eating a tomato plant
   c. bats and moths
   d. monarch and viceroy butterflies
   e. lupines and blue butterflies

4. *What is the function of aggressive mimicry?*
   a. to hide a prey from a predator
   b. to warn a predator that a prey is dangerous
   c. to warn a predator that a prey is distasteful
   d. to keep prey from recognizing a predator
   e. to startle a prey when it sees a predator

5. *What is coevolution?*
   a. two species selecting for traits in each other
   b. individuals of two species living together
   c. the presence of two species in the same community
   d. two species evolving separately through time
   e. individuals of two species learning how to coexist with or to hunt with each other

6. *By the competitive exclusion principle, coexisting species*
   a. can use the same resources
   b. cannot eat exactly the same things
   c. cannot have identical ecological interactions
   d. cannot be exactly the same size
   e. cannot be closely related to one another

? Review Questions

1. Define ecological *community*, and list three important types of community interactions.

2. Describe four very different ways in which specific plants and animals protect themselves against being eaten. In each, describe an adaptation that might evolve in predators of these species that would overcome their defenses.

3. List two important types of symbiosis; define and provide an example of each.

4. Which type of succession would occur on a clear-cut (a region in which all the trees have been removed by logging) in a national forest, and why?

5. List two subclimax and two climax communities. How do they differ?

6. Define *succession*, and explain why it occurs.

Applying the Concepts

1. Herbivorous animals that eat seeds are considered by some ecologists to be predators of plants, and herbivorous animals that eat leaves are considered to be parasites of plants. Discuss the validity of this classification scheme.

2. An interesting interspecific relationship exists between the tarantula spider and the tarantula hawk wasp. This wasp attacks tarantulas, paralyzing them with venom from their stingers. The wasp then lays eggs on the paralyzed spider. The eggs hatch, and the young eat the living, immobilized tissues of the spider. Discuss whether this relationship between spider and wasp exemplifies parasitism or predation.

3. An ecologist visiting an island finds two very closely related species of birds, one of which has a slightly larger bill than the other. Interpret this finding with respect to the competitive exclusion principle and the ecological niche, and explain both concepts.

4. Think about the case of the camouflaged frogfish and its prey. As the frogfish sits camouflaged on the ocean floor, wiggling its lure, a small fish approaches the lure and is eaten, while a very large predatory fish fails to notice the frogfish. Describe all the possible types of community interactions and adaptations these organisms have selected for. Remember that predators can also be prey and that community interactions are complex!

5. Design an experiment to determine whether the kangaroo is a keystone species in the Australian outback.

6. Why is it difficult to study succession? Suggest some ways you would approach this challenge for a few different ecosystems.

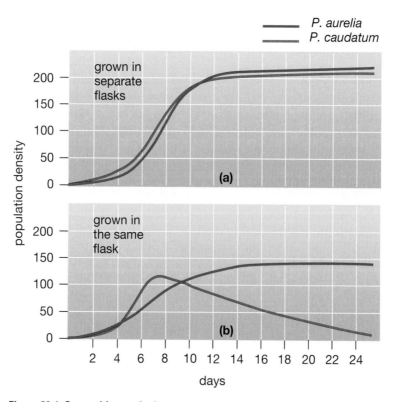

Figure 39-1 **Competitive exclusion**

© 2003 Prentice Hall, Inc.

NOTES

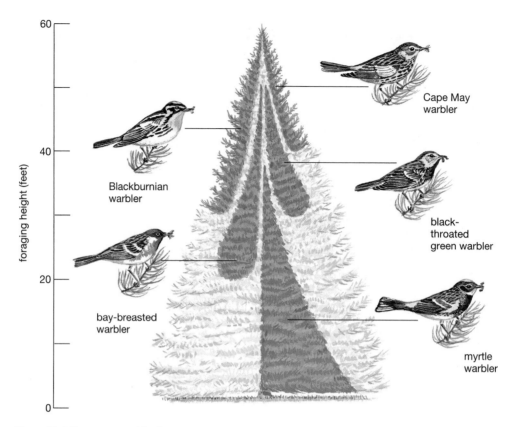

Figure 39-2 Resource partitioning

Figure 39-16 Primary succession

© 2003 Prentice Hall, Inc.

NOTES

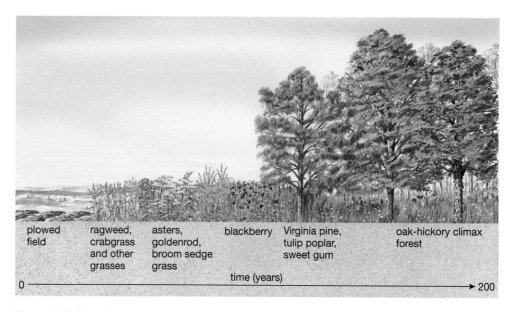

Figure 39-17 **Secondary succession**

© 2003 Prentice Hall, Inc.

NOTES

CHAPTER 40 How Do Ecosystems Work?

Thinking Through the Concepts

Multiple Choice

1. *Why do scientists think that human-induced global warming will be more harmful to plants and animals than were past, natural climate fluctuations?*
   a. because temperatures will change faster
   b. because the temperature changes will be larger
   c. because species now are less adaptable than species in the past
   d. because ecosystems are now more complicated than they used to be
   e. because the temperature changes will last longer

2. *The major source(s) of carbon for living things is (are)*
   a. coal, oil, and natural gas
   b. plants
   c. CO_2 in the atmosphere and oceans
   d. methane in the atmosphere
   e. carbon in animal bodies

3. *Why would you expect there to be a smaller biomass of big predators (lions, leopards, hunting dogs, etc.) than of grazing mammals (gazelles, zebra, elephants, etc.) in the African savanna?*
   a. too little cover for the predators to hide in
   b. the inefficiency of energy transfer between trophic levels
   c. like domestic cats, large predators are susceptible to hair balls
   d. many predators occur in social groups, thus limiting their numbers
   e. because grazers are better adapted to moving long distances, they can better follow the rains

4. *What is the one group of organisms that is able to fix atmospheric nitrogen into forms usable by living organisms?*
   a. plants
   b. fungi
   c. insects
   d. bacteria
   e. viruses

5. *The biological process by which carbon is returned to its reservoir is*
   a. photosynthesis
   b. denitrification
   c. carbon fixation
   d. glycolysis
   e. cellular respiration

6. *As a black widow spider consumes her mate, what is the lowest trophic level she could be occupying?*
   a. third
   b. first
   c. second
   d. fourth
   e. fifth

? Review Questions

1. What makes the flow of energy through ecosystems fundamentally different from the flow of nutrients?

2. What is an autotroph? What trophic level does it occupy, and what is its importance in ecosystems?

3. Define *primary productivity*. Would you predict higher productivity in a farm pond or an alpine lake? Defend your answer.

4. List the first three trophic levels. Among the consumers, which are most abundant? Why would you predict that there will be a greater biomass of plants than herbivores in any ecosystem? Relate your answer to the "10% law."

5. How do food chains and food webs differ? Which is the more accurate representation of actual feeding relationships in ecosystems?

6. Define *detritus feeders* and *decomposers*, and explain their importance in ecosystems.

7. Trace the movement of carbon from its reservoir through the biotic community and back to the reservoir. How have human activities altered the carbon cycle, and what are the implications for future climate?

8. Explain how nitrogen gets from the air to a plant.

9. Trace a phosphorus molecule from a phosphate-rich rock into the DNA of a carnivore. What makes the phosphorus cycle fundamentally different from the carbon and nitrogen cycles?

10. Trace the movement of a water molecule from the moment it leaves the ocean until it eventually reaches a plant root, then a plant stoma, and then makes its way back to the ocean.

Applying the Concepts

1. What could your college or university do to reduce its contribution to acid rain and global warming? Be specific and, if possible, offer practical alternatives to current practices.

2. Relate fossil fuel consumption to (a) the loss of aquatic life in lakes in the Northeast and Canada and (b) the lengthening of the growing season in Europe. Trace each step from the burning of gasoline in a car or power plant to the change in question.

3. Define and give an example of *biological magnification*. What qualities are present in materials that undergo biological magnification? In which trophic level are the problems worst, and why?

4. Discuss the contribution of population growth to (a) acid rain and to (b) the greenhouse effect.

5. Describe what would happen to a population of deer if all predators were removed and hunting was banned. Include effects on vegetation as well as on the deer population itself. Relate your answer to carrying capacity as discussed in Chapter 38.

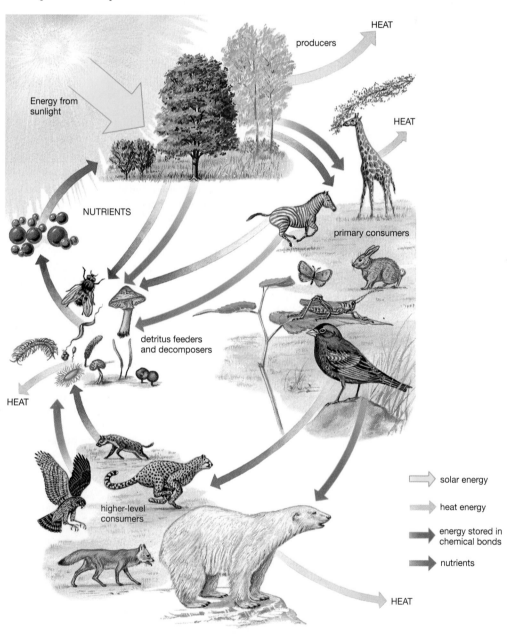

Figure 40-1 Energy flow, nutrient cycling, and feeding relationships in ecosystems

© 2003 Prentice Hall, Inc.

NOTES

Figure 40-3 Ecosystem productivity compared

© 2003 Prentice Hall, Inc.

NOTES

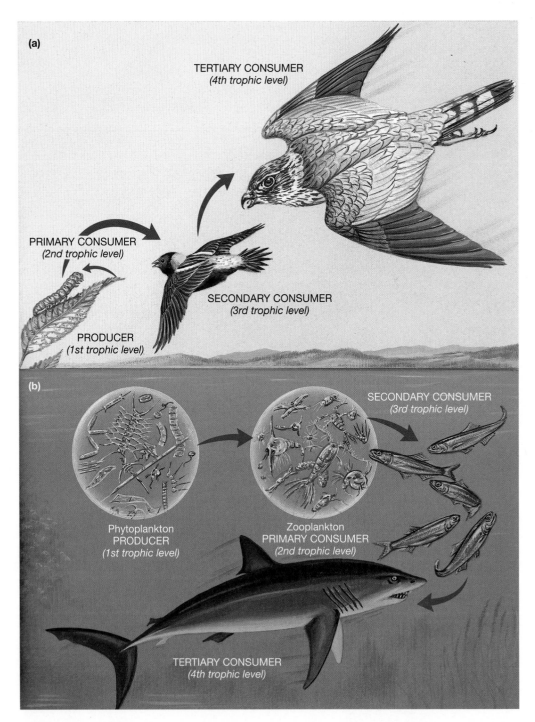

Figure 40-4 Food chains

© 2003 Prentice Hall, Inc.

NOTES

Figure 40-5 A food web

© 2003 Prentice Hall, Inc.

NOTES

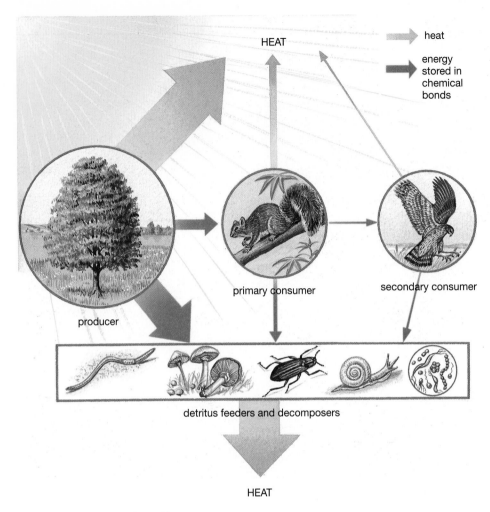

heat

energy stored in chemical bonds

HEAT

producer

primary consumer

secondary consumer

detritus feeders and decomposers

HEAT

Figure 40-6 Energy transfer and loss

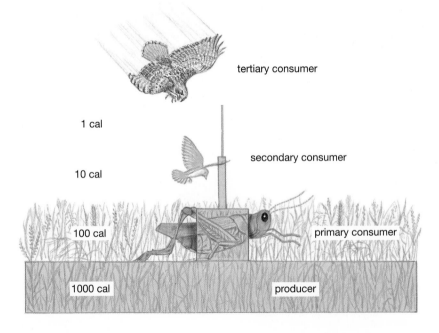

tertiary consumer

1 cal

secondary consumer

10 cal

100 cal

primary consumer

1000 cal

producer

Figure 40-7 An energy pyramid for a prairie ecosystem

© 2003 Prentice Hall, Inc.

NOTES

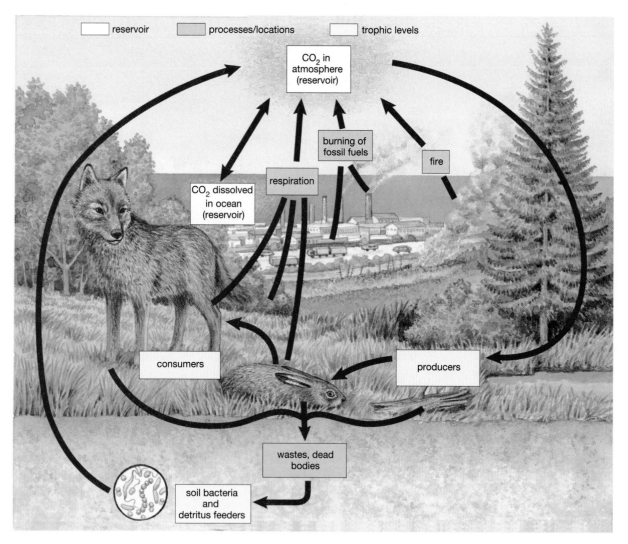

Figure 40-8 The carbon cycle

© 2003 Prentice Hall, Inc.

NOTES

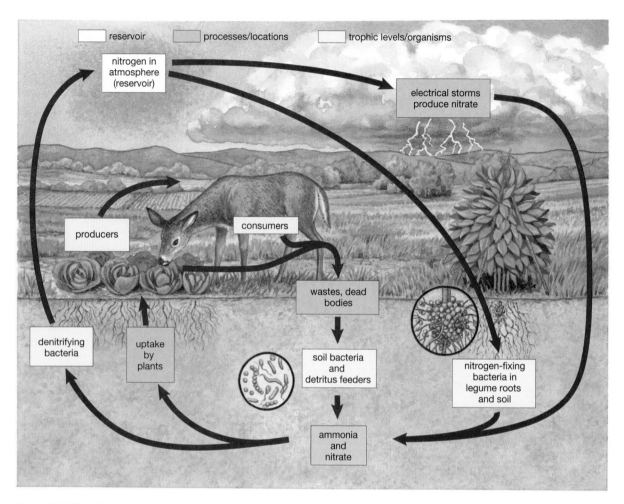

Figure 40-9 The nitrogen cycle

© 2003 Prentice Hall, Inc.

NOTES

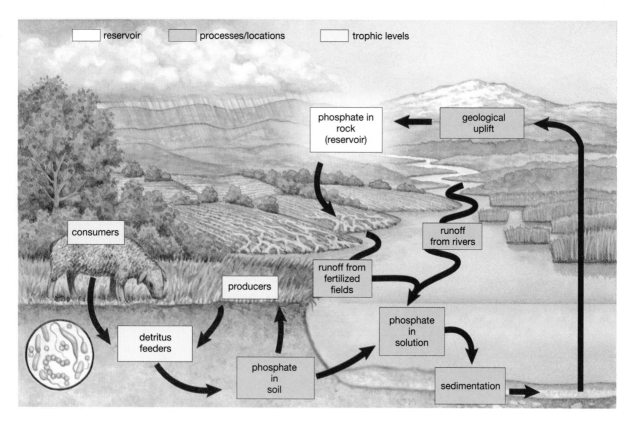

Figure 40-10 The phosphorus cycle

© 2003 Prentice Hall, Inc.

NOTES

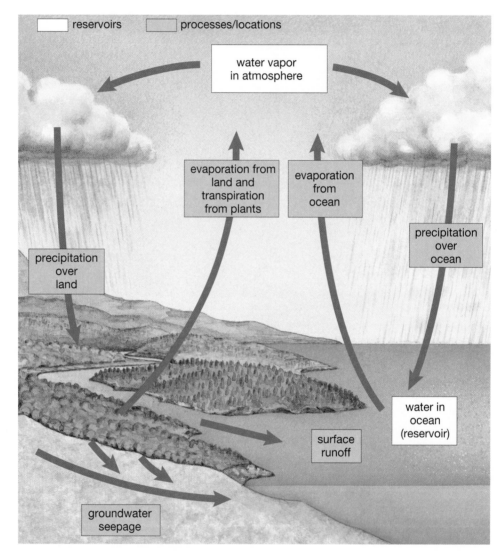

Figure 40-11 The hydrologic cycle

© 2003 Prentice Hall, Inc.

NOTES

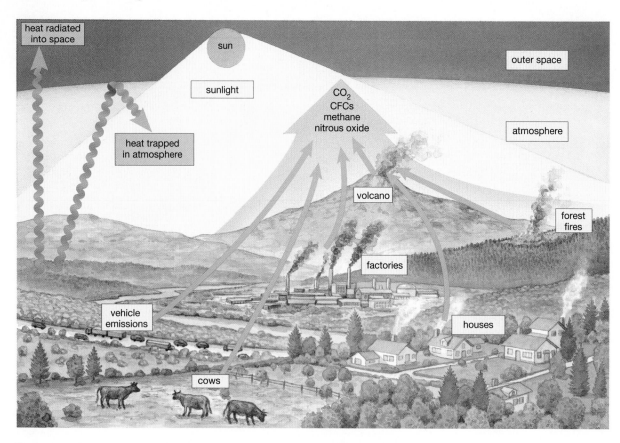

Figure 40-15 Increases in greenhouse gas emissions contribute to global warming

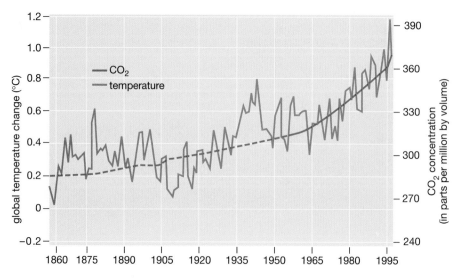

Figure 40-16 Global warming parallels CO$_2$ increases

© 2003 Prentice Hall, Inc.

NOTES

CHAPTER 41   Earth's Diverse Ecosystems

Thinking Through the Concepts

Multiple Choice

1. *Most plant species fit into only a few morphological types. Which type would you think is most restricted by temperature and rainfall?*
a. trees
b. shrubs
c. grasses
d. perennial herbs
e. annual weeds

2. *In which biome is the smallest fraction of carbon and nutrients present in the soil?*
a. tropical rain forest
b. savanna
c. tundra
d. grassland
e. coniferous forest

3. *How do mountain ranges create deserts?*
a. by lifting land up into colder, drier air
b. by completely blocking the flow of air into desert areas, thus preventing clouds from getting there
c. by forcing air to first rise and then fall, thus causing rain on one side of the mountains and desert on the other
d. by causing the global wind patterns that make certain latitudes very dry
e. by causing very steep slopes that are subject to erosion

4. *What is the primary reason that plants from distant, but climatically similar, places commonly look the same?*
a. common ancestry
b. adaptation to the same physical conditions
c. adaptation to similar herbivores
d. continental drift
e. effects of past climate change

5. *Which of these biomes has been increased in area by human activities?*
a. savanna
b. temperate rain forest
c. grassland
d. coniferous forest
e. desert

6. *What biome has the richest soil and has largely been converted to agriculture?*
a. tundra
b. coniferous forest
c. grassland
d. tropical rain forest
e. deciduous forest

? Review Questions

1. Explain how air currents contribute to the formation of the Tropics and the large deserts.

2. What are large, roughly circular ocean currents called? What effect do they have on climate, and where is that effect strongest?

3. What are the four major requirements for life? Which two are most often limiting in terrestrial ecosystems? In ocean ecosystems?

4. Explain why traveling up a mountain takes you through biomes similar to those you would encounter traveling north for a long distance.

5. Where are the nutrients of the tropical forest biome concentrated? Why is life in the tropical rain forest concentrated high above the ground?

6. Explain two undesirable effects of agriculture in the tropical rain forest biome.

7. List some adaptations of (a) desert plants and (b) desert animals to heat and drought.

8. What human activities damage deserts?

9. How are trees of the taiga adapted to a lack of water and a short growing season?

10. How do deciduous and coniferous biomes differ?

11. What single environmental factor best explains why there is shortgrass prairie in Colorado, tallgrass prairie in Illinois, and deciduous forest in Ohio?

12. Where are the world's largest populations of large herbivores and carnivores located?

13. Where is life in the oceans most abundant, and why?

14. Why is the diversity of life so high in coral reefs? What human impacts threaten them?

15. Distinguish among the limnetic, littoral, and profundal zones of lakes in terms of their location and the communities they support.

16. Distinguish between oligotrophic and eutrophic lakes. Describe (a) a natural scenario and (b) a human-created scenario under which an oligotrophic lake might be converted to a eutrophic lake.

17. What is the reason and importance of the spring and fall overturn in temperate lakes?

18. Distinguish between the photic and aphotic zones. How do organisms in the photic zone obtain nutrients? How are nutrients obtained in the aphotic zone?

19. What unusual primary producer forms the basis for hydrothermal vent communities?

20. On the basis of the location of the worst atmospheric ozone depletion, which biomes are likely to be most affected by increased UV penetration?

Applying the Concepts

1. List at least six differences between human-dominated and undisturbed ecosystems, and discuss in some detail how these differences can be minimized.

2. In which terrestrial biome is your college or university located? Discuss similarities and differences between your location and the general description of that biome in the text. If you are living in a city, how has the urban environment modified your interaction with the biome?

3. During the 1960s and 1970s, many parts of the U.S. and Canada banned the use of detergents containing phosphates. Until that time, almost all laundry detergents and many soaps and shampoos had high concentrations of phosphates. What environmental concern do you think prompted these bans, and what ecosystem has benefited most from the bans?

4. Because ozone depletion is expected to get worse, not better, for decades to come, biologists have tried to assess which types of species will be most susceptible to increased UV penetration. Two of the groups that may be most vulnerable—ocean plankton and long-lived birds and mammals—are quite different from each other. Try to think of what makes each of these groups so susceptible to increased UV radiation.

5. Understanding the ways in which the four basic requirements for life determine where different biomes occur can help us predict the consequences of global warming. Global warming is expected to make most areas warmer, but it is also expected to change rainfall in ways that are hard to predict—some areas will get wetter, and others drier. Our ignorance of how rainfall will change is not very important in understanding shifts in more northerly biomes, but it is very important for our understanding of changes in tropical areas. Look at Figure 41-8 and explain why this is true.

6. More-northerly forests are far better able to regenerate after logging than are tropical rain forests. Try to explain why this is true. HINT: The cold soils of northern climates greatly slow down decomposition rates.

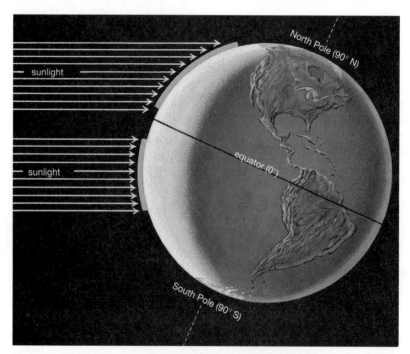

Figure 41-1 Earth's curvature and tilt produce seasons and climate

© 2003 Prentice Hall, Inc.

NOTES

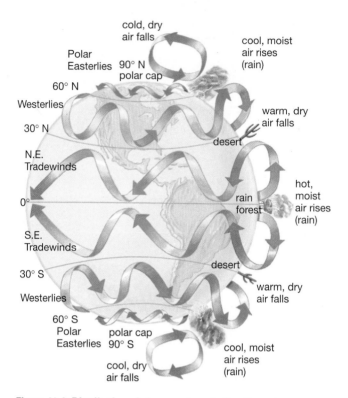

Figure 41-2 Distribution of air currents and climatic regions

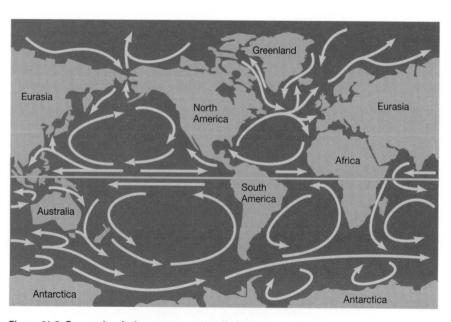

Figure 41-3 Ocean circulation patterns are called gyres

© 2003 Prentice Hall, Inc.

NOTES

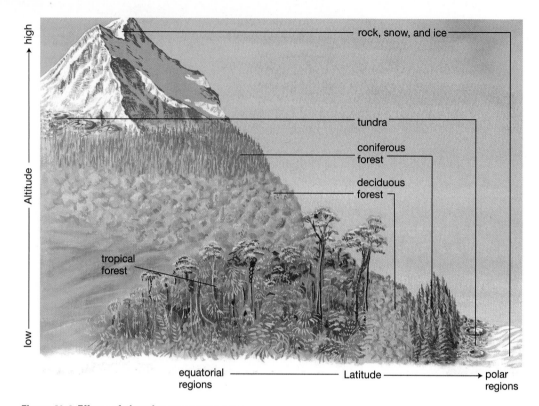

Figure 41-4 Effects of elevation on temperature

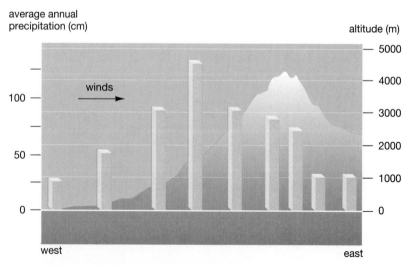

Figure 41-5 The rain shadow of the Sierra Nevada

© 2003 Prentice Hall, Inc.

NOTES

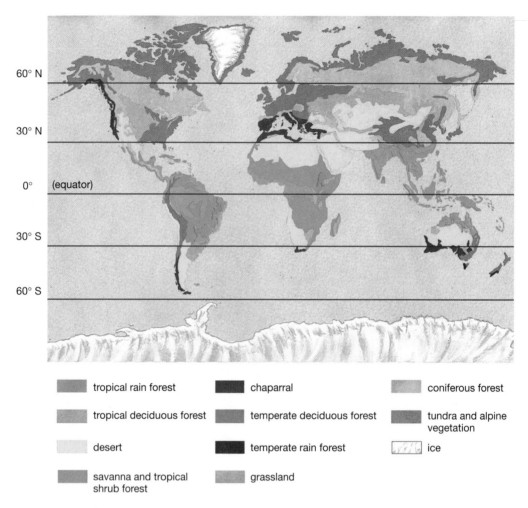

60° N

30° N

0° (equator)

30° S

60° S

tropical rain forest

chaparral

coniferous forest

tropical deciduous forest

temperate deciduous forest

tundra and alpine vegetation

desert

temperate rain forest

ice

savanna and tropical shrub forest

grassland

Figure 41-7 The distribution of biomes

© 2003 Prentice Hall, Inc.

NOTES

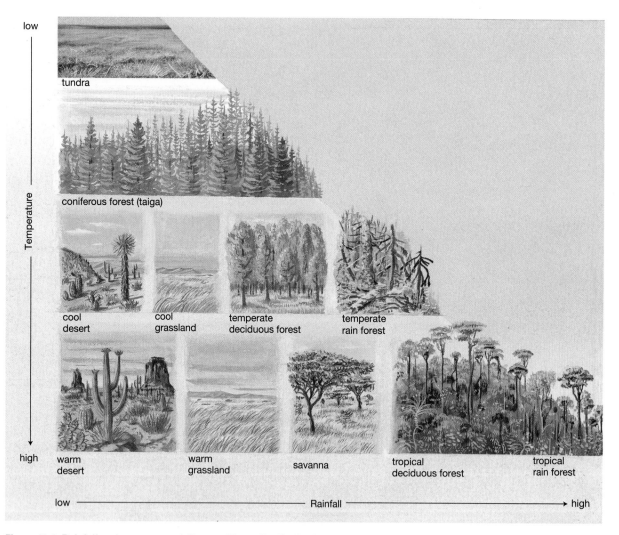

Figure 41-8 Rainfall and temperature influence biome distribution

© 2003 Prentice Hall, Inc.

NOTES

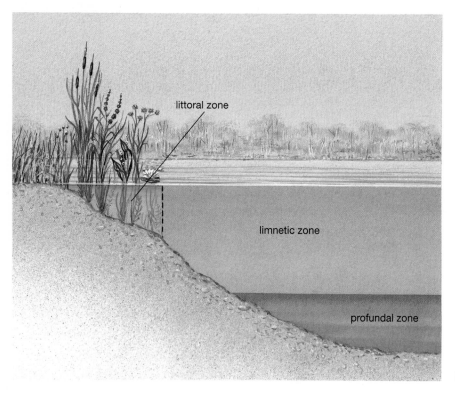

littoral zone

limnetic zone

profundal zone

Figure 41-24 Lake life zones

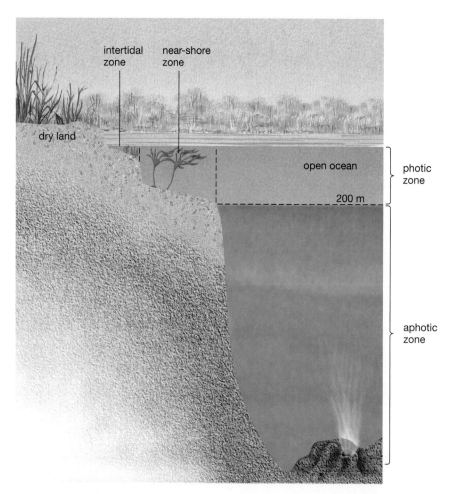

intertidal zone

near-shore zone

dry land

open ocean

photic zone

200 m

aphotic zone

Figure 41-25 Ocean life zones

© 2003 Prentice Hall, Inc.

NOTES

Photo Credits

03-02a   Dr. Jeremy Burgess/Science Photo Library/Photo Researchers, Inc.
E11-01   Courtesy of the Roslin Institute
19-18   Cabisco/Visuals Unlimited
20-04b   Breck P. Kent/Breck P. Kent
20-04c   Carolina Biological Supply Company/Phototake NYC
21-09   Dr. William M. Harlow/Photo Researchers, Inc.
21-09   Gilbert S. Grant/Photo Researchers, Inc.
23-09   Ed Reschke/Peter Arnold, Inc.
23-09   E.R. Degginger/Animals Animals/Earth Scenes
23-16a   D.C. Cunningham/Visuals Unlimited
23-16b   Stephen J. Krasemann/Photo Researchers, Inc.
34-09b   Manfred Kage/Peter Arnold, Inc.